ARCHEOLOGY OF MISSISSIPPI

Archeology of Mississippi

By

Calvin S. Brown

With a New Introduction

By

Janet Ford

University Press of Mississippi
Jackson and London

First published in 1926 for the Mississippi Geological Survey by the University of Mississippi

Copyright © 1992 by the University Press of Mississippi
All rights reserved
Manufactured in the United States of America
Print-on-Demand Edition
The paper in this book meets the guidelines for permanence and durability of the Committee on Production Guidelines for Book Longevity of the Council on Library Resources.

Library of Congress Cataloging-in-Publication Data

Brown, Calvin S. (Calvin Smith), 1866-1945.
   Archeology of Mississippi / by Calvin S. Brown : with a new introduction by Janet Ford.
     p.   cm.
   Originally published: 1926.
   Includes index.
   ISBN 0-87805-602-5. — ISBN 0-87805-603-3 (pbk.)
   1. Indians of North America—Mississippi—Antiquities.
2. Mississippi—Antiquities.   I. Title.
E78.M73B76   1992
976.2'01—dc20

92-28657
CIP

British Library Cataloging-in-Publication data available

CONTENTS.

	PAGE
Preface to the 1926 Edition	vii
Introduction	xi
Chapter I. Mounds and Earth-works	1
Mounds in General	1
In Lafayette County	4
In North-east Mississippi	9
Stone-Heaps or Cairns	12
The Ingomar Mounds	14
In Lowndes County	21
In Oktibbeha County	23
Nanih Waiya	24
Some Scattered Mounds	28
On the Gulf Coast	30
In the Vicinity of Natchez	33
In Copiah County and Vicinity	47
In Warren County	48
On the Yazoo River	53
On the Sunflower River	70
In Issaquena and Sharkey Counties	76
In Washington County	80
In Bolivar and Other Counties	90
In Clarksdale and Coahoma County	96
In Panola, Tunica, and De Soto Counties	113
Chapter II. Arrow-heads, Spear-heads, and Perforators	125
Chapter III. Axes and Celts	146
Chapter IV. Ornamental, Ceremonial, and Problematic Stones	161
Discoidal Stones	161
Spuds, or Spade-shaped Stones	170
Boat-Stones	173
Gorgets	176
Plummets and Sinkers	184
Beads	188
Banner-Stones	193
Rectangular Tubes	203

	PAGE
Cigar-shaped Stones	203
Cones	204
Egg-shaped Stones	205
Carved Stones	205
Miscellaneous	208
Chapter V. Agricultural and Domestic Implements	209
Chapter VI. Pipes	235
Chapter VII. Shell, Bone, and Copper	273
Chapter VIII. Pottery	286
Chapter IX. Post-Columbian Material	348
Index	367

PREFACE TO THE 1926 EDITION.

The author has attempted to give in this volume a systematic idea of the different types of Indian remains found in the state of Mississippi. Believing that illustrations are more effective than descriptions he has given as many pictures of artifacts as circumstances permitted. It is believed that every illustration in the book represents an object from this state.

The author wishes to express first of all his deep and lasting obligation to Dr. E. N. Lowe, State Geologist, for the invitation to write this book and for constant encouragement during the course of its preparation.

He wishes also to thank Dr. Dunbar Rowland, Director of Archives and History, of Jackson; Mr. Victor C. Barringer of Monroe, La.; Dr. J. A. K. Birchett of Vicksburg; Mr. Charles W. Clark of Clarksdale; Mr. J. E. Gift of Corinth; Mr. Fred Schubach of Memphis; and Mr. Andrew Learned, Mr. George Kelley, and Mr. W. A. Harris of Natchez; all of whom have helped to make archeological specimens accessible to the writer.

Two efficient collectors, Mr. Brevoort Butler of Enola, and Mr. E. R. Ballard of Winona, have passed from the field of action.

Mr. Will Ticer of New Albany, Mr. Ben H. McFarland of Aberdeen, the G. B. Hansell estate of Nettleton, Mr. F. T. Bessac of Natchez, and Mr. H. K. Williams of Haynes Bluff, have given to the Survey good collections of archeological material, and hence made permanent contributions to their state. Others have made smaller donations.

The directors of the great museums thruout the country have cooperated with that spirit of helpfulness which is characteristic of scientific men.

Mr. Daniel of Jackson, Mr. Major and Mr. Barrow of Oxford,

with their skill in photography, have contributed to the artistic appearance of the book, as have also Miss Pauline Wright (now Mrs. Nichols), Prof. Raymond Mathews, and Mr. Charles A. Barton with their skill in drawing.

To all these, and to many others who have given their aid in some form or other, the author expresses his gratitude.

Among the more helpful publications touching the archeology of Mississippi or adjacent territory, the following may be especially mentioned:

1. SQUIER AND DAVIS: Ancient Monuments of the Miss. Valley, Washington, 1848.
2. JONES, CHARLES C.: Antiquities of the Southern Indians, New York, 1873.
3. JONES, JOSEPH: Aboriginal Remains of Tennessee. Smiths. Contrib. to Knowl., Vol. 22, 1876.
4. THOMAS: Mound Exploration, 12th Ann. Rept. of Bu. of Am. Ethn. Washington, 1894.
5. THRUSTON: Antiquities of Tennessee, Cincinnati, 1897.
6. MCGUIRE: Pipes and Smoking Customs of the American Aborigines, Washington, (1898) 1899.
7. CULIN: The Dickeson Collection of Am. Antiquities, Philadelphia, 1900.
8. HOLMES: Aboriginal Pottery of the Eastern United States, 20th Ann. Rept. of Bu. of Am. Ethn., Washington, 1903.
9. PEABODY: Exploration of Mounds, Coahoma County, Miss., Vol. III, no. 2, Papers of the Peabody Museum of Am. Arch., Cambridge, Mass., 1904.
10. MOORE: Certain Aboriginal Remains of Mobile Bay and Miss. Sound. Philadelphia, 1905.
11. MOORE: Certain Mounds of Arkansas and Mississippi, Philadelphia, 1908.
12. MOORE: Some Aboriginal Sites on Mississippi River, Philadelphia, 1911.

13. SWANTON: Indian Tribes of the Lower Miss. Valley, Bull. 43, Bu. of Am. Ethn., Washington, 1911.

In the description of mounds and earth-works in the first chapter of this book the author has drawn freely from his predecessors in the field, Mr. Cyrus Thomas, Dr. Charles Peabody, and Mr. Clarence B. Moore. It seems desirable to summarize here in convenient form all that has been done in the investigation of the mounds of the state, even tho the account should run to considerable length. Unaltered quotations have been indicated by quotation marks, but many condensed descriptions have not been so indicated: the indebtedness however has been acknowledged in every case. Thruout the book mounds and other earth-works are named preferably by towns and geographical designations rather than by land owners, for the reason that geographic designations are more permanent.

In giving the dimensions of objects the scale refers always to linear measurements unless otherwise stated.

Of the three hundred and fifty-four illustrations used in this book more than three hundred are here published for the first time: the source of the others is acknowledged.

The sympathetic reader will keep in mind that the material on which this study is based is scattered in many collections both public and private and is in many cases difficult of access, and that the book has been written under the stress of more pressing obligations, and that the progress of its preparation has often been interrupted. Such as it is the author gives it to the people of Mississippi and to the archeologists of the world in the hope that it will increase the knowledge of the prehistoric life of the state and of America.

CALVIN S. BROWN.

JANUARY, 1924.

INTRODUCTION.

Perhaps the most overworked phrase used to introduce books being reissued is, "this volume is a classic." Never, however, has the phrase been more applicable than in the case of *Archeology of Mississippi*. No other book covers the antiquities of Mississippi so thoroughly. Very few, in fact, so comprehensively cover the archaeology of *any* area of the United States at such an early date. Although written for the lay reader of the 1920s, even today this is the first sourcebook consulted by professionals working in the state—if they can find a copy. The illustrations in the book are the only photographic records of certain important cultural sites that have since been drastically altered or destroyed.

Brown's work continues to benefit the nonprofessional who is interested in archaeology. His clear descriptions, excellent illustrations, and information on location of sites and artifacts provide comparative data valuable in assessing finds. Even the reader who is not an avocational collector will be impressed with the artistry of the artifacts and the number and scale of the earthen monuments produced by the prehistoric inhabitants of Mississippi and reproduced in this book. This is not a book to be read from cover to cover so much as a store of delightful discoveries to be made in increments. It bridges the gap between reference and popular art books in a way few volumes can. The full range of artifacts is covered; the reader will find the mundane and misshapen as well as the rare and gracefully beautiful. Thus this new edition, which is a faithful reproduction of the text and illustrations in the original one, meets an important need for both professional archaeologists and non-professionals interested in the state's prehistoric past.

That *Archeology of Mississippi* is still relevant is remarkable given the changes that southeastern archaeology has undergone since its original 1926 publication date. The recovery of most of the Indian artifacts before the turn of the century was accomplished by men who dabbled in the field. During the nineteenth century doctors and lawyers gathered into erudite private "academic associations" dedicated to the study of a variety of subjects. The Davenport [Iowa] Academy of Science, repository of two of the artifacts which Brown pictures (Fig. 59 & Fig. 327), for example, was established in 1867 "as a part of a general program to develop knowledge of local flora, fauna, geology, and archaeology" (McKusick 1970:2). Such groups produced volumes filled with illustrations of the most bizarre or attractive artifacts and reports of varying accuracy. The Davenport Society, as a matter of fact, is best known in archaeological circles for a set of fraudulent artifacts. By the turn of the century, however, these academies were superseded by people whose profession or whose consuming passion was archaeology. Local individuals continued to collect and exchange information, but largely ceased to publish their findings widely. An early chancellor of the University of Mississippi, Dr. R. B. Fulton, for example, in 1887-88 solicited information by mail regarding location and content of Indian sites in various counties, but apparently published nothing on the subject. American archaeology as a discipline, however, was still in its infancy. Most professionals of the era had begun their careers in one of the sciences, switching to archaeology at a later date. Their numbers were limited, and not equally distributed geographically. The "passionate" archaeologists were even less numerous, since they required not only the desire, but the personal wealth to pursue their interests.

Ancient Monuments of the Mississippi Valley, by Squier and Davis (1847), contains second-hand reports of Mississippi earthworks, and Cyrus Thomas' (1894) work in identifying the moundbuilders contains references to excavations performed in the state by agents of the Smithsonian Institution. In reality, however, by 1926 very little first-hand work had been reported in the state. The major works published about Mississippi archaeology were written by Clarence B. Moore, a wealthy "passionate" archaeologist from Philadelphia, Pennsylvania, and by Charles Peabody and Warren K. Moorehead from the Department of Archaeology of Phillips Academy and the R. S. Peabody Museum in Andover, Massachusetts. Moore's books, which were handsome and abundantly illustrated, were expeditiously published, but Moore had conducted little research in Mississippi. Brown, nevertheless, reproduced appropriate portions of Moore's publications, including plates of Mississippi pottery. Brown also borrowed descriptions, site maps and drawings directly from the earlier Thomas publication. Lacking a photocopy machine, he mutilated several of these now irreplaceable volumes to include both illustrations and text in his handwritten manuscript—sacrifice for a good cause, I suppose. In every case Brown has given proper credit to his source.

Peabody and Moorehead were not so diligent in publishing as Moore. Peabody dug at the Oliver site in Coahoma County and published a brief account in 1904. Brown's Fig. 18 map of the site is not only "Redrawn from Peabody, plate vii," but is an improvement over the original illustration. Peabody also dug at the Alligator site in Bolivar County in 1918. *Archeology of Mississippi* contains more information on this excavation than any publication by Peabody. In his "Postscript," Brown refers to Moorehead's work in the Natchez area and to his anticipation of a report. Moorehead summarized his investigations in five pages of a larger report not published until 1932. In this report, he refers the reader to Calvin Brown's *Archeology of Mississippi* for illustrations of the kind of artifacts common in the area (Moorehead 1932:165). Brown visited Peabody at Alligator, noting where he had dug and what he had found. He also visited Moorehead in Natchez and obtained for the Survey's collection the majority of the artifacts recovered (Moorehead 1932:165).

For his illustrations, Brown culled the collections of all of the major museums and not a few minor ones to assure that at least some easily accessed record of artifacts taken out of the state would be preserved. His journals and notebooks indicate that he contacted all the collectors he could find in the state and everyone that he heard might have a collection including artifacts from Mississippi. He tracked down collections that had been sold and viewed endless numbers of reported sites and collections, photographing and/or sketching as he went and recording copious cross-indexed notes about each.

In short, Calvin Brown carefully and completely investigated, summarized and authenticated all archaeological work completed at that date in Mississippi. Publication of *Archeology of Mississippi* conveniently marks the end of an era.

About the time of publication, the tenor of archaeology in the state began to change as people trained specifically in the discipline came to the forefront. In 1925, as Brown notes in his "Postscript," Henry B. Collins, associated with the United States National Museum, Smithsonian Institution, began a series of excavations. At about the same time, Moreau B. Chambers and James A. Ford were hired by the Mississippi Department of Archives and History to conduct a survey of archaeological sites. Collins took over the training of these two young men, particularly that of native son Ford, who would eventually raise the professional quality of study yet another notch (Blitz 1988:6). The Chambers and Ford survey results were never published, although much of the data recovered was used by Ford in a subsequent publication (Ford 1936). Both men went on to make substantial contributions to Mississippi archaeology.

The subsequent development of a comprehensive archaeological program, however, was somewhat slower in Mississippi than in neighboring states. Major investigation of much of the Southeast under the direction of people trained specifically in the field of archaeology occurred in the 1930s. Throughout the country the Work Projects Administration employed thousands of people left jobless by the Great Depression in the excavation of mounds under the direction of professionals or graduate students in archaeology. Although

Collins continued small-scale excavations in the state, Mississippi remained substantially untouched by the large-scale WPA archaeology. It was not until the 1940s that there was an extensive, systematic archaeological program initiated in the state with the establishment of the Lower Mississippi Survey by Ford, Philip Phillips, and James B. Griffin (see Phillips, Ford, and Griffin 1951). As a result, a chronology of artifact types and categories, which Collins had begun, was further defined. In the ensuing decades interests turned to the finer points of anthropological explanation of the distribution of sites and artifacts.

Because Brown's volume preceded establishment of chronological ordering, he organized his chapters according to artifact categories—domestic implements, pipes, pottery, and the like. The reader, therefore, cannot use this book as an accurate guide for chronological placement of the artifacts. This limitation is not serious since those knowledgeable in the area are aware of proper chronological context. Brown's categories may even make the book more logical for some non-professional readers. The real joy for all is the quantity and quality of illustrations. Brown's original prints, housed at the University of Mississippi, show the care he took to produce the volume. He often had more than one version of a drawing done, so that he could choose the one that best emphasized the detail he wished to highlight. He photographed sites from several angles, selecting the one he thought most representative. For example, his Fig. 6 illustration of Nanih Waiya is taken from the south, but he had additional views from the three other sides from which to choose. He tried to see that all artifacts were reproduced either in the natural size of the object or in some fraction thereof so that the reader could easily visualize the actual size. He was careful to see that the outlines of objects were accurate and undistorted by shadows or support structures. He was just as meticulous with the technical treatment of his text. The manuscript reveals multiple galley proofs of the title page and chapter headings, in attempt to select the most impressive type size and font.

The volume is not perfect. There is an occasional editorial error, such as a reference on page 3 to Fig. 15, when Fig. 17 is meant. Subsequent investigation has also corrected some of Brown's interpretation of artifacts. For example, the artifact to the far left in Fig. 141 is identified as a piece of cane used in drilling stone. Upon examination, however, the cane exhibits a stain usually produced by the presence of copper. In addition, the spiral markings which Brown considered striations scratched into the cane by boring are, instead, slightly raised. They were probably produced by copper wiring which had been wrapped around the cane. The Trudeau site (Brain 1979:196) and the Oliver site have both produced pieces of cane wrapped with copper coils dating to a period after European contact. Also, 1990 excavations by the University of Mississippi on a historic Chickasaw site in Tupelo yielded a wooden dowel wrapped with copper wire in a similar manner (Yearous 1991:43). Brown's cane fragment was found inside a buried historic period brass kettle, confirming that it, like the other objects wrapped with copper wiring, dated to the postcontact period. Brown infers that the cane was used to produce drill cores similar to those also pictured in Fig. 141. The drill cores actually date to a much earlier time period. Brown could not have known about the discrepancy in dating; his logic simply fell victim to the knowledge available at the time. Of course, subsequent work has enabled us to sort many of the artifacts into categories according to time and style.

Archeology of Mississippi becomes more interesting still when the man who produced it is examined. Calvin Smith Brown, Jr., marked the end of an era as much as his book did. In today's world of specialization it is rare to find a man who shows such excellence in so many diverse fields as did Brown, a true Renaissance man. Born near Glass, in Obion County, Tennessee, on February 13, 1866, he completed his undergraduate work at Vanderbilt in 1888 and continued his education there, in the meantime serving as an instructor of English Language and Literature. He earned an M.S. in 1891 and a D.Sc. degree in Geology a year later. His main interest was in paleobotany and his dissertation was entitled, *The Coal Flora of Tracy City* (Tennessee). Although his ultimate profession was not to be in this field, Brown retained an interest in geology and in both fossil and modern flora, publishing the article, "The Petrified Forest of Mississippi" in *The Popular Science Monthly* in 1913, and the books, *The Lignite of Mississippi* in 1917 and *Botany of Tishomingo State Park* in 1936. A later, undated manuscript archived at the University of Mississippi is titled, "Landscaping with Native Plants" and he landscaped the area around his Oxford home with native flora.

Brown pursued studies in Paris and Leipzig before continuing his education in the United States. His second graduate degree, a Ph.D. in Comparative Literature from the University of Colorado (1899), led to his "official" occupation and additional publications. Before going to Mississippi, he taught English at Rutgers College, and modern languages at the University of Missouri. He studied in Spain, Italy, and Greece in 1903-1904 and joined the faculty of the University of Mississippi in 1905, eventually becoming chairman of the Department of Modern Languages and teaching Romance languages and German until his death in 1945.

In the context of his work with Comparative Literature and languages, he edited works on Tennyson, Sheridan, and a publication entitled, *The Later English Drama*. He also edited *Latin Songs, Classical, Medieval and Modern, with Music,* in 1914. He even had an original poem published in 1898. He was Phi Beta Kappa and a fellow of the American Association for the Advancement of Science.

Brown's accumulated notes and notebooks, also housed at the University of Mississippi, show a fascination with language and a sense of humor not reflected in his publications. He collected a large number of tongue twisters, humorous poems, word games, and palimdrones in English, Latin, and Greek. Phrases whose meanings could be changed by inflection ("Do you take this woman for better . . . or for worse") abound in his notes. He collected newspaper clippings whose messages were less than clear. ("Wanted—a steady young man to look after a garden and care for a cow who has a good voice and can sing in the choir.")

His interest in archaeology was apparently stimulated through his association with another scholar and Renaissance man, Dr. E.N. Lowe, the director for the Mississippi Geological Survey. Lowe was responsible for Brown's appointment as an archaeologist for that agency, under whose auspices *Archeology of Mississippi* was published. Lowe's Letter of Transmittal, reproduced in *Archeology of Mississippi,* notes that all of Brown's work was done on his own time, when not committed to his primary occupation at the University.

Brown took his appointment as archaeologist seriously. He had already begun his own collection of Indian artifacts, fully intending to bequeath it to the University eventually, and in 1916 he began obtaining a collection of artifacts for the Geological Survey to be housed at the University. He persuaded collectors from all over the state to donate their artifacts to the Survey. For his own collection, the Geological Survey Collection, and each contributor's collection, he kept a perfect catalog of artifact description and source. Today, all of those collections as well as his catalog, notes, photographs, and glass negatives remain at Ole Miss and they still provide archaeologists with raw material for analysis and comparison. Some are especially notable. The Davies collection of Mississippian period pottery, much of which is pictured in *Archeology of Mississippi,* is famous among southeastern archaeologists as one of the finest of the time period.

Not all of Brown's collections were prehistoric. Around the turn of the century he became interested in an eccentric potter, George Ohr, known as "The Mad Potter of Biloxi." He corresponded with Ohr and, after Ohr's death, with his widow. Eventually he obtained a collection of Ohr's pottery for the University. While Ohr's work was at that time appreciated by few persons other than Brown, today Ohr pottery is highly regarded as masterpieces of design and technique, well ahead of its time.

Calvin Brown had many interests. Never a passive student, he contributed significantly to many fields of study. *Archeology of Mississippi* is a classic volume; it was produced by a man who was, himself, a classic. The inscription on his tombstone in St. Peter's Cemetery in Oxford reads, "UBER ALLEN GIPFELN IST RUH." That is the first line of Goethe's eight line poem now called *Wanderer's Night Song #2,* that speaks of the unity of heaven and earth and man and assures the wanderer that when nature rests, so, too, shall he. The epitaph is remarkably apt for this inquisitive wanderer through nature and knowledge, Calvin Smith Brown.

Janet Ford is a professor of anthropology at the University of Mississippi, where she is curator of the Calvin S. Brown Collection.

REFERENCES CITED.

Brain, Jeffrey P.
    1979 *The Tunica Treasure.* Papers of the Peabody Museum of Archaeology and Ethnology, Harvard University, 78.

McKusick, Marshall
    1970 *The Davenport Conspiracy.* State Archaeologist Reports, 1. Iowa City.

Blitz, John H.
    1988 Henry Collins and Southeastern Archaeology. *Mississippi Archaeology*, 23 (1):1-11.

Ford, James A.
    1936 *Analysis of Indian Village Site Collections from Louisiana and Mississippi.* Anthropological Study No. 2, Department of Conservation, Louisiana Geological Survey, New Orleans.

Moore, Clarence B.
    1905 *Certain Aboriginal Remains of Mobile Bay and Mississippi Sound.* Journal of the Academy of Natural Sciences of Philadelphia, 13 (2):279-299.
    1908 *Certain Mounds of Arkansas and of Mississippi; Part I. Mounds and Cemeteries of the Lower Arkansas River; Part II. Mounds of the Lower Yazoo and Lower Sunflower Rivers, Mississippi; Part III. The Blum Mounds, Mississippi.* Journal of the Academy of Natural Sciences of Philadelphia, 13:480-600.
    1911 *Some Aboriginal Sites on Mississippi River.* Journal of the Academy of Natural Sciences of Philadelphia, 14:367-478.

Moorehead, Warren K.
    1932 "Explorations near Natchez, Mississippi," in *Etowah Papers.* Yale University Press, New Haven.

Peabody, Charles
    1904 "Exploration of Mounds, Coahoma County, Mississippi." Papers of the Peabody Museum of American Archaeology and Ethnology, Harvard University III:2:27-57.

Phillips, Philip, James A. Ford and James B. Griffin
    1951 *Archaeological Survey in the Lower Mississippi Alluvial Valley, 1940-47.* Papers of the Peabody Museum 25, Cambridge, Mass.

Squier, Ephraim G. and E. H. Davis
   1847 *Ancient Monuments of the Mississippi Valley.* Smithsonian Contributions to Knowledge, vol. I. Washington, D.C.

Thomas, Cyrus
   1894 *Report of the Mound Explorations of the Bureau of American Ethnology. Twelfth Annual Report of the Bureau of Ethnology, 1890-91,* pp. 17-722.

Yearous, Jenny Dee
   1990 *Meadowbrook: An Eighteenth Century Chickasaw Village.* M.A. Thesis, University of Mississippi, University.

ARCHEOLOGY OF MISSISSIPPI

CHAPTER I.

MOUNDS AND EARTH-WORKS.

MOUNDS IN GENERAL.

The State of Mississippi abounds in those ancient remains known as Indian mounds or tumuli. They are found most frequently along the streams and in the valleys and lowlands, but also occur in the uplands and among the hills. In size, shape, and structure they vary greatly.

Many of the mounds, especially the smaller ones, are conical in shape, and usually rounded at the top; tho some of the conical mounds are truncated or have flat tops. Many of the larger mounds are rectangular or four-sided and have flat tops. The inclination of the sides varies from a very gentle slope in some to a very steep slope in others. In some cases the approach or roadway leading up the side of a large mound can still be recognized. In a few mounds the outline of the base is quite irregular; tho so far as I have observed, it in no case represents the shape of man or of the lower animals; I have observed no effigy mounds in Mississippi.

The size of the mounds varies from scarcely perceptible swellings of the ground less than a foot high to immense hillocks fifty or sixty feet in elevation, with an area of one-fifth of an acre on top. The famous Nanih Waiya has a base 218 by 140 feet and is 22 feet high. The large mound at Oliver, excavated by Dr. Peabody, measures 190 feet from north to south and 180 feet from east to west and has a vertical height of 26 feet. The Ingomar rectangular mound is about 222 by 165 feet and is 27 feet high. The largest of the Leland mounds is nearly 200 feet long, about 175 feet wide, and 30 feet high. The largest mound of the Anna group near Natchez is 50 feet high. The great central mound of the Winterville group is 55 feet high; and the great central mound at Mound Place near the mouth of Lake George is 55 or 60 feet high. The Selsertown plateau or platform with its superincumbent mounds is much greater in cubic contents than any of these, but it is not entirely artificial.

Mounds are found singly or in groups. The single mounds are usually small and conical. In the smaller groups of mounds there are three or four, in the largest many more. The Ingomar group in Union County contains or did contain fourteen. The Edmonds group contains fifteen, including several less than two feet high. The Winterville group contains fifteen mounds. The Lake George group near Holly Bluff, Yazoo County, contains twenty-five or more mounds within the enclosure and two outside. A few groups are surrounded by earth-walls and moats or ditches, as the Lake George group just mentioned.

The mounds are generally composed of soil or earth similar to that surrounding them. In some cases the pits or excavations from which the earth was taken for the construction of the tumuli may still be seen, as in the Batesville group and the Lake George group. In most cases, however, there now remains no depression to show the site from which the earth was taken. Perhaps in many cases it was taken up over a relatively large area and to a very small depth, the laborers thus getting the dirt in the easiest way. In addition to the local soil or earth used in the construction of the mounds, there are sometimes found ashes, burnt clay, shells, and refuse matter.

As to the purpose or object of the mounds, that was different in different cases. Some were used for burial purposes, as is evidenced by the fact that skeletons of human beings are still found in them. Frequently where there are a number of mounds together one of the smaller ones is a burial tumulus. Since many mounds are at present used for cemeteries, some by the white people, others by the negroes, care must be taken not to confuse an intrusion burial with an original burial. Some of the mounds seem to have been used as residence sites and are therefore called domiciliary mounds. Evidence of this use is presented by the burnt-clay floors and in other ways, as well as by the testimony of early travelers. Some mounds may have been used in military operations, as certainly earth-walls were. The embankments at Philipp in Leflore County (fig. 15) seem to be of this nature; they are long and irregular and run parallel with the Tallahatchie River, ending near two sloughs. Some mounds may have been used as signal or look-out stations. Some may have been used in religious or other ceremonials. Finally, some may have been used as refuge places in times of high water; certain it is that some of these ancient mounds have been used very effectively by the present inhabitants and their cattle in times of overflow. A few mounds have been built for this purpose in recent years by white people.

As to the contents of the mounds, they may be largely surmised from what was said about the purpose of the mounds in the preceding paragraph. Most of them contain nothing, except perhaps potsherds and fragments of flint and such other refuse as was lying about on the surface when the mound was being constructed. Some contain beds of ashes, charcoal, and burnt clay. Posts and pieces of wood are sometimes found. The burial mounds contain skeletons or parts of skeletons and sometimes beads, pottery, stone implements, and other objects of ancient workmanship. The mounds do not contain treasure; gold and silver were virtually unknown to the Amerind in this part of the country upon the coming of the white man.

As to the age of the mounds, some date back centuries before Columbus, no doubt; others are more recent; and some were built, in part at least, after Columbus, as is shown by the fact that they contain objects of European or Caucasian manufacture. It is probable that some mounds are the result of additions extending over considerable lapse of time. There is no reason for supposing that the mounds were built by any other race than the Indians. Early European travelers saw them in use. The White Apple mounds near Natchez are historic. A great national council of the Choctaws was convened at Nanih Waiya under the leadership of Greenwood Laflore in 1828.[1]

The word mound as here used signifies a structure of earth intentionally thrown up as such; the mounds of Europe and Asia and of the Cliff-dwellers' country in the United States often represent the remains of a structure or village more or less crumbled or covered with dust.

In addition to the true mounds there are also found in Mississippi refuse-heaps and shell-heaps similar to the kitchen middens of Northern Europe, stone-heaps or cairns, and also earth-walls, enclosures, fortifications, and cemeteries.

IN LAFAYETTE COUNTY.

The little mound shown in figure 1 is located in Lafayette County one mile west of the south-west corner of the University property. It is a typical small conical mound, seven and a half feet high and fifty feet in diameter. It stands on the brow of a hill and overlooks a long valley. On top of it are growing trees of medium size. About it have been found flint arrow-points, fragments of pottery, hammer-stones, and part of a mortar or maize grinder. A slight opening was made in the north-eastern part of the mound before 1906. A large hole was dug into the south-western part a few years ago, probably in 1917, by some unknown person. Apparently nothing was found, for when I repaired the mound in 1918

---

[1]Halbert: Nanih Waiya, in Pub. Miss. Hist. Soc., vol. II, Oxford, Miss., 1899.

there was almost no sign of potsherds, flints, or other foreign substances, only the soil itself, which had been thrown out.

Figure 2 shows a somewhat larger mound at Cornish, Lafayette County, as it appeared in December, 1913. It was then 12 or 14 feet high. Since the photograph was taken the mound has been partially cut down and a residence built upon

FIG. 1. Small conical mound, near the University of Mississippi, height 7.5 feet, April 28, 1912. C. S. B.

it by Dr. Webster. Nothing of consequence was found in removing the upper part of this mound.

Two miles down the Yokona valley from the mound just mentioned, not far above Oliver bridge, and about 10 miles south-east of Oxford, are the Slaughter mounds, a group of four standing in an open field. The most northerly one is the tallest, being about 17 or 18 feet high, and is slightly elongated toward the east (fig. 3). This mound has been partially tunneled from the south. The other three mounds have been plowed over and no doubt considerably flattened. Near the mounds, especially to the east of the smaller ones, quantities of potsherds, flints, and hammer-stones abound, and rarer pieces may be found occasionally. One of the axes

FIG. 2. Mound at Cornish, Lafayette Co., height 12 to 14 feet, Dec. 12, 1913. C. S. B. Now occupied by a house.

(no. 189) pictured in a later chapter was found in this field by Miss Kathleen Baldwyn.

At the confluence of Harrison Creek and Tallahatchie River in the northern part of Lafayette County, there is a considerable mound between the two streams near the creek side; apparently it is rectangular, tho at the time of each of my visits the vegetation was so rank that it was difficult to study the mound. It is nearly enclosed by the creek, a depression, and a slough. The land on three sides is subject to overflow.

About 1890 a mound was demolished by treasure hunters in the Tallahatchie bottom north-west of Oxford some distance east of the Teckville bridge. It was probably 8 feet high, judging from a small portion of the mound which still stands. It is said that in earlier times there was a semi-circular rampart of earth passing to the south of the mound and connecting east and west with water, thus forming an enclosure.

FIG. 3. Mound near Oliver bridge, Lafayette Co., 17 or 18 feet high, Dec. 12, 1913. C. S. B.

At the juncture of the Clear Creek valley and the Tallahatchie valley on the Haley place are two mounds, partly opened many years ago by Dr. Joseph Jones. From this vicinity came the fine stone vessel, first figured by Dr. Jones[1] in his *Antiquities in Tennessee,* and illustrated in figure 172 of this book.

Squier and Davis, on the authority of the Rev. R. Morris of Mount Sylvan Academy, Lafayette Co., described seventy years ago two groups of earth-works in western Lafayette Co., and gave diagrams of the same.[2]

---

[1] Jones: Explor. of the Aborig. Remains of Tenn. (called thruout Antiquities in Tennessee), Washington, 1876, p. 144, fig. 85.
[2] Squier and Davis: Anc. Mon. of the Miss. Valley, Washington (1847) 1848, pp. 110 and fol., and pl. 38, nos. 2 and 3.

The former (no. 2) is situated in T. 4 S., R. 7 W. [T. 7 S., R. 4 W.?] upon a bluff above a small creek, five miles south-east of Tallahatchie River, and consists of an embankment of earth about 3 feet high and an exterior ditch of corresponding dimensions; the side next to the creek is not entrenched, being protected by the high bluff. Within the work are several low mounds [four in the diagram]. The area of the enclosure is 5 acres.

The latter (no. 3) is situated on the left bank of Clear Creek, near Mount Sylvan, and occupies a high point of land, the bluff on the right being 40 feet high. The enclosure is quadrangular in form and consists of an embankment or earth-wall 30 feet wide at base, 12 feet wide on top, and about 3 feet high, with a gate-way in the western wall. There are no mounds within the enclosure, but there are three small ones outside, one near the gate. At the foot of the bluff there are abundant springs of water.

The present writer has not succeeded in locating either of these enclosures, tho his search has been by no means thoro. Neither the embankments nor the mounds were high, and the plow could easily have leveled them in the seventy years that have elapsed since they were described.

About a mile and a half south by south-east of Oxford there is a camp-site in the Temple field, where good diminutive triangular points and the usual fragments may be found.

About three miles north-west from Oxford at Davidson spring on the College Hill road is a camp-site, where I have found two mortars, a notched ax, and many flaked points.

Near Bay Springs between Quick's upper and middle lakes about ten miles north-east of Oxford there is a camp-site abounding in fragments of pottery and flint, with some shells and bones. Here I have found good small triangular points, a number of hammer-stones, and other artifacts. Workmen report the plowing up of bones. There is plenty of spring water nearby. There is another Indian site on the hill occupied by the Hickey garden.

Many other mounds and camp-sites exist in the county, but I shall not attempt to enumerate all. It is likewise impossible to enumerate all the earth-works and sites thruout the state; in the following pages, however, I call attention to many of these, some on my own authority, some on the authority of others who have made earlier reports on different localities.

IN NORTH-EAST MISSISSIPPI.

All the counties of north-east Mississippi show mounds and other remains of Indian occupation.

Moore[1] found one small mound in the extreme north-east corner of the state in his expedition up the Tennessee River. It is about one mile west-south-west from Hubbard Landing, near the residence of Mr. R. L. Hubbard, to whom it belongs; the height is about 4 feet; the diameter 30 feet; the central part has been completely dug away.

There is a small mound west of the road near Keownville, about nine miles north-east of New Albany, Union Co., which has been partially opened. A camp-site or burying-ground three miles south-west of New Albany shows numerous crude hammer-stones, mortars, and other artifacts. Here was found the large brass kettle containing a quantity of late ornaments and implements, described in the chapter on post-Columbian material.

About Tupelo, Lee Co., and in adjacent counties, Indian graves of comparatively recent date are encountered. These sometimes contain objects of silver, bronze, and iron, even of glass and chinaware. In 1916, the workmen grading for the new home of Mr. Robert Clark two miles south of Tupelo encountered human bones and trade beads.

---

[1]Moore: Aborig. Sites on Tenn. River, Philadelphia, 1915, p. 234.

About Tupelo are also remains of ponds or reservoirs on tops of hills, which are said to have been found there by the oldest white inhabitants, and which are called "Indian reservoirs." Mr. William Robins showed me one on his farm about a mile south of Tupelo and spoke of three others within his knowledge.

Some interesting material was obtained from a grave near Nettleton, and presented to the Survey by the Hansell family. Here there is a large camp-site heavily strewn with fragments of shells, pottery, and stone.

Several mounds and burial fields are reported in the vicinity of Aberdeen, Monroe Co. Mr. Ben H. McFarland gave the Survey a small collection of material from this territory.

Samuel A. Agnew, of Guntown, Lee Co., writing to the Smithsonian Institution[1] in January, 1868, mentions a number of mounds in the north-eastern part of the state, a list of which is here given for record:

No. 1, 10 ft. high, on land of Joseph Agnew, on Camp Creek, south-eastern Tippah Co.

No. 2, about 10 ft. high, 6 miles west of Ellistown, Pontotoc Co., near James Wiley's.

No. 3, 6 or 8 ft. high, 5 miles south-east of New Albany, in Pontotoc Co., near John M. Simpson's; contained human bones.

No. 4, on north side of Tallahatchie bottom on road from New Albany to Ripley [Union Co.]; top flattened for a residence.

No. 5, 10 to 15 ft. high, between Butchiecunifila and Oconitahatchie Creeks, about 10 miles south-west of New Albany, near William Parks's; quadrangular, with flat top.

---

[1] Agnew: Ann. Rept. of Smiths. Inst. for 1867, Washington, 1868, pages 404, 405.

No. 6, in Tishomingo Creek bottom, 5 miles west of Guntown, Lee Co., near Dr. Selman's; area of summit from a quarter to a half acre.

No. 7, 10 ft. high, on same creek, near Duncan Clark's.

No. 8, 10 ft. high, in same vicinity, near T. A. Sullivan's.

No. 9, on Fane place, in same neighborhood, surface cultivated; silver thimble plowed up on it in 1860.

No. 10, near Birmingham, Lee Co., on Longbridge farm, surface cultivated, dug into 8 or 10 years ago, yielding pieces of pottery. Silver ear-rings taken from ancient graves nearby.

No. 11, 2 miles above Baldwin [Prentiss Co. ?], 50 yards from the Mobile and Ohio railroad, of considerable size, dug into.

No. 12, 8 ft. high, 6 miles south-east of no. 11, on Michenor's, near Manatachie Creek.

No. 13, large mound near Knight's mill, Lee Co., with dwelling and well on it.

No. 14, 8 ft. high, 2 miles east of Ellistown. Union Co., near Dr. Maas.

No. 15, 8 or 10 ft. high, 1 mile south of Guntown, Lee Co., on Mean's farm, cultivated.

No. 16, group of 7 or 8 mounds, in Twenty-mile Creek bottom, 8 to 15 miles east of Guntown.

No. 17, mound reported in Yorribie Creek bottom, 3 miles south of Birmingham, on John A. McNiel's place, 100 ft. high [!].

No. 18, two other large mounds near no. 17 in the same creek bottom.

Agnew also mentions seeing nearly twelve years earlier, between John's Creek and Friendship Church in Pontotoc Co., remains of ancient ditches or embankments enclosing plots of ground in the shape of parallelograms, which he did not examine closely.

STONE-HEAPS OR CAIRNS.

In March, 1918, in company with Dr. Lowe, State Geologist, and Mr. Will Ticer, I examined seven stone-heaps in the vicinity of Dumas, Tippah Co., in the hills forming the head-waters of the Hatchie and the Tallahatchie.

On a high ridge five or six miles north-east of Dumas, ten miles west of Booneville, and fourteen miles east by

FIG. 4. Stone-heap or cairn in the Hatchie Hills, Tippah Co., height 4 feet, 1918. C. S. B.

south-east of Ripley, we examined a fine cairn or stone-heap, located directly on one of the Ripley-Booneville roads (fig. 4). It is about 4 feet high and elliptical in shape, the longer axis east and west being 34 feet, the shorter north and south being 25 feet. It stands on a very sharp ridge, commanding a view of five to eight miles to the west thru a valley. The heap is made of small pieces of iron sandstone, which is abundant in the vicinity. These pieces seem to show no signs of artificial shaping. Holes in the top of the cairn show that it has been entered. Mr. Joe H. Bartlett, our excellent guide, says he has known the cairn for fifty years.

There is a second cairn about one mile east or southeast of the first. The average height is about 4 feet and the axes 34 feet and 30 feet, the longer axis being north-east by south-west. This cairn has a longitudinal opening thru the middle, from which a skeleton is said to have been taken fifteen or twenty years ago. The stones and everything are of same character as in the preceding heap.

Three-fourths of a mile from Noah Morgan's shop twelve miles west of Booneville is a tall isolated peak commanding a fine view in almost every direction. On the very top is a cairn five feet or more high, of iron sandstone. It has been opened to the bottom. The diameter is perhaps slightly smaller than in the case of the other two. It is a beautiful cairn with beautiful location, but unfortunately mutilated.

Another quite small cairn is on a round (possibly artificial) hill-top. This heap is probably artificial, tho that is not so certain as in the preceding cases.

A fifth cairn, quite small, is found near Mr. Bartlett's house.

A sixth cairn, small and typical, near Mr. Bartlett's, is probably two feet high and 18 or 20 feet in diameter. The situation is rather low down on the hill slope. The stones have been pretty well cleared from the surface of the hillside for some distance about the cairn.

The seventh cairn is situated on a high hill just east of the ditched channel of the Hatchie River about a mile or a mile and a half south of Mr. Bartlett's. This one was apparently of about the size of the first and second or a little larger, but has been badly torn up. A large tree seems to have been growing in the edge of it. It is located high up on the hill but not on the very highest point.

The seven stone-heaps or cairns which we examined that day had all been disturbed. Mr. Bartlett, who has lived all his life of sixty-two years in the vicinity, says he knows of probably half a dozen more, all of which have been opened.

Mr. J. E. Pearce of Ripley tells me that he knows of several stone-heaps in Tippah Co., one twelve miles north of Ripley on his father's farm.

Wailes[1] made the following note in 1854: "A few miles north of Ripley in Tippah Co., on a ridge where ferruginous sandstone abounds, fulgorites are numerous, and appear to have been collected, with other fragments of the rock, and piled up so as to form a mound, supposed to be one of the monumental tumuli of the aborigines, and similar in character to the cairns of Scotland."

Two stone mounds or stone-heaps along with other interesting mounds are reported in Alcorn Co., about twenty miles south-west of Corinth and near Kossuth.

A letter received in July, 1926, as the proofs of this book were being read, tells of stone mounds or cairns, 3 to 5 feet high, five miles from Belmont, Tishomingo Co.

Further investigation of the cairns of north-east Mississippi should be made. It is a pity that so many of them have been mutilated.

THE INGOMAR MOUNDS.

There is an interesting group of earth-works near Ingomar in Union County, (fig. 5), tho much of its former character has been destroyed by cultivation and exploration. This ancient monument is located about one mile south-west from the station in Ingomar and is within the corporation of that town, its more exact location being the south-east quarter of sec. 12 and the north-east quarter of sec. 13 of T. 8 S, R. 2 E. It is a short distance north of Okanitahatchie Creek.

---

[1]Wailes: Agriculture and Geology of Miss., Jackson, Miss., 1854, p. 220.

This group of earth-works was explored in 1885 by Gerard Fowke and a full account published by Cyrus Thomas[1] in 1894. That account is condensed in the following description:

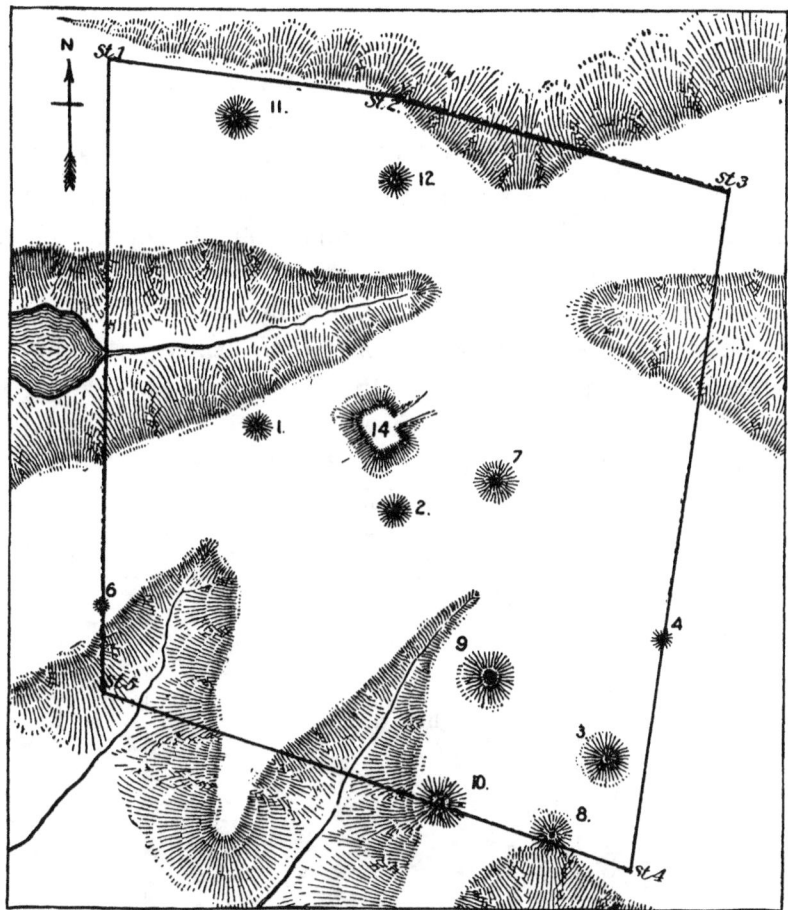

FIG. 5. Ingomar mounds, Union Co., area of enclosure about 70 acres. From 12th Ann. Rept. of Bu. of Am. Ethn., 1894, p. 268.

There are fourteen mounds belonging to the group, twelve of which are together, the other two (not shown in the figure) being one east and the other west, about half a

---

[1] 12th Ann. Report of the Bu. of Ethn., Washington, 1894, pages 267-78.

mile from the large mound, which is the most prominent of the group. The general level of the field is about 50 feet above the creek bottoms to the north and south.

The large mound, no. 14, is a flat-topped quadrilateral. At the bottom, the sides beginning with the south-east measure 153, 210, 177, and 234 feet; on the top 87, 124, 94, 119 feet. From these measurements it will be seen that the slope of the sides is not uniform. On the north-east side is a graded way 20 feet wide at the top and running out 45 feet from the base. This figure, 20 feet, probably represents its original width on top along the whole length, tho it is now much worn down. The height of the mound is 27 feet.

The smaller mounds were located by bearings from the center of the large mound, but the distances to all except 11 and 12 were measured from the south corner; for 11 and 12 the measurements were from the north corner. Mounds 5 and 13 are not shown on the plot.

Mound number	Bearing in degrees	Distance in feet	Diameter in feet	Height in feet
1	N. 88 W.	352	64	14
2	S. 10½ E.	165	100	4
3	S. 34½ E.	1056	120	6
4	S. 53½ E.	891	54	2
5	S. 80 E.	half mile	50	4
6	S. 58 W.	792	28	3
7	S. 66½ E.	330	120	7
8	S. 23 E.	1155	120	6
9	S. 23½ E.	693	150	7
10	S. 9½ E.	990	160	8
11	N. 24½ W.	891	120	4
12	N. 2½ E.	561	90	3
13	N. 70 W.	half mile		plowed level

All the mounds except the first have been plowed over until they are probably 3 to 5 feet lower than when built.

Before the soil had been cultivated an embankment could be traced around the twelve central mounds which was about 2 feet high and ten feet wide, with a ditch on the outside entirely around. The ditch was mostly and in some places entirely filled up. At present no trace of it remains and the embankment can be seen only for a few rods on the west and north sides, where it has not been plowed over. It was cut thru in several places and showed no trace of wood; this however is not positive evidence that no palisades existed, for it may have been washed down farther than the posts would have been sunk, the area being much worn by drains. The earth forming it is the same as the surrounding soil, and was probably thrown inward from the ditch.

The line of the wall is shown as it was traced out by Mr. Parks, the first permanent settler of the country, and may not be correct, especially on the southern line; as laid down here it runs over mounds 8 and 10. Beginning at the northwest corner the bearings and measurements of the earth-wall are as follows:

From station	Bearing in degrees	Distance in feet
1 to 2	S. 83 E.	792
2 to 3	S. 74 E.	957
3 to 4	S. 7¾ W.	1930
4 to 5	N. 77¾ W.	1505
5 to 1	N. 1 E.	1937

The enclosure is thus virtually a quadrilateral with the north boundary 1749 feet long and containing about 70 acres.

In the space inclosed by mounds 3, 4, and 9 is a cemetery, as shown by the bones and numerous fragments of pottery plowed up. Some arrow-points, beads, and a number of pitted stones were found scattered about on the surface. The arrow-points are all small and chipped from water-worn pebbles of jasper. With one skeleton exhumed here were found an iron pipe, some silver ornaments, copper beads, wrought nails, and a piece of glass.

A pond of 5 or 6 acres begins at the western line of the

embankment. The earth put into the larger mound was probably taken from this place, as all the different sorts of earth used in the mounds are to be found in the field or adjacent swamps.

In exploring the mounds the dirt was in every case removed down to the original soil and far enough outwardly to make it certain that the limit of the mound was reached. Trenches varying in width from 6 to 10 feet were carried to the center and space cleared out about the center sufficient to show that nothing of interest remained.

Mound 1, located west of the large central mound, was the most prominent of the smaller ones. Four trenches were led to the center of this mound (fig. 166 in the Bureau report). In it were found human skeletons, shell beads, fragments of thick red pottery, ashes, charcoal, traces of wood, quartz pebbles, and holes below the surface level filled with ooze. The arrangement of the earth in this mound indicates that the original mound was much smaller than it is now and that the skeleton in the ashes was at the center. Afterward the mound was added to on the eastern side. The lenticular masses show that the dirt had been carried in baskets or skins and thrown in without any attempt at stratification in the older part of the mound. The masses were from 12 to 18 inches across and from 4 to 6 inches thick. The lower side, as they lay in the mound, was always darker in color than the upper side. Occasionally a little charcoal or a fragment of bone or pottery occurred in the mound.

In mound 2 nothing was found except a small piece of pottery of very neat design that had probably been dumped in with the dirt. The dirt was in layers of regular thickness, as tho it had been spread when deposited. On the south-east edge was a layer of mingled dirt and charcoal 6.5 feet across, from 2 to 4 inches in thickness; a large amount of broken pottery was found scattered thru it, but no ashes.

At a distance of 75 feet west of the center of mound 3 was a fire-place, on the original surface, covered with a foot of dirt that had been washed down from the mound. Along with pieces of pottery and animal bones was a piece of iron that had apparently been a brace for a saddle-bow; this was 8 inches under the top of the ashes and below most of the pottery found. In the trench on the west side was found one blade of a pair of scissors. Three feet above the surface at the center was an ash bed, 6 inches thick in the middle, 6 feet in diameter, curving upward or dish-shaped and running to an edge on every side. It rested directly upon earth that had been dumped like that in the first mound, and was in very thin layers as tho many successive deposits had been made and spread out. Within an inch of the bottom was a small piece of greenish glass, apparently broken from a glass bottle. Resting upon the ashes, tho of less extent, was a mass 12 inches thick of charcoal, dirt, ashes, and broken pottery, in which lay an iron knife and a thin silver plate stamped with the Spanish coat of arms (figure 173 in the Bureau report). At the top was a thin layer of charcoal where a fire had been extinguished. There was a want of conformity between this mass and the surrounding dirt, which shows it may have been of later origin; that the mound had been opened after its completion and afterward restored to its former shape; but the bed of ashes was undoubtedly as old as the mound itself, so that altho the iron knife and silver plate offer no positive proof as to age, the piece of glass is strong evidence that the mound was constructed after its builders had dealings with the whites. It may be remarked that this group is located in the area occupied by the Chickasaws.

Mound 4 was made thruout of a heavy gray clay, such as forms the ground to the north of it. The embankment ran, according to local belief, directly over this mound; it was therefore closely examined for any signs of palisades, but none were found; nor is there now the slightest indication here of either wall or ditch.

Mound 5, not shown in the plot, is outside the enclosure to the east. A wide trench thru it exposed thirteen skulls, with a few fragments of other bones. They were all within ten feet of the center and arranged in three layers, the first on the original surface, the second nearly two feet above, and the third at about the same distance above that. The skulls belonged to persons of different ages, from the child whose first teeth were beginning to appear, to the aged individual whose teeth were worn to the gums. With the oldest was a burnt clay pipe, the only relic found in the mound. The bones were put in without regard to position; a skull and a rib, for example, or a femur and a jawbone lying together. All the skulls were of one shape and that very like the modern Indian skull.

Mound 6, like mound 4, was on the supposed line of embankment, but no trace of wood in the mound or of a ditch outside could be seen. Probably mounds 4 and 6 were at a break in the embankment forming a passage way thru it.

Mound 7 showed the same marks of dumping as in mounds 1 and 3. More charcoal and burnt dirt were found in this than in any other mound opened, but they seem to have been thrown in simply because it was convenient. The arrangement and material of the mound show that dirt had been carried in from different places at the same time. One burial, apparently intrusive, was found.

Mound 8 was built partly on the slope of the ravine to the west. Near the center were some shreds of a coarse woven cloth. Six feet north of the center, in the original soil, was a hole 18 inches across and 14 inches deep, the sides burnt hard as a brick, filled with charcoal and dirt. Seven feet north-east of the center was a similar but smaller hole. The gray layer of clay at the bottom of the mound was undisturbed over both these spots, showing that the mound was built after this part of the field had been occupied.

The remaining mounds were not opened. Of those opened only no. 1 and no. 5 were found to be burial mounds.

Such was the Ingomar group of earth-works in 1885 as described in the report of the Bureau of Ethnology. The present writer made a brief visit to this ancient site in September, 1918. The great central mound is still almost intact, a fine example of the truncated pyramid type. The sides are very steep and difficult of ascent. The approach or ramp on the north-east side is not so prominent as in the early account. Mounds 1 and 7 do not appear to have been entirely cultivated since the explorations, the excavations being still clearly traced. Mound 2 is in cultivation and quite flat. The location of the pond on the west is evident, tho the land is in cultivation. Nothing of the wall or moat was seen from the central mound.

IN LOWNDES COUNTY.

In 1901 Mr. Clarence B. Moore made a trip of investigation down the Tombigbee River, the greater part of the territory covered being in Alabama. He lists the following mounds and camp-sites in Lowndes Co., Mississippi[1]:

Mound at Butler's Gin, James Cox.
Mounds at Chowder Spring, Mustin, and Halbert and Vaughn.
Mound at Halbert Lake, P. M. Halbert.
Camp-sites at Moore's Bluff, J. W. T. Hairston, and W. Snowton.
Camp-sites at Blue Rock Landing, A. B. Mybrick.
Mound and camp-sites near Wild Cat Bend, J. W. T. Hairston.

---

[1] Moore: Certain Aborig. Remains on the Tombigbee River, Philadelphia, 1901.

Camp-site at Union Bluff, T. B. Franklin.
Mound opposite Union Bluff, J. W. T. Hairston.
Camp-site at Jim Creek, William Baldwin.

Several of these are described at some length by Mr. Moore, whose descriptions are here condensed:

There is an oblong mound in a cultivated field about 200 paces south-south-east from Butler's Landing, Lowndes Co., on property of Mr. James Cox. It is 8 feet high, with basal dimensions of 128 feet and 180 feet, and plateau dimensions of 80 feet and 137 feet. It has houses upon it. No investigation was allowed.

In a cultivated field, about 250 yards north-north-east from the Chowder Spring Landing, on property of William S. Mustin, Esq., is a mound of circular outline, 5 feet 8 inches high, 80 feet across the base. Part has been under cultivation; on the other portion is a small log cabin. Considerable excavation in various parts showed the mound to be of sandy clay. This mound was probably domiciliary.

About 100 yards north-north-east from the preceding, in woods bordering the field, is a mound of sandy clay on property of Messrs. Halbert and Vaughn. Wash of freshets has made its outline irregular. It is 5 feet 3 inches high and 90 feet by 104 feet across the base. The mound was largely dug into by us to the base, including central parts, resulting in the finding of several bunched burials and a number of isolated bones. One small rude clay pot with a loop-shaped handle at either side of the rim was found unassociated.

In the Burrell field, about one-half mile in a straight course north-east from Wild Cat Bend, is a mound on the property of J. W. T. Hairston, Esq. It is of clayey sand, 3 feet 2 inches high, and 60 feet by 70 feet across the base. This mound was largely excavated without result. In the same field was a dwelling-site, apparently, in which one skeleton was found.

The Coleman mound, well known through all the district, probably originally was a parallelogram in shape, but the washing of high water has made the outline irregular. It is about one mile in a northerly direction from Union Bluff, Lowndes Co., on property of J. W. T. Hairston, Esq. It is of the regular domiciliary type. At present there are a number of houses on it.

IN OKTIBBEHA COUNTY.

Prof. W. N. Logan describes briefly several mounds and burial-grounds in Oktibbeha Co.; from his report[1] the following account is condensed:

One mound is located on the W. D. Walker place in the western part of Starkville; it is now only a few feet high and about 30 feet across, tho no doubt formerly much higher; Indian pottery, arrow-heads, and bones have been taken from excavations made in this mound.

An Indian burial-ground, from which pottery, arrow-heads, and skeletons have been exhumed, is situated on a small divide on the Aiken farm, two miles north of Starkville. A similar burial-ground is situated about three miles north-west of the Aiken place. A third is located on the south side of Catalpha Creek about two miles south-east of Sessumsville, on the Askew farm.

A mound 15 or 20 feet high and about 90 feet in diameter is located on the White farm about half a mile north of the junction of Walker and Hollis Creeks; from it artifacts and skeletons have been taken. A large mound, from which bones, the teeth of a mammoth, beads, and other relics are said to have been taken, is situated on the north side of Lake Harmon. An Indian battle-field and burial-ground has been found on the Curry farm a few miles north-west of Starkville.

---
[1]Logan: Geology of Oktibbeha Co., 1904, page 20.

NANIH WAIYA.

The famous Nanih Waiya, which Halbert designates the sacred mound of the Choctaws, stands in Winston County about ten miles south-east of Noxapater (fig. 6). The name signifies in Choctaw "slanting hill." It is a typical rectangular mound, 218 feet long by 140 feet wide at the base, thus covering seven-tenths of an acre. The axis is north-west by south-east. The dimensions of the flat top are 132 feet by 56 feet, the area being one-sixth of an acre. The height is 22 feet, in some places nearly 25 feet. The slopes of the mound are covered with trees; the top seems to have been cultivated. A heavy rain set in during my survey of the site, July 6, 1917, and prevented a completion of my study.

I visited the site again on August 3, 1923, and located one section of the earth-wall or rampart near the residence, more than half a mile from the great mound. This section of the wall is now 2.5 to 4 feet high and about a hundred yards long. The resident on the farm states that four sections of the earth-wall still exist. The low mound about 250 yards to the north-east of the great mound is now about 7 or 8 feet high, and very much spread by cultivation. Artifacts are scarce.

The great Nanih Waiya retains its original height and is still in a state of excellent preservation, tho the small mounds and the wall have been much reduced. This historic mound should be preserved for all time to come.

An early account of Nanih Waiya is that of B. L. C. Wailes, who visited the mound on the fifth of December, 1854. The following data are arranged from his manuscript field notes of that date (page 151):

I visited the Indian mounds and entrenchment in the fork of Nanawaya and Tallahaya, identified by tradition as the place of origin or the birth-place of the Choctaws, who held it in superstitious reverence as their mother. The height of the principal mound is at least 50 feet; it is a parallelogram with

FIG. 6. Nanih Waiya or Slanting Hill, Winston Co. height 22 feet. Photograph by B. N. Powell; courtesy of W. A. Love.

corners rounded by plowing; dimensions 180 or 200 feet east and west by perhaps 100 or 105 feet north and south.

Some 200 yards to the north of the high mound is a cone covering more extent, but only about 10 feet high. Some small mounds nearly obliterated are between the two large ones.

The wall or entrenchment goes around three sides of the mound and in many places in the woods has trees of 4 feet diameter growing upon it. The height in the most elevated places is near 10 feet, the width 30 or 40 feet; in other places it dwindles away to a slight embankment; in the clear land east of the mounds it can scarcely be traced owing to the constant plowing. Many gaps or gate-ways have been left in the wall, some of them 100 feet wide. The enclosure embraces about a section or square mile.

Such is Wailes's account of this ancient monument in 1854. The common tendency to over-estimate the height of mounds may be noted in both his and the later account by Halbert[1], which I here quote at some length:

"Nanih Waiya is situated on the west side of Nanih Waiya Creek, about 50 yards from it, in the southern part of Winston County, and about 400 yards from the Neshoba County line. The mound is oblong in shape, lying north-west and south-east, and about 40 feet in height. Its base covers about an acre. Its summit, which is flat, has an area of one-fourth of an acre.

"The mound stands on the south-eastern edge of a circular rampart, which is about a mile and a half in circumference. In using the word 'circular' reference is made to the original form of the rampart, about one-half of which is utterly obliterated by the plow, leaving only a semi-circle.

---

[1]Halbert: Nanih Waiya, the Sacred Mound of the Choctaws, Pub. of the Miss. Hist. Scciety, Vol. II, Oxford, Miss., 1899, p. 223.

This rampart is not, or rather was not, a continuous circle, so to speak, as it has along at intervals a number of vacant places or gaps, ranging from 20 to 50 yards wide. According to Indian tradition, there were originally 18 parts or sections of the rampart, with the same number of gaps. Ten of these sections still remain, ranging from 50 to 150 yards in length. All the sections near the mound have long since been leveled by the plow, and in other places some of the sections have been much reduced. But on the north, where the rampart traverses a primeval forest, it is still five feet high and twenty feet broad at the base. The process of obliteration has been very great since 1877, when the writer first saw Nanih Waiya. Some of the sections that could then be clearly traced in the field on the west have now utterly disappeared. In regard to the rampart, it was, no doubt, surmounted by palisades. As to the gaps in the rampart, the writer is convinced that these gaps were left designedly as places for the erection of wooden forts or towers, as additional protection to the town.

"About 250 yards north of Nanih Waiya is a small mound, evidently a burial mound, as can safely be stated from the numerous fragments of human bones that have been exhumed from it by the plow and the hoe. The great number of stone relics, mostly broken, scattered for hundreds of yards around Nanih Waiya, shows that it was the site of prehistoric habitations. In addition to this the bullets and other relics of European manufacture evidence the continuity of occupancy down within the historic period.

"The magnitude of these ancient works—the mound and the rampart—together with the legendary traditions connected with them, leads one irresistibly to the conviction that this locality was the great center of Choctaw population during the prehistoric period. It should here be stated that the symmetry of the mound has been somewhat marred by a tunnel which was cut into it in the summer of 1896 by some treasure-seekers, who vainly hoped to unearth some wonderful bonanza from out the deep bosom of Nanih Waiya.

"All the modern Choctaws living in Mississippi look upon Nanih Waiya as the birth place and cradle of their race. She is 'ishki chito', 'the great mother'. In the very center of the mound, they say, ages ago, the Great Spirit created the first Choctaws, and through a hole or cave, they crawled forth into the light of day. Some say that only one pair was created, but others say that many pairs were created. Old Hopahkitubbee (Hopakitobi), who died several years ago in Neshoba County, was wont to say that after coming forth from the mound the freshly-made Choctaws were very wet and moist, and the Great Spirit stacked them along on the rampart so that the sun could dry them."

The reader is referred to the version of the creation legend quoted later on in this book in the chapter on post-Columbian material.

J. F. H. Claiborne[1], the historian, who in 1842-3 presided over a Board of Commissioners established by the United States to inquire into and adjudicate the claims of the Choctaws, records that "all the very aged Choctaws, on being interrogated as to where they were born, insisted that they came out of Nana-Wyyah. Many of the Choctaws examined by the Commission regarded this mound as the mother or birth-place of the tribe, and more than one claimant declared that he would not quit the country as long as the Nana-Wyyah remained."

SOME SCATTERED MOUNDS.

A handsome little mound about three-fourths of a mile south of Coffeeville, Yalobusha County, may be seen from the train, if the traveler looks to the east. It is about 11 feet

---

[1]Claiborne: Miss. as a Province, Territory and State, Jackson, 1880, p. 519.

high and 200 feet in circumference at the base, and stands upon level ground.

Near the Culley homestead about four miles east of Madison station, Madison Co., and about twelve miles from Jackson on the Natchez Trace, is a mound, which has been spread and lowered much by plowing. It is only 3 or 4 feet high. I saw a number of bones, teeth, pebbles, and flakes of flint, but no potsherds. Many skeletons are said to have been plowed from the mound.

At Pocahontas, Hinds Co., there are two mounds, the larger in plain view from the railroad. This large mound is elliptical or oblong in shape, being 600 feet in periphery at base. The plateau is level and measures 100 feet long by 50 feet wide, the longer axis being approximately north and south. It is without trees and has been cultivated. The height is apparently 26 to 30 feet. The sides have not been cultivated; they are steep and covered with trees. No depression corresponding to the great quantity of earth in the mound was found. Fragments of pottery are abundant; flakes of flint are apparently few. Human bones are reported to have been plowed up near the mound.

The other mound at Pocahontas is diametrically across town from the one just described and stands about 400 yards away from it, just back of the Baptist church. It is circular in form and much smaller, being about 233 feet in circumference and about 9 feet high. It has been considerably disfigured by digging. Large liquidambers (sweet-gums) and a plane-tree (sycamore) stand on top of it.

The station called Indian Mound near the Alabama line in Clarke Co. takes its name from a group of small aboriginal mounds. I saw five in 1917, ranging from 20 to 36 inches high; they are round and uniform in character. The little boy who conducted me about said there was another near their house. He reported that he and his cousin had dug a skeleton from one of the mounds. I saw very few fragments of artifacts of any kind. This group of small uniform mounds is unique.

ON THE GULF COAST.

Shell-heaps as well as other mounds exist along the southern coast of Mississippi. These shell-mounds are not so large or so rich in artifacts as those of Florida. In 1916 I made a hurried trip along the coast and located a few of these ancient refuse-heaps.

On the farm of Mr. Joseph Mauffray two and a half miles from the town of Bay St. Louis, Hancock Co., where Jordan River runs into the bay, I saw a number of shell-heaps, apparently from 8 to 12 inches thick, on some of which were found fragments of pottery. These heaps are often quite near the edge of the water. From one of these a skeleton was said to have been recently exhumed. Other large shell-heaps are reported in the vicinity, some much thicker. There are still a number of mixed-blood Indians about here and at Dillville, some of whom still speak Choctaw.

Near Delisle, Harrison Co., there is a fine example of a large artificial shell-bank, tho much of it has been hauled away for road material. It is a hundred yards long or more and from 2 to 6 feet high. Human remains seem scarce. There are two other large shell-heaps in this vicinity, one near the mouth of Wolf River, the other two miles west of Delisle on the bay at what is known as Shell Beach. A mile or two east of Delisle there is an earth mound perhaps 14 or 16 feet high.

At Biloxi, Harrison Co., and in that vicinity there formerly existed a number of shell-heaps, some of which have since been completely or partially obliterated. Dr. William G. Hinsdale made some investigations among these about the year 1886. There were found many fragments of pottery; many disks of clay, some of which were perforated; relatively few artifacts of shell; no celts. The following account of the remains about Biloxi is taken from personal letters to the author:

On the channel side of Point Cadet near the Biloxi canning factory are scattered hearths and their accompanying shell-mounds. Excavation brought to light many fine fragments of pottery, one bone awl, and a few other artifacts.

At the extreme tip of Point Cadet are the remains of a large shell-heap now mostly washed away. The beach is paved with shells and pottery, and after a storm many fine pieces are cast up by the sea. In front of the place at low tide may be seen many stumps of trees.

Just back of the Biloxi light-house is a small rivulet upon the farther bank of which is an acre or more covered by a thin deposit of oyster and gnathodon shells; in some places it is between three and four feet thick. There are also a few low refuse-heaps overgrown with cedar trees. In places the ashes are deep, especially adjoining the hearths. An hour or more spent in excavating resulted in the discovery of quantities of broken clay vessels, turtle and alligator bones, scales and bones of fishes, a shell bead and one other worked shell object.

A sand mound near this shell-heap was excavated some years ago by some one who is said to have obtained entire clay vessels which were buried with the skeletons.

On the Back Bay is a shell-heap, which owing to the encroachment of the tides has been partly washed away, leaving a vertical exposure. There are many hearths of calcined shell about three feet in diameter. There were found fragments of clay vessels, pottery disks about the size of a silver dollar, and in the water in front of the deposit stemmed arrow-points of jasper.

Near the western extremity on the north side of Deer

Island, off the coast of Biloxi, is a long irregular shell-heap varying in thickness from a few inches to 15 feet. The thickest portion is at the east end, where it is also widest (about 150 feet). About 300 feet west of the ship-way is a circular hut-ring about 20 feet in diameter. Excavations at the summit of the deposit near the ship-way brought to light great quantities of human bones. Relics were not abundant and for each object found a ton of shells had to be turned over. Among the finds were clay disks and bird-heads, and perforated oyster shells.

Mr. James Brodie who lives north of Biloxi across the bay has done collecting in this vicinity; he tells me that he has sent much material to Edinburgh, Scotland.

Mr. Scuyler Poitevent conducted me to an Indian shell-bank not far from his house on the bay near Ocean Springs, Jackson Co. This heap is 18 inches deep, and is situated directly on the edge of an inlet, which has washed away much of the heap. Fragments of pottery were in evidence.

Mr. Clarence B. Moore[1] undertook in 1905 the investigation of mounds from the south-eastern corner of the state along Mississippi sound, but abandoned the work at Biloxi because of poor success in finding artifacts and because his advance agent reported no mounds of importance west of that place. The mounds investigated were:

Mound near Mary Walker Bayou, Jackson Co.
Seven mounds near Graveline Bayou, Jackson Co.
Three mounds near Belle Fontaine Point, Jackson Co.
Mound on Tchula Cabawfa River, Harrison Co.

A summary of Moore's work on these mounds follows:

On the south side of Mary Walker Bay near its mouth, in Jackson Co., is the residence of Mr. David Saucier. About 100 yards in a north-westerly direction from the house is a

---

[1]Moore: Certain Aborig. Remains on Mobile Bay and Miss. Sound, Phila., 1905.

mound of sand of circular outline, 3.5 feet in height and 56 feet in diameter. A thoro investigation showed this mound to have been domiciliary in character.

Back from the bluff that overlooks the sound at this place, not far from the eastern side of Graveline Bayou, are seven mounds of sand, on property of Mr. J. I. Ford. All these mounds are circular in outline with the exception of the largest, which is oblong, with basal dimensions of 93 feet east and west and 81 feet north and south, and height of about 6 feet. The summit-plateau measures 50 feet east and west and 38 feet north and south. Each of the seven mounds was carefully examined without discovery of human remains. A few bits of earthen-ware were found, only one bearing decoration.

About two miles in a north-westerly direction from Belle Fontaine Point, Jackson Co., are three mounds on property of Mr. S. G. Ramsey. One of these mounds, used as a modern place of burial, was not investigated, but as it resembles the other two, which investigation showed to be domiciliary, it is doubtless of the same kind.

A mound in Harrison Co. said to be on state land, stands in the pine woods about six miles north of Biloxi, being about 200 yards from the eastern bank of Tchula Cabawfa River and about half a mile above Hawley's Bluff on the opposite side of the river. This mound is of clay and has a rounded but irregular outline, with basal diameters of 450 feet north and south and 290 feet east and west, and height of 11 feet. This mound, evidently domiciliary, was dug into to a reasonable extent without material result.

IN THE VICINITY OF NATCHEZ.

Adams County including the region about Natchez is rich in Indian legend and history and likewise in Indian monuments and remains; here lived in the days of the early colonists the celebrated Natchez tribe.

Mounds are abundant. At Foster, the first railroad station north-east of Natchez, there is a considerable mound with a residence upon it. In the northern part of the county are the Anna group and the Selsertown earth-works. Twelve miles south of Natchez stand the mounds which mark the site of the White Apple village. Skeletons have been unearthed on the Washaway plantation on the Homochitto near Kingston in the southern part of the county.

Dickeson[1] describes from personal observation in 1842 and 1843 the Bernard mounds three miles east of Natchez, near St. Catherine's Creek, the Quitman mounds eight miles north of Natchez on the low ground near the river, and the Lewis mounds ten miles from Natchez, and mentions many others in his list of specimens.

There are several good collections of Indian relics in and about Natchez, and many pieces have been taken from this vicinity to museums outside the state.

Moore investigated in 1910 a small mound near Ellis Cliff in the southern part of Adams County, some distance below Natchez, and gives the following account[2]:

"About one mile in a southerly direction from Ellis Cliff, on rising ground forming a part of the hills that here approach the river, was the remnant of a small mound which has been dug into previous to our coming. Investigation of the parts remaining yielded two burials and parts of two others. One skeleton lay closely flexed on the back, the knees being drawn up toward the chin. Another was closely flexed on the right side. Two skeletons which had been interred side by side, closely flexed on the right side, had lost heads and shoulders by the making of another grave in aboriginal times. No artifacts were present with these burials."

The White Apple mounds are situated on Second Creek

---

[1] Culin: The Dickeson Col. of Am. Antiq., Phila., 1900.
[2] Moore: Some Aborig. Sites on Miss. River, Phila., 1911, p. 377.

in Adams County about 12 miles south of Natchez, not far from Laurel Hill and the Cliffs. I visited these mounds on August 15, 1916, when the vegetation was very rank and the conditions for observation least favorable. The two mounds still standing are of the conical type. The first mound measured 500 feet in circumference at the base; the second measured 131 feet in longer diameter on the top. This second mound stands directly on the bank of the creek and much of it has been cut away by the water. The heights of these two mounds were not measured, but were estimated at 12 to 18 feet. About the mounds are still to be seen numerous fragments of flint and pottery.

Dr. M. W. Dickeson, who visited the White Apple village site in 1844, left a somewhat fanciful drawing of three mounds, since published by the University of Pennsylvania[1]. He states that the largest was about 25 feet high and that near it were indications of other small structures.

White Apple village was one of the chief villages of the Natchez Indians and figures prominently in the early history of the settlements about the city of Natchez. The Natchez Indians were first visited by the French in 1682, at which time the tribe probably numbered about 6000 people. They were an agricultural people and had developed considerable skill in the arts. They wove cloth, made excellent pottery and stone implements, and erected mounds of earth. They were sun-worshipers and practiced head-flattening. Their chief was called the great Sun. The Natchez engaged in three wars with the French, the last one in 1729 proving fatal to their nationality; in 1730 they abandoned their villages and were dispersed; a few remained in the vicinity; some were sold into slavery in Santo Domingo; many were received by the Chickasaw tribe and later were further dispersed[2].

[1]Culin: The Dickeson Col. of Am. Antiquities, Philadelphia, 1900.
[2]Handbook of American Indians, Bull. 30, Washington, 1907, 1910.

In 1907, Swanton found five Indians who could still speak the Natchez language, living near Braggs, Oklahoma, then in the Cherokee nation not far from the Creek nation. Most of them could speak also Creek and Cherokee. The oldest of the five, said to have been over 80 years old, died in the spring of 1908[1].

Persons interested in the history of the Natchez Indians should consult such books as Du Pratz's *Histoire de la Louisiane* (1758) and Swanton's *Indian Tribes of the Lower Mississippi Valley* (1911).

The Selsertown earth-work (fig. 7) is located on the Emerald Mound plantation in Adams County near the Jefferson County line, about twelve miles north-east of Natchez. It is about three-quarters of a mile or a mile from the site of the extinct village of Selsertown, and twice that distance from the present railroad station of Stanton. This celebrated prehistoric earth-work is unique in that it consists of a vast elevated plateau on which stand the different mounds. My survey of this ancient site was made in March, 1917, and is as follows:

	At base of plateau	On top of plateau
Length on south side,	670 feet	....
Length on north side,	650 feet	....
Length thru middle,	700 feet	596 feet
Width on east end,	400 feet	300 feet
Width on west end,	500 feet	406 feet
Area of earth-work	7 acres	5 acres

The length thru the middle both at base and on top is greater than on either side. The axis is almost east and west. The elevation of the main plateau varies from 21 to 44 feet, being least on the south side, which ranges from 21 to 23 feet; and greatest on the west end, which reaches 44 feet, not including the tall mound which stands upon the platform at that end. The elevation at the east end is from 24 to 37 feet, not

---

[1]Swanton: Indian Tribes of the Lower Miss. Valley, Bull. 43, Washington, 1911.

including the low mound at that end; at the north side from 26 to 42 feet. These variations are not surprising when it is remembered that the level of the base upon which the plateau stands is quite irregular and that the top is by no means level.

The outline of the plateau was no doubt originally more regular than it is at present, for it has long been in cultivation and erosion has been at work. A deep and wide ravine has eaten far into the northern side of the platform and there are smaller ones on the south and east edges. The

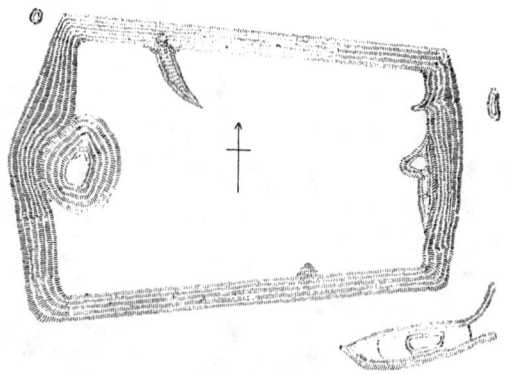

FIG. 7. Selsertown plateau, Adams Co., scale 1 inch to 300 feet.

southern slope and the top of the plateau are now in cultivation; the other three slopes are largely in wood and thickets. On the southern slope near the ravine quantities of burnt earth with cane impressions are to be seen. As already remarked the surface of the plateau is quite uneven.

At present two mounds stand upon the plateau, one at the west end and one at the east end. The one at the west is of the truncated conical type, measuring 475 feet in circumference at base and 28 feet in altitude (fig. 8). The flat top is somewhat elliptical, with the longer axis north and south. It has been cultivated, but is now grown up in small trees. The top has had a deep hole sunk into it. According to Mr. James D. Middleton[1], the last digging was made in behalf of Dr. Joseph Jones of New Orleans, who was not however present in person. The depth reached was not more than 15 or 16 feet, about half the distance to the base of the mound. The result is not known with certainty. Adding the height of the circular mound, 28 feet, to that of the plateau

FIG. 8. Selsertown plateau and mound on the west end of it, looking from the mound on the east end, March, 1917. C. S. B.

at the west, 44 feet, it will be seen that the total height of the earth-work is here 72 feet. The eastern mound is very much smaller than the western and is quite irregular in outline. The main part of it is a rather flat conical mound not more than six or seven feet high; along the eastern edge it takes the form of an embankment and extends at a reduced height some distance toward the south. Here were found the five fine stone pipes pictured in figures 218-226 and other arti-

[1]Twelfth Ann. Rept. of Bu. of Ethn., Washington, 1894, p. 266.

facts. Many fragments of pottery and flint and some small concretions may be seen here.

In the opinion of the present writer, the Selsertown plateau is not to be regarded as entirely artificial. The Amerinds took advantage of a natural elevation and merely shaped it to suit their purposes, the faces being built up and filled in at places and the spurs of the hills being cut away at other places, thereby making the shape of the platform more regular and the slope of the sides steeper. The largest cut is found at the south-east corner, where a depression 60 feet wide runs between the plateau and the unremoved lower part of the spur, making a square turn toward the north at the corner of the platform. Other cuts may be seen at the east end and at the north-west corner. The writer sank many trial-holes on the slopes and on the surface of the plateau to test the character of the soil; in many places made earth was found, but the core of the plateau seems to be original undisturbed loess. An examination would probably show that the great wash on the north side is largely due to a fill at that place.

It is difficult to say now where the original approach or approaches were. The narrow sunken way leading up on the east end near the north-east corner may have been one. A rather gentle inclination at the south-west corner has long been used by the farmers as an approach to the top of the plateau.

Mr. James D. Middleton[1], who made a careful survey of the Selsertown group in 1887 and submitted his findings and drawings to the Bureau of Ethnology, reports two other mounds on the platform, situated near the middle of the north and south margins. They were circular and quite small, the northern one being two feet high, the southern one only a foot and a half high. Squier and Davis[2] forty

---
[1] Twelfth Ann. Rept. of Bu. of Ethn., Washington, 1894, pages 263-7.
[2] Anc. Monuments of the Miss. Valley, Washington, 1848, p. 118.

years earlier, in 1847, reported eight mounds besides the two end mounds; they were regularly placed at various points and measured from 8 to 10 feet in height. They also state that the group was surrounded by a ditch at its base, averaging perhaps 10 feet in depth. This is hardly probable, in the opinion of the present writer, tho there may have been ponds of water at the base.

The Anna or Robson group of mounds is located in

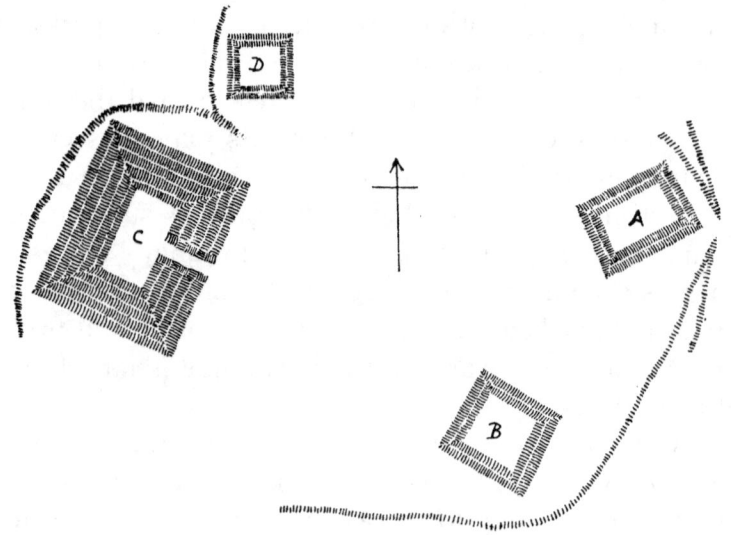

Fig. 9. The Anna or Robson mounds, north of Natchez. Scale 1 inch to 300 ft.

Adams County 10 or 12 miles north of Natchez. There are four of these mounds standing in the loess foothills, just above Anna, the tallest being 50 feet high. The arrangement of the mounds is shown in figure 9. The public road passes between mound A and the other three, cutting away part of mound D. The ground here is uneven. Mounds C and D stand on the edge of the bluff and there are deep ravines behind A and B. Thus the bluffs and ravines practically make an enclosure for this group of mounds.

These four mounds are all of the truncated pyramid type; all are quadrilateral, tho none is exactly square.

Mound A is deeply covered with canes, bushes and briers, so that exact measurements are difficult; the top is about 28 feet above the level, about 114 feet long, 60 feet wide on the south-west and 80 feet on the north-east.

FIG. 10. Tallest Anna mound, C, height 50 ft. Taken March 16, 1917, from mound B. C. S. B.

Mound B is 13 feet high and 100 feet north and south by 90 feet east and west. It has suffered considerably from erosion.

The great mound C (fig. 10) is 50 feet high on the side away from the bluff, that is, at its lowest. The top is flat and covered with canes and other vegetation; the east edge measures 135 feet, the west 127, the north end 72 feet, the south 64. The surface is thus about one-fifth of an acre, which is about the same as the surface of A and likewise of B. The slope of the sides is very steep. There may still be seen the remains of an approach up the eastern side, 75 feet from the south-east corner. The approach is about 10 feet wide and the inclination is somewhat gentler than that of the rest of the mound. This tall mound stands right on the edge of the bluff and would have made an excellent observation tower. The Mississippi River is about two miles distant and is visible from the mound at high water. Several trial-holes were made in the sides of the mound and showed fragments of pottery and bones.

D is the smallest of the four mounds, being only 6 feet high, and measuring about 60 by 75 or 80 feet before being partly cut away by the road. Several trial-holes in this mound as well as the wall exposed by the road revealed numerous fragments of pottery, flakes of flint, and bones. The earth is largely black, and often banded.

From the margin of A to the margin of B is 275 feet; from the margin of B to the margin of C is 530 feet. No one of these mounds has its basal lines oriented exactly with the cardinal points or running parallel with those of any of the other three mounds. The surface of the intervening fields and lots is strewn with many evidences of prehistoric occupation.

In addition to the four large mounds shown in the diagram (fig. 9) there are two other small mounds covered with canes, bushes, and vines beyond the ravine from mound A.

This is a magnificent group of mounds, and should be preserved.

A group of earth-works located a short distance east of Natchez was investigated in 1842 by Dr. M. W. Dickeson[1], a Philadelphia showman and archeologist, whose methods

---

[1]Culin: The Dickeson Col. of Am. Antiq., Philadelphia, 1900, p. 116.

MOUNDS AND EARTH-WORKS.   43

and conclusions were, perhaps not always strictly scientific. His description of the earth-works is condensed as follows, the original drawing being omitted:

On the plantation of Thomas Bernard, three miles east of Natchez and near the margin of the St. Catharine, are several mounds. They are now, after some fifty years cultivation, almost razed to the surface of the ground, with the exception of a few small ones which have been protected by a meagre growth of oak and persimmon. Our attention was first called to three basin-shaped depressions, seventeen feet in diameter and five feet deep, arranged to form a triangle. Cleansing these of their rubbish, we found a large, square, coarse-grained sandstone mortar, hollow on both sides, and later, in each of the other basins, a smaller and less perfect mortar. Several small stone ornaments, four stone beads and eleven arrow-heads were all we discovered in removing the detritus. Similar depressions were discovered, a few months after, at Ellis Cliffs some fifteen miles distant. They also lay close to the side of the St. Catharine and were similarly lined with clay and inlaid with pebbles. In one of them we found several curiously formed stones and a few arrow-points.

Five years prior to our visit Mr. Bernard's' gardener dug up a small mound completely filled with bones in the rear of his garden and about 400 feet from the system of structures.

We next examined the vestiges of two walls (banks) of earth, some thirty-eight yards long, lying parallel to each other, fifteen yards apart. There are two small oval mounds at either end equidistant between. Immense quantities of broken pottery, arrow and javelin points and an occasional ornament of jasper are picked up from the surface. At the eastern end of the banks we dug up two small jars filled with fine large pearls which fell into powder as soon as they became dry. There are two more banks of a crescent shape and eight feet wide and on one side are traces of a ditch six feet wide from which a portion of the material has been taken to construct the segments. West of the basin-shaped depression there seems to have been a large swale or basin, no doubt artificially constructed for a reservoir. A small ravine now cuts through it into the St. Catharine and has to a great extent destroyed its original form. A great many pipes have been found in the vicinity of these structures.

The Quitman mounds, located 8 miles north of Natchez between the Misissippi River and the bluffs, just opposite the lower end of Fairchild's Island, were investigated by Dr. Dickeson in 1843, and his description and drawings were published by the University of Pennsylvania in 1900. According to his map, there are eight mounds in all, one rectangular, the rest circular or oblong; one stands upon the bluff, the others are in the valley. The mounds, or some of them, seem to have been entirely obliterated by immense quantities of soil carried down from the hillsides; they were located by the dark rich loam filled with fragments of human bones, teeth, and pottery.

Thru one of these mounds a trench two feet wide was dug. It contained 24 skeletons, lying on their backs with heads to the east and hands extended along the chests. Their heads were flattened lengthwise. All the mounds in the immediate neighborhood and in the adjoining burial-places in the same bottom contained crania flattened in conical form.

The Lewis mounds, ten miles from Natchez on the plantation of Mr. F. Lewis, were investigated by Dr. Dickeson in July, 1843. Many skeletons and many specimens of pottery were found, as were also shell ornaments and flint projectiles. Good terra-cotta vessels with incised scroll designs are pictured in Culin's plates 14 and 16 (figs. 344 and 345 in this book). Some of the human bones showed burning. The number and size of the mounds comprising this group are not stated.

Other mounds from which Dr. Dickeson enumerated archeological material (now in the museum of the University of Pennsylvania) were: the Chamberlain group above Natchez, mounds on the plantation of Col. Adam Bingamon near Natchez, Kibby's mounds, Ellis Cliff mounds, Stower's mounds, Elliott's mounds, Race Course Mounds, Dr. Dunbar's, William Conner's, Gillespie's, Allen Grafton's, Railey's, Minor's, Mrs. Postlewait's, and a mound at Washington belonging to Col. Wales [Wailes?].

The Ferguson mounds in Jefferson County furnished a number of the artifacts collected by Dr. Dickeson in the early days and now deposited in the museum of the University of Pennsylvania. Dr. Dickeson examined this group in 1846; the following description is condensed from his account of the investigation[1].

The Ferguson mounds are situated on the summit of the range of bluffs bordering on the Mississippi, some eighteen miles above the town of Natchez. The system is composed of seven conical mounds, five of them arranged to form a flattened circle, and the others a short distance above. Immediately in front of them are two large basins, the sides of which are regularly finished. In the centre of these depressions, quantities of skeletons surrounded by curious objects are dug up. Extensive roads diverge from this system of mounds, one touching the great Seltsertown mound.

The four largest mounds stand equidistant from each other, on the summit of the bluff. The largest, fifty-six feet in height, overlooks a series of small lakes between the Mississippi and the bluffs, and commands a view of the river in both directions for many miles, as well as some eight or ten miles across into Louisiana.

---
[1]Culin: The Dickeson Col. of Am. Antiq., Philadelphia, 1900, p. 122.

We divided our force of laborers and set them at work digging into the mound from the top and sides. A short distance brought them to the skeletons, all flatheads. Our time being limited, we paid but little attention to the stratification, and simply endeavored to get as many relics as possible. In the large mound we sunk a shaft eight feet wide and fifteen feet deep. From this mound was excavated a stone pipe (plate 12 of Culin, figure 227 in this book) carved to represent a flathead Indian in a sitting posture holding a pipe in his hands.

In the side of one of the small mounds we found at the head of a skeleton three finely finished vases filled with ashes and curiously wrought ornaments.

I made drawings of several finely carved pipes which were found in the mounds. Their possessors would not part with them. In former times a great number of green stone and syenite axes have been picked up in the adjacent fields, but very few have been found in the mounds themselves.

Moore[1] mentions a mound about 12 feet high near Rodney, Jefferson Co., and another about the same height near Grand Gulf, Claiborne Co. The first had been partly washed away, the second was dug into without results.

The preceding account of the archeological remains in the Natchez territory was written some years before Mr. Warren K. Moorehead conducted extensive investigation in that field in January and February of 1924. Tho the present writer took some small part in those operations, being present three days in the field at Selsertown and Anna, no attempt is made to incorporate the results of those investigations in this book; it is reserved for Mr. Moorehead to publish a detailed account of his studies in the Natchez territory.

---

[1] Moore: Some Aborig. Sites on Miss. River, Philadelphia, 1911, page 368, note 1.

IN COPIAH COUNTY AND VICINITY.

Dr. Thomas B. Birdsong, formerly of Hazelhurst, did considerable collecting in Copiah Co. and adjacent territory. His material was sold to Mr. Victor C. Barringer of Monroe, La. Dr. Birdsong wrote me as follows in 1917:

"Col. Louis J. Dupree and I about the year 1904 spent many days investigating the mounds of Bayou Pierre in Copiah Co. and the western borders of the county into Claiborne Co., as well as the eastern portion of Copiah in the valley of Pearl River, and across it into Simpson Co. Most of the things were actually exhumed from the mounds, tho some pieces were given to me by people who had plowed them up in the fields upon or near the mounds.

"Near Rockport, close to Pearl River, we went into a group of five mounds in a cluster, the central one yielding several fine pieces of pottery and many skeletons. One of this group was almost flat with the surface, and upon digging a little in its center we found the remains of a fire; we brought out the sharpened point of a stake from below where it had been burnt to the ground. Two mounds only I found on the side of hills; all the rest were in low places, valley and creek bottoms. In two we came upon copper findings: copper beads and two spool-shaped things which might have been used as ear-pendants.

"My pieces were all from Mississippi; I had specimens from the counties of Copiah, Simpson, Lawrence, Claiborne, Adams, and Hinds; tho I did no digging in Adams or Hinds."

The author of this book has not seen the "Copiah Wall," near Brandywine, which gets into print from time to time as an archeological wonder, but the opinion of Dr. Charles Peabody[1], Dr. E. N. Lowe, and other competent observers, is that it is a purely natural geological formation.

---

[1] Peabody: Expl. of Mounds, Coahoma Co., Miss., Cambridge, Mass., 1904, p. 56.

IN WARREN COUNTY.

Locust Mound, on Horseshoe Lake, Warren Co., less than 4 feet high, was dug into by Mr. Clarence B. Moore[1] with negative results.

A mound near Oak Bend Landing, Warren Co., was opened in 1910 or 1911 by Moore, who gives a full account of his investigations, here condensed as follows:

A few feet from the water's edge at Oak Bend Landing is a mound of irregular outline, about 50 feet and 60 feet in basal diameters, and about 3 feet high. Persons long resident in the neighborhood report the mound, which they say once was considerably higher, to have been graded to serve as a foundation for a house, and subsequently to have suffered additional loss in height through wash of water. The house had disappeared at the time of our visit, but a cistern was present in the mound. Trial-holes in this mound came at once upon human remains, and two days were devoted by us to the investigation of what probably had been a small burial mound.

Unfortunately much digging into this mound had been done by others, as there was great disturbance of bones and of artifacts, in places, and numerous corroded nails of iron were found, which presumably had been left on the surface of the mound at the time of the demolition of the house. Twenty-eight burials were noted by us, mostly belonging to the bunched variety, but a few burials of adults extended on the back, and the skeletons of several children also were present in the mound. Three individual burials had the skulls covered by inverted bowls which fitted the skulls like caps.

Some of the bunched burials were extensive, one having no fewer than thirty skulls (many in fragments) and a great quantity of other bones. The skulls of the bunched burials, as a rule, were heaped together at one side of the burial.

---

[1]Moore; Some Aborig. Sites on Miss. River, Philadelphia, 1911, p. 368, p. 378.

In most instances singularly few artifacts lay with the bunched burials considering the number of individuals these burials represented. Burial no. 7, a large bunched burial with many skulls, had associated with various parts of it: twelve earthenware vessels; fragments of corroded sheet-brass or copper; glass beads; a rude disk of bituminous coal about 2.5 inches in diameter; powdered hematite in two places. A feature of this burial was the presence of several toy vessels of earthen-ware, put in near bones of children. The mound is post-Columbian.

Burial no. 13 was the skeleton of an adult, extended on the back. At the head was an earthen-ware vessel in fragments; at the feet a bottle. On the chest of the skeleton and extending to one side of it lay a small bunch of human bones with which no skull was found. Lying above this bunch, but possibly deposited for the lower burial also, were a number of objects in line, overlapping each other to some extent, as follows: an imperfect flint arrow-head; a chisel wrought from a flint pebble; a polished celt of flint, 4 inches in length; two celts of sedimentary rock, 5.25 inches, and 6.75 inches in length, respectively; a tool or weapon of iron or of steel, about 5 inches in length, badly corroded; and, together, five lance-points and knives of flint, two broken; one leaf-shaped implement of flint, 3.5 inches long; and a bit of rock-crystal.

Burial no. 20, a bunch having eleven skulls, including two of adolescents, was accompanied with two earthen-ware vessels. Near a skull, not on each side of it, but placed together, were two disks of indurated clay, each about 1.24 inch in diameter and three-quarters of an inch in thickness (fig. 4, Moore; fig. 338, Brown). Presumably these objects were ear-plugs.

Burial no. 26, of the bunched variety, having twenty-five skulls, had in association four vessels of earthen-ware, one arrow-head of flint and three pebbles. With this burial also was a circular object of indurated clay, 1.3 inches in diameter, centrally perforated, concave on both sides. The two faces of this object which perhaps was an ear-plug are polished.

Burial no. 28 consisted of a single skull over which was an inverted bowl. Besides the covering bowl stood another vessel, and near the skull and just below the rim of the bowl over it were two chisels wrought from pebbles of flint.

A few objects lay in the mound apart from burials: a small celt of diabase; a chisel made from a flint pebble; an ornament 1.25 inch in length, fashioned from the axis of a marine univalve *(Fulgur),* including a small part of the whorl, perforated longitudinally; a flat pebble about 3 inches in length, chipped on opposite sides near the smaller end.

Forty-six vessels of earthen-ware, mostly in small fragments, were recovered from this mound. The ware, as a rule, is inferior to that found in the mound near Glass, only two miles distant. Ten of the vessels are without decoration; most of the others bear incised or trailed designs, some however crude and scanty. One fragment of a vessel which apparently had been coated with red pigment was the only evidence encountered of the use of paint in the decoration of earthen-ware in this mound. A specimen of this pottery is given in figure 5 [fig. 337 of this book].

The group of mounds near Glass, Warren County, a short distance below Vicksburg, was investigated by Moore in 1911. The published account of his work[1] is condensed in the following description:

About one mile north by north-east from Glass, a station on the Yazoo and Mississippi Valley Railroad, on the plantation of Mrs. J. P. Cline, are four mounds forming a very irregular circle with a diameter of about 420 feet. Some distance north of these mounds is another, much spread and

---

[1] Moore: Some Aborig. Sites on the Miss. River, Phila., 1911, pp. 381-388.

worn, on which is a house. None of these mounds was erected as a place of refuge in time of flood, for altho they are on ground subject to occasional overflow, they are not ten minutes' journey from the hills which approach the river at this place.

The largest mound of the group composing the so-called circle is 30 feet in height and is still rather symmetrical, tho wash of rain has already scarred the upper part. The basal diameter north-east and south-west is 180 feet; south-east and north-west it is 167 feet. The diameters of the summit-plateau in the same directions respectively are 60 and 64 feet. Fourteen trial-holes in this plateau failed to come upon artifact or bone.

Two other mounds of the four composing the circle have been greatly mutilated. One, about 6 feet in height originally, has been partly cut away in making a road, while the other, curtailed on one side by the same road, has been in part washed away on the opposite side by a small bayou, and has been leveled to a considerable extent to serve as a foundation for a building which formerly stood upon it. Both these mounds were dug into by us without results.

The fourth mound of the circular group has a height of 15 feet; its basal diameters are 149 feet and 128 feet. This mound, however, has been under cultivation practically over its entire surface, and a narrow spur, protected from the plow by a tree, projects from a corner of the summit-plateau a distance of 13 feet, thus showing that the plateau has been worked away through cultivation by at least that number of feet on one side. Trial-holes in the summit-plateau of the mound in question came upon several vessels of earthen-ware, all near the surface. Consequently it was decided to dig completely thru that part of the plateau (about three-quarters of its present area) where indications of graves were found. Human remains were encountered but twice; in both instances accompanied with deposits of pottery. In other instances artifacts were present, singly and in groups, where no burials were apparent, tho beyond question they had been present but had disappeared thru decay.

There came from this mound, in addition to vessels of earthen-ware: several polished pebbles, evidently smoothing-stones for pottery; a discoidal stone roughly shaped from a pebble; a flat pebble chipped toward one end, on two opposite sides, probably to facilitate attachment to a handle; a small quantity of powdered hematite used for paint.

Associated with pottery and lying side by side, were two cylinders of yellow clay material, crumbling and in many fragments. We were unable to determine the length of these cylinders, which fell into many fragments on removal, but the deposit as it lay in the ground, was 15 inches in length. Each of these cylinders possessed one rounded end. The character of the end opposite the rounded one we were unable to determine, though we think it likely that the objects had been what is known as spade-shaped implements and that their upper parts had crumbled away.

Thirty-five vessels of earthen-ware were scored by us as coming from this mound; tho the count was of necessity imperfect, as only two whole vessels were encountered. The ware from this place contains little if any shell-tempering. It is fairly thin and of medium excellence. The principal feature about the pottery from this place is the great proportion of decorated vessels; in fact but one wholly undecorated vessel was found in the mound. [See figures 332 to 336.]

Various slight rises of ground in different parts of this plantation, on which were a few scattered signs of aboriginal occupancy, were investigated, but without success. Probably burial places at these sites had been destroyed in the course of long cultivation.

ON THE YAZOO RIVER.

Mr. Clarence B. Moore in 1908 did considerable exploration among the mounds of the lower Yazoo River and of the Sunflower River[1]. His work up the Yazoo River extended from Vicksburg to Racetrack Landing above Greenwood and up the Sunflower to Lake George. On the lower courses of those rivers dwelt in early historic times the Yazoos, Ofos, and other smaller tribes. Moore's poor success in finding aboriginal objects in that region led him to the conclusion that the placing of artifacts with the dead was not widely practiced there. He enumerates the following mounds and sites investigated on the Yazoo River:

Three mounds at King's Crossing, Warren Co.
Dwelling-site below Haynes Bluff, Warren Co.
Three mounds near Haynes Bluff Landing, Warren Co.
Two mounds near Leist Landing, Issaquena Co.
Two mounds near O'Neill's Landing, Yazoo Co.
Mound near Stella Landing, Yazoo Co.
Mound near Clark's Ferry, Yazoo Co.
Dwelling-site near Monterey's Landing, Yazoo Co.
Mound at Caruthers' Landing, Yazoo Co.
Dwelling-site at Koalunsa Landing, Yazoo Co.
Mound near Parker's Bayou, Holmes Co.
Five mounds at the Fort Place, Yazoo Co.
Mound near entrance of Tchula Lake, Holmes Co.
Mound on Tchula Lake, Holmes Co.
Four mounds at the Peaster Place, Holmes Co.
Mound at Belzoni, Washington Co.
Mound above Belzoni, Holmes Co.
Mound near Welsh Camp Landing, Holmes Co.
Mound near entrance of Wasp Lake, Washington Co.
Six mounds near Wasp Lake, Washington Co.

[1] Moore: Certain Mounds of Arkansas and Mississippi, Philadelphia, 1908.

Two mounds near Silent Shade Landing, Holmes Co.
Two mounds near Carey Middleton Gin, Holmes Co.
Two mounds near head of Honey Island, Holmes Co.
Mound near mouth of Yalobusha River, Leflore Co.
Three mounds on the Lucas Plantation, Leflore Co.
Mound at Racetrack Landing, Leflore Co.

I follow the course of Moore's journey up the river, adding at times the results of observations by myself and others. Moore gives the following description of the first group of mounds:

At King's Crossing, about four miles north of Vicksburg, in full view from the Yazoo and Mississippi Valley Railroad, are three mounds, and what may be parts of other mounds.

Mound A, on property belonging to Miss M. C. Collier, resident on the place, was used as a fortification by the Confederates during the siege of Vicksburg, and cannon-balls may still be seen partly imbedded in its clay. The mound evidently belongs to the domiciliary class so abundant thruout southern United States. At the time of our visit the mound was about 25 feet in height and showed much irregularity in shape, though doubtless formerly it had been a symmetrical oblong. Its basal measurements north and south and east and west were respectively 157 feet and 173 feet. The diameters of the summit-plateau in the same directions were 74 feet and 92 feet.

Mound B, about 100 feet east of mound A, on property of Mr. T. D. Major, residing nearby, was much spread by long cultivation. Its height was 5 feet 5 inches; its base, of irregular outline, was 96 feet north and south and 84 feet east and west. Fourteen trial-holes were put into this mound (which probably was domiciliary), without result.

Nine trial-holes were dug without success into soil blackened with organic matter, somewhat to the north of the mound, evidently a former dwelling-site.

Mound C, about 250 feet east by north from mound A, on property belonging to Miss Collier, has been almost cut to pieces—in the first place for use as a fortification, and later, it is said, by treasure seekers.

The present author visited these mounds in 1916. Many fragments of pottery, stone, shell, and bone are to be seen upon them. A number of artifacts are said to have been taken from mound C at the time the railroad was built, and sent to the North.

On the dwelling-site half a mile south of Haynes Bluff, Warren Co., Moore found a limestone pendant about the size and shape of a hen's egg (fig. 1, Moore; fig. 115, Brown).

On the plantation of Mr. H. K. Williams, resident on the place, about one-half mile in a north-east direction from Haynes Bluff Landing, on ground sloping toward the river, he investigated a symmetrical mound, evidently domiciliary. This mound, to some extent impaired by wash of water at its north-east angle, has a roadway leading out from its southern side. Its height from the western side is 30 feet 2 inches; from the eastern side, 28 feet 5 inches. The mound is practically square, the base being about 185 feet in each direction. The summit-plateau is 75 feet square.

Fourteen trial-holes were put down, resulting in the discovery of a few fragments of bones of lower animals, mostly of deer, and a bone identified as being part of a tibia of a wild turkey. There were also some bits of earthen-ware, shell-tempered as a rule, a few having a fine black polish on each side.

In the neighborhood of this mound are three elevations, one of which he believed to be a knoll that has served as a dwelling-site; the other two, remnants of mounds. In one of these, just below the surface, was a skeleton having small glass beads at the neck.

Mr. H. K. Williams has kindly presented to the Mississippi Geological Survey a small collection of archeological material from the vicinity of Haynes Bluff, including celts, circular stones, flint points, and trade beads. The Davenport Academy of Sciences has a fine flint knife 8.25 inches long from the large mound at Haynes Bluff (fig. 59).

I continue to follow Moore's trip up the Yazoo River, and condense from his published report:

On the property of Mr. Samuel Leist, near Leist Landing, Issaquena County, are two mounds; an elevation in a field, probably a dwelling-site; and the remnant of a low mound, on which stands a house. One of the mounds, which serves as a refuge for cattle in flood-time, is about 400 yards in a westerly direction from Leist Landing. Its height, taken from the eastern side, is 29 feet 4 inches. Its basal outline is circular in a general way, but somewhat irregular owing to cultivation of the field and to wash of water in times of overflow. The sides of the mound also have been impaired thru wash of rain and trampling of cattle in all probability. The diameter of the mound is about 174 feet. There is but little summit-plateau. Eleven trial-holes were put down in the upper part of the mound; with the exception of three recent burials in coffins, nothing was encountered in this mound.

On the bank of the Little Sunflower River, which here approaches the Yazoo, and about half a mile north-west from the mound just described, is a curious platform covered with loam filled with evidence of long occupancy, averaging 8 feet in height except at the southern end, where it is 14 feet high. Its outline is irregularly oblong, its basal diameter north and south being about 305 feet, east and west about 245 feet. Fourteen trial-holes thru dark loam to yellow

MOUNDS AND EARTH-WORKS. 57

clay, showing that the plateau had been built and then occupied, yielded no object of importance.

A mound about 12 feet high with houses upon it near Miller's Landing, Sharkey County; a small mound near Sweet Home, Yazoo County; mounds near Big Mound Landing and Sycamore Landing, Yazoo County; and a mound near Friedlander Landing, Yazoo County, were listed.

A considerable collection of artifacts from Warren and Yazoo Counties was made by Mr. C. F. Causey of Eldorado. The fine effigy pipe shown in figures 228 and 229 and the little stemless pipe shown in figure 197 are from this vicinity. May the mounds about Eldorado be those referred to in the Smithsonian Report of 1874, page 370, as being twenty miles below Satartia? I have not examined them.

Dr. Eugene A. Smith in his manuscript notes of 1870 mentioned some remains of aboriginal works at Satartia, Yazoo Co., just at the edge of the town towards the hills.

Four miles down the valley road from Satartia he visited two mounds. A landslide from one of these had exposed fragments of human bones and teeth; a skull protruding crumbled so readily that it was impossible to remove it whole. Arrow-heads and other implements abounded. The present writer visited in 1906 two mounds on Mr. Smith's place on the valley road from Satartia to Phœnix, which are no doubt the mounds mentioned by Dr. Smith. Both these mounds were then much worn away by water.

Mr. L. H. Coody of Phœnix writes that there are several small mounds and a camp-site on his farm, and that he has plowed up two skeletons and abundance of broken pottery.

The two small mounds near O'Neill's Landing, Yazoo Co., were examined by Moore with negative results. The one in the woods was completely demolished.

The conical mound 7 feet high and 49 feet in diameter standing in a cultivated field about 100 yards south-west of

Stella Landing, Yazoo Co., yielded a layer of shells all the species of which are still common to the region, two adult skeletons, and part of a child's skeleton, about the neck of which were a number of shell beads.

Mounds near Enola Landing, Oak Valley Landing, Rialto Landing, and Tarsus Landing, Yazoo Co., were reported but not excavated.

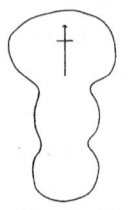

Fig. 11. Outline of mound, Champlin Group, reduced from Thomas.

A number of mounds near Yazoo City were not visited by Moore because he was informed that they had already been opened. He suggests that these are probably the Champlin mounds, opened and described by the Bureau of American Ethnology.

The Champlin mounds in Yazoo Co. were investigated by agents of the Bureau of American Ethnology and an account of the work was published by Cyrus Thomas[1] in 1894, here condensed as follows:

The Champlin group, consisting of four mounds, is situated about the center of Yazoo County, two miles north of Yazoo City and two miles east of Yazoo River. The mounds stand on low swampy land, about half a mile from the hills, and during the flood of 1882 were surrounded by water. The large mound is of the form shown in figure 162 [figure 11 in this book], the other three are conical and smaller. The dimensions of the large mound were found by careful measurement to be as follows:

> Length at base from north to south 106 feet.
> Width of northern section 50 feet, height 14 feet.
> Width of middle section 36 feet, height 8 feet.
> Width of southern section 38 feet, height 11 feet.

It was explored down to the original surface and found to be

---

[1]Thomas: Mound Explorations, 12th Ann. Rept. Bu. of Am. Ethn., Washington, 1894, pp. 260-63.

composed thruout of dark earth similar to the surrounding soil.

In the southern portion at the depth of three and a half feet were three adult skeletons, all extended at full length. One lay with the face up and head north; about the neck and waist were a number of shell beads. Another lay also with face up but head to the west; close by the head was a nicely polished celt. The other lay on the left side, with the head north; by the head was a polished celt and immediately in front of the face a small water bottle. There were also in the southern section about half way between the top and the original surface the skeleton of an adult and the skeleton of a very young child, neither accompanied by artifacts. The adult skeleton lay extended on the left side with head south; the earth immediately around it was burned hard, the bones also showing signs of fire. At the bottom of the southern section of the mound were the remains of six skeletons. These had doubtless been buried after the flesh was removed, as the bones of each had been taken apart and placed in a heap, the parts of one skeleton forming one heap.

In the central and northern parts of the mound were found numerous skeletons; also celts, beads, and pots. An image vessel is shown in figure 164 [not reproduced in this book]. None of the burials in this mound were in inclosures or coffins of any kind, except two instances where bark covering was used. All the skeletons having no relics buried with them had the heads compressed showing frontal pressure and backward elongation. The others, those with ornaments or instruments accompanying them, had heads of the usual type. Altho this fact seems to indicate that individuals of two different tribes were buried here, it seems evident that they belonged to the same era.

Mound no. 2 stands 1,300 feet east of the large one and is a regular cone, 58 feet in diameter and 13 feet high. The main body was composed of dark swamp soil like that of the surrounding land, but at the bottom was a central, conical core of yellow clay, 12 feet in diameter and 3 feet high. The nearest point where the clay could have been obtained is half a mile away. About 3 feet beneath the apex were a few human teeth and slight traces of other bones, with which were associated a few beads made of deer horn. Immediately below the surface, on one side, an ornamented water bottle was discovered.

Mound no. 3, about 700 feet from no. 2, is oval in outline, rounded on top, 35 feet long north and south, 27 feet wide, and 3 feet high. This was not explored.

No. 4, which is 275 feet due south of no. 3, is similar in form and size to the latter. It was explored and found to be composed thruout of dark swamp soil. Nothing was discovered except a few coals.

Moore found nothing of special significance in the mounds near Clark's Ferry and at Caruthers' Landing, or in the dwelling-sites near Monterey Landing and at Koalunsa Landing, all in Yazoo Co. At the latter landing are shell deposits of considerable thickness yielding human bones. Low mounds were reported at Belle Prairie Landing and at Beech Grove Landing, Yazoo Co. The low mound near Parker's Bayou, Holmes Co., was said to have been erected recently as a refuge for cattle against high water.

A group of mounds on the Fort place on the river in Yazoo County is described by Mr. C. B. Moore as consisting of a central mound with each of the four corners directed toward a smaller mound, the distances being:

    east-south-east, 120 feet
    south-south-west, 195 feet
    west-north-west, 120 feet
    north-north-east, 90 feet.

The angles are so regular that Mr. Moore considers the

circumstances as perhaps indicating attention by the aborigines to the cardinal directions. The large central mound has been altered for a house-site; the four satellites have been altered either by cultivation or by presence of a road.

Trial-holes sunk into the mound near the mouth of Tchula Lake, about 300 yards north-west from the landing on Honey Island in a cultivated field, and into the mound on the west bank of Tchula Lake about 3 miles from its mouth, yielded no special returns.

On the Peaster Place on the western side of Tchula Lake in Holmes County, on property belonging to Mr. R. L. Peaster, Moore investigated four aboriginal mounds.

Mound A, a symmetrical mound in sight of the bank of the old river, about 150 yards in an east-south-east course from the landing, has a height of 9 feet 4 inches, and a diameter at base of 58 feet. Forty-seven burials were found from just below the surface to a thin layer of dark material 9 feet down, on which were three fire-places, one having fish-scales near it. The form of twenty-six of these burials was not determined.

Burial no. 1, 1 foot 8 inches down, was a skeleton of an adult, lying at full length on the back, the skull south-south-west. This skeleton, from the skull to the pelvis inclusive, had lain on a bed of fire and the bones were badly affected by the heat, which had burnt the adjacent clay to a red hue.

Burial no. 2, 10 inches down, was an adult skeleton extended at length on the back, the head directed south-east. This skeleton, from the upper part of the chest down to and including the feet, had lain on the same fire as skeleton no. 1, the legs of skeleton no. 2 crossing the chest of the other skeleton.

Altho such parts of both these skeletons as had been exposed to heat showed markedly the effects of fire, the bones remained entire and were not reduced to small calcined fragments, as is the case when cremation among the aborigines has been successfully carried out.

Burial no. 5 consisted of the skeleton or of a large part of the skeleton of an adult, arranged in a bunch. Immediately above this bunch was a small layer of calcined fragments of bone which had belonged to a somewhat smaller skeleton than the one below it.

The foregoing burials, which were all superficial, were the only ones bearing marks of fire that were met with by us in this mound.

Burial no. 17 was 9 feet down, that is to say on the base of the mound, the trunk on the back, the face turned to the right. Nine other burials were lying on the right side, closely flexed; two were lying on the left side, closely flexed; one was lying face down, closely flexed. The skulls found in the mound showed no fixed orientation.

Mainly with burials were a number of arrow-heads or knives, and four lance-heads, all of chert. These points with one exception were rather rudely made, many showing breakage, thus leading to the belief that imperfect objects had been utilized for interment with the dead. One heart-shaped lance-head of dark gray chert would be a fine example of aboriginal workmanship were it not for the absence of the point.

Lying with a burial was a celt 5.4 inches long, having a graceful flare on one side of the edge. This hatchet was given to Mr. Peaster. The earthen-ware in this mound showed no evidence of shell-tempering, but was poor in quality, and when found was spongy from moisture.

Mound B, in a cultivated field, about one mile from mound A in a south-east by east direction, is 2 feet 7 inches high and 40 feet in diameter. Eleven trial-holes were put down, some of which came upon human remains. Two feet from the surface was an urn-burial consisting of a skeleton presumably, the decaying remains of a skull and some long-bones being noted, which, after the removal of the flesh, had been taken apart and arranged in a heap on the ground. This heap had been covered, or rather almost covered (for a few ends of long-bones projected), by a large inverted bowl of most inferior ware, which upon removal fell into many small fragments paste-like in consistency. This bowl had no decoration except a grotesque representation of a human head extending above the rim. Near the projecting bones was a small celt.

Mound C, about 285 feet south-east by east from mound B, is a circular rise of the ground 2 feet 4 inches high and 40 feet in diameter. Trial-holes yielded nothing.

Mound D is in a cultivated field, about one-half mile north-west from mound A; its height is 3 feet, its diameter 83 feet. Trial-holes exposed two skeletons of adults, at full length on the back, parallel one to the other. At the skull of one was an inverted vessel of inferior ware, badly broken, bearing an incised decoration (fig. 2; fig. 328 in this book). On the other side of the head was part of a vessel in fragments.

Moore mentions but does not describe the mounds at Holly Landing and at Silver City. The author visited these mounds in June, 1912, and made the following observations.

About two miles down the Yazoo River from Silver City, Yazoo County, are the Holly mounds, on the larger of which stands an old-time residence facing the river. A cistern in the back yard is dug in the mound. The height and form of the mound were no doubt changed to prepare for the building and premises. About 300 feet east of this is a second mound, with a circumference of 308 feet at the base, and a height of about 11 feet. The negroes use the base of this mound for burial purposes. Very few pottery or flint fragments were noticed here. Near the river there is apparently part of a third mound.

There is a large mound at Silver City, Yazoo County, whose present form is entirely different from its original form. It is situated on the Yazoo River just below the source of Silver Creek. In 1897 in order to make a refuge against anticipated high water the top was cut from this mound and an apron or platform built entirely around the mound. As the mound now stands it is 475 feet in circumference above the apron, 140 feet on top north-west by south-east, and 92 feet north-east by south-west. The present height of this mound is 15 feet; the amount cut down from the top according to local information was about 12 feet; hence the original height of the mound was about 27 feet. Two fine oaks three and a third and five feet in diameter respectively were left undisturbed. No skeletons, bones, or flints were found, tho some shells were encountered. Shells may still be seen on the west side. Scattered about the mound are many potsherds.

There are two smaller mounds nearby in cultivation; one located south 10° east about 225 feet distance from the center of the large mound is about 4 feet high; another located south 20° west about 300 feet away is approximately 5 feet high. There are other elevations in the vicinity that may be small mounds.

Three-eighths of a mile up the Yazoo River are shell heaps two to five feet thick, containing many fragments of pottery and some charcoal.

At Midnight, seven miles down Silver Creek from Silver City, is a large mound with one small satellite. The large mound is 12 feet high on the west side and 16 feet high on the east side, the difference being due to the slope of the ground. The smaller mound stands about 360 feet distant slightly to the north of west and has its surface covered with great quantities of pottery fragments.

A mound near Springwood Landing was reported by Moore's agent, but not visited by that archeologist.

Moore describes the mound at Belzoni, Washington Co., as 11 feet high and 165 feet long at bottom and 96 feet long at top east and west by 125 feet wide at bottom and 56 feet wide at top; it is visible from the river and about a quarter of a mile north-east of the landing. Part of the eastern end has been hauled away to utilize the shells. Twelve trial-holes were put down; one exposed six post-holes in line, about 30 inches below the surface; these were about 2 feet deep and 3.5 to 4 inches in diameter. No doubt an aboriginal building had once stood on the mound before its final increase in height.

About one mile above Belzoni on the opposite side of the river in Holmes Co. stands a mound at the water's edge 5.5 feet high and 14 feet in diameter. Eleven trial-holes were sunk without result.

On the Montgomery property about three-quarters of a mile south-south-east from Welsh Camp Landing, Holmes Co., a circular mound 7.7 to 9 feet high and 47 feet in diameter was dug down and subsequently rebuilt. In all seventeen burials were found, at depths varying from 1 foot to 8 feet 8 inches—those at the greatest depth being four skeletons in a circular grave at the center of the mound. Of these four skeletons, with skulls in three directions, three lay on their left sides and one on the right side. Three were closely flexed, the knees being drawn up well toward the chin. One had the legs at right angles to the body. The predominating form of burial in this mound, where determination was possible, was that of close flexion. Arrow-heads, lance-heads, and knives were encountered in the mound.

About one-half mile west from the entrance to Wasp Lake, Washington Co., is a mound 3.5 feet high with circular base of 48 feet diameter, standing in a field belonging to S. H. McClintock. Fourteen trial-holes brought to view no human remains, tho two broken vessels of inferior ware were found.

About 5 miles up Wasp Lake, on the west side, somewhat less than a mile above Jaketown, are six mounds in the immediate vicinity of the landing and a number of smaller mounds some distance away. Two are large quadrangular mounds with summit-plateaus and evidently domiciliary; one, a low flat mound; another thru which a road has been cut; while two are mounds from 3 to 5 feet in height, which have been considerably reduced in diameter to make way for a railroad. One of these mounds apparently had contained many burials. Spread over the neighboring fields were many fragments of shell and numerous bits of earthen-ware, some of the latter shell-tempered and some not. Nearly all were undecorated, tho some bore a beautiful bright red pigment on both sides, which proved to be red oxide of iron.

Near the Tchula road from Silent Shade Landing, and in full view from the highway, are two mounds within a few feet of each other.

Mound A to the north, on property belonging to Mr. Robert E. Warfield, of Tchula, Miss., is 5 feet 7 inches high and 50 feet in diameter. An excavation was made by us 16 feet by 10 feet, with perpendicular walls. As usual, the outer part of the mound proved to be soft, the inner part hard and tenacious. Only seven burials were encountered. Nineteen inches down was a deposit of calcined fragments of human bones; on top of part of this deposit was a small undecorated bowl of inferior ware, in fragments.

Two skeletons at full length on the back, almost in a condition to crumble into dust, lay side by side 3 feet 8 inches down, the heads directed south-west. Near the skull of one were two small undecorated vessels of ordinary shape, and of inferior porous ware, both in fragments. With these vessels were two hammer-stones. The second skeleton also had near the skull a vessel similar to the others. On the chest was an ornament of wood, rotten thru and thru, which had been coated with sheet-copper, a few fragments of which still adhered. This circular ornament, flat on one side and convex on the other, had a diameter of 2.5 inches, a thickness of three-quarters of an inch. Near the surface of the mound were two undecorated pots of crude ware, found in fragments.

Mound B, on property of Mr. S. S. Hudson of Vicksburg, Miss., is 4 feet 10 inches high and 46 feet in diameter. An excavation with perpendicular walls, 10.5 feet by 10 feet, and 5 feet 7 inches in depth, was sunk in the central part of the mound. Some human bones and some broken vessels of earthen-ware were found.

About one-half mile east-south-east from the landing at the Carey Middleton gin, on property of Mr. Carey Middleton, are two mounds in a cultivated field, about three hundred yards apart.

Mound A, 6 feet 3 inches high, much spread by cultivation, has a diameter of 64 feet. A hole 9 feet by 12 feet was carried down into undisturbed ground below, revealing decayed human bones and teeth.

Mound B, north-east by east from Mound A, is 5 feet 10 inches high and has a present diameter of 60 feet, no doubt much increased by the cultivation of the mound. An excavation 9 feet by 11 feet was made to a depth of somewhat more than 6 feet, disclosing fragments of calcined human bones.

Not far from the Carey Middleton mounds is another which our agent informs us is somewhat larger than the ones investigated.

Our agent reported a mound near Montgomery Landing, Holmes Co., which we did not visit, not having been able to obtain permission to dig.

Near the head of the Yazoo River side of Honey Island

on the plantation of Mr. A. W. Evans, about half a mile north-east by east from the landing at Golddust, are two mounds in a cultivated field, in full view of each other, both much spread by cultivation. One, largely of sand, has a height of 4 feet 4 inches and diameters of 78 feet and 64 feet. The other mound, partly of sand, 2 feet 10 inches high, with diameters of 38 feet and 54 feet, has somewhat below the surface a great deposit of mussel-shells, mostly badly crushed. Some less broken than the rest have been determined by Dr. H. A. Pilsbury as *Quadrula pyramidata, Q. plicata, Lampsilis fallaciosus,* all shell-fish still found in the Mississippi Valley.

Two mounds near Sheppardtown Landing, Laflore Co., described by our agent, were passed by us without a visit.

There are a number of mounds near Shell Bluff Landing, Laflore Co., on properties belonging to Messrs. W. G. Poindexter and F. M. Southworth. These mounds so nearly resembled others in which we had been unsuccessful that we decided not to delay our journey.

Two small mounds near Phillipston Landing, Leflore Co., on property belonging to Mr. F. M. Southworth, were not investigated by us for the same reason that those at Shell Bluff Landing were not dug into.

Two mounds near Oakwood or Roebuck Landing, Leflore Co., belonging to Mr. Herman Aron, were likewise not visited by us.

On property of Mr. S. J. Stein, of Greenwood, Miss., at the roadside, about one-quarter of a mile north-north-east from the landing, at the union of the Yalabusha and the Yazoo Rivers, Leflore Co., is a mound almost circular in basal outline, with height of 3.5 feet and diameter of 46 feet. A central excavation 10.5 feet by 8.5 feet by 4 feet deep yielded neither bone nor artifact.

In a cultivated field, a short distance from Ashwood Landing, Leflore Co., on property belonging to Mr. W. C. George, of Greenwood, Miss., is part of a mound, the remainder having disappeared through cultivation and through wash of rain.

Two small mounds, said by our agent to be about 1.5 mile from Star West Landing, Leflore Co., and owned by Mr. P. M. Aldridge, of Greenwood, Miss., were not dug into.

On the plantation of Dr. J. H. Lucas, of Greenwood, Miss., about 5 miles above Greenwood, Leflore Co., on the west side of the river, all in sight from the bank, are three mounds. The northernmost is a remnant immediately on the bank. The next, in a cultivated field, has a small modern cemetery upon it. The third, in the same field, much spread by plowing, is 6 feet 4 inches in height, and 82 feet across its circular base. Fourteen trial-holes were sunk without result.

In sight from Racetrack Landing, Leflore Co., on property of Mr. S. F. Jones, is a mound with irregular circular base, 107 feet in diameter, 20 feet across the circular summit plateau, and 24 feet in height. The mound, tho furrowed by rain and somewhat cut by cultivation at the base, is still symmetrical and presents an imposing appearance. Three trial-holes in the summit-plateau, each 5 feet in depth, were without result.

On our way up the river our hopes had been buoyed by reports which our agent had heard of a carved vessel of stone, with a top of like material, which, it was said, had been taken from the mound at this place. The rumor turned out to be without any basis whatsoever, nothing, we were assured by Mr. Jones, having been taken from the mound.

At this point on the Yazoo River, there being no report from mounds farther up to justify hope of greater success in returns, the investigation of the river banks and the adjacent territory was abandoned by us, altho abundant work had been mapped out by our agent as far as Sharkey, about 70 miles above by water.

ON THE SUNFLOWER RIVER.

Mr. Moore's investigations on the lower Sunflower River included the following mounds and sites[1]:

Mound near Anderson Landing, Sharkey Co.
Mound near Bachelor Retreat Landing, Sharkey Co.
Three mounds near Wrong-end-up Landing, Yazoo Co.
Three mounds at Spanish Fort Landing, Sharkey Co.
Mound at Fairview Landing, Yazoo Co.
Mound on Fairview Plantation, Yazoo Co.
Three mounds at Stalonia Landing, Sharkey Co.
Many mounds near George Lake, Yazoo Co.

In woods about one-quarter of a mile south-east from Anderson Landing, Sharkey County, on property probably belonging to Messrs. George T. Houston & Co., is a mound 6 feet 7 inches in height and 62 feet across its circular base. This mound, which gave evidence of former, but apparently somewhat superficial, investigation, was dug out by us in the central part, the excavation being 7 feet 6 inches, by 12 feet, by 7 feet 4 inches deep, the sides of the hole being carried squarely down.

Near the surface were disturbed human bones with which were fragments of a vessel of yellow ware without shell-tempering. This vessel is no. 1, figure 3, in Moore's book and figure 329 in this book. About 3 feet 9 inches from the surface was a small undecorated bowl of dark ware (vessel no. 2), in fragments, with mere traces of a skull and teeth nearby. Six feet 9 inches down, presumably on the base of the mound, near what were probably traces of human bones, was vessel no. 3 (fig. 4, Moore; fig. 330, Brown). While we were engaged on other and more superficial work in the mound, an undecorated vessel in small fragments was encountered.

---

[1] Moore: Certain Mounds of Arkansas and Miss., Philadelphia, 1908, page 586.

A mound at Pecan Grove, Sharkey Co., was not dug into by Moore because of the presence of a house on it.

By the roadside, in sight of Bachelor Retreat Landing, Sharkey Co., on property of Mr. John Ross, is a mound much worn by cattle, rain, and overflow. The present diameter of the circular base is 60 feet; the present height 3 feet 7 inches. Fourteen trial-holes resulted in the discovery of decaying human bones.

In woods about three-quarters of a mile east from Wrong-end-up Landing, on property of Mrs. J. E. Edwards, is a circular mound with diameter of base and plateau respectively 72 and 28 feet, and altitude of 7 feet 9 inches. Nine holes were made in the summit and sides, revealing badly decayed human bones.

Two other mounds about one-quarter of a mile in a northwesterly direction from the one just described served as foundations for pens for domestic animals in flood-time and were not dug into.

My investigation of the ancient works at Spanish Fort was conducted in June, 1917, about nine years after Moore's. I observed the following:

All indications point to Indian origin for this enclosure, tho the name of Spanish Fort attaches to it. It consists of a rough semicircle (fig. 12) north of the Sunflower River with an earth-wall from 5 to 10 feet high and 40 to 60 feet wide and a moat just outside of the wall with the same dimensions and form inverted. No embankment runs along the river front, which encloses the fort on the south. There are four brief breaks in the wall, but none in the moat. The breaks in the earth-wall may have been filled by stockades. There is a modern burying-ground on each end of the wall near the river. That the wall is rapidly weathering down may be plainly seen at the enclosed graves. The area of the enclosure is about 45 acres. Within the enclosure toward the south-east is a semicircular refuse-heap or dwelling-site accumulation several feet thick and rich in shells and potsherds. The shells seem to be the same as those found in the river at the present time. Moore did considerable digging in this heap without return. Medium-sized mounds flank the enclosure at a distance of about 300 yards both up and down the river; only the two nearer are shown in the drawing.

From Spanish Fort my route led me up the railroad; Moore's led up the river.

At Mr. Blooms's a little more than a mile south of the

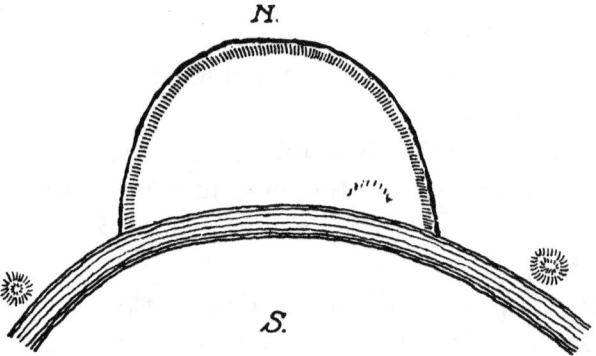

Fig. 12. Indian enclosure at "Spanish Fort," Sharkey Co., area about 45 acres.

village of Holly Bluff there is a group of three large mounds and several small ones. Mr. Bloom's house stands on a mound between the railroad and the river. The largest mound of the group is apparently about 9 or 10 feet high and stands west of the railroad. These are perhaps the mounds described by Moore as the Stalonia Landing group. Considerable digging by Moore in the largest mound of the Stalonia group was fruitless.

Somewhat less than a mile below Holly Bluff there are two medium-sized mounds.

The mound in the village of Holly Bluff is said to be of recent creation for the protection of stock against high water.

What is probably the most wonderful group of mounds and earth-works in the state (quite different in character from Selsertown) exists about half a mile from the union of Lake George with Sunflower River. The place lies south of the lake on property belonging to Mr. W. A. Henry and is known as Mound Place. It is a large field of mounds and depressions surrounded by an earth-wall and outer moat. The wall

FIG. 13. Large central mound, Holly Bluff Group, on Lake George, Yazoo Co., height 55 to 60 feet. C. S. B.

is now from 4 to 7 feet high and was no doubt higher when in use. On the north side along the water front there is no earth-wall. The ditch is more or less filled at most places.

Within the enclosure are a number of ponds and depressions, from which earth was no doubt taken for the erection of the tumuli; in fact the whole surface of the enclosure is uneven, tho it lies in a flood-plain that is normally quite level.

The great central mound (fig. 13) is 55 or 60 feet high,

commanding a view of the whole fortification. It is approximately square and its sides run approximately with the cardinal directions. The area of the base is about one and three-quarter acres, the area of the uneven summit-plateau about one-fifth of an acre. This fine mound has suffered greatly from erosion and the trampling of cattle, and it is at present difficult to locate the original approaches. I fancied that I traced zig-zag ramps up the north and east sides of the mound. Moore, who examined the mound nine years earlier, says that the approaches were up these sides.

The second mound in size stands south-west from the great mound, has a rectangular base and an altitude of 22 or 23 feet; the area of the summit is nearly the same as that of the great mound. It seems to have a direct right approach up the north side.

Twenty-five or more mounds, many irregular in shape, may be counted within the enclosure, and two others between the enclosure and the Sunflower River. Almost all the mounds within the enclosure have been cultivated, and no doubt the forms of many have been altered. The residence occupies one mound on the lake front; other mounds hold houses or barns. Vast quantities of potsherds strew the fields and mounds, with smaller quantities of flint-flakes, shells, and burnt earth. The fine celt shown in figure 74 was picked up on one of the medium-size mounds during my visit. This and other mounds seem to be burial mounds, for we took out a number of human bones in a short while, and the plows bring up quantities of bones and potsherds. A report from the place since my visit says that the workmen in running a road thru one of the mounds found many human bones and some pieces of pottery.

This is a magnificent work of antiquity and should be completely surveyed and mapped and preserved for future generations.

The home of Brevoort Butler, the collector, was near the Holly Bluff mounds; some of his material was found among them.

Moore found on one of the low mounds an earthen-ware pipe "probably representing a wolf or dog" (fig. 6, Moore; fig. 207, Brown). Thirteen trial-holes sunk into this mound by him were without reward. His other digging among the mounds yielded only two skeletons.

Moore in his journey round the river between Spanish Fort and Holly Bluff found several mounds near Fairview landing and mentions two reported near Maybon Landing.

"In sight from Fairview Landing, on property of Mr. William G. Childers, of Satartia, Miss., in a cultivated field, are three mounds in line, but short distances apart. The largest, much spread, had been considerably dug into previous to our visit, and the smallest mound is in use as a cemetery. Neither of these mounds was dug into by us. The third mound, lying between the other two, is conical and fairly symmetrical. Its height is 11 feet 6 inches; its basal diameter, 75 feet. A moderate amount of digging in this mound showed that it, too, had been used as a cemetery in recent times.

"Near Fairview Landing is a mound belonging to Mr. S. S. Hearn, which we did not investigate, owing to the presence of a house upon it.

"In sight from an arm of the river that here encircles a small island, at the upper end of Fairview plantation, partly cut away by the road, is a small mound also belonging to Mr. S. S. Hearn. The height of this mound is 3 feet; its diameter, 35 feet. Our investigation was unrewarded.

"Two mounds reported by our agents as near Maybon Landing were not visited by us, permission to dig not being forthcoming."

IN ISSAQUENA AND SHARKEY COUNTIES.

Dr. Eugene A. Smith in his manuscript notes of 1870 mentioned two groups of mounds in Issaquena Co.: a group of four or five mounds, one quite high, just back of Mr. Campbell's in section 30 of T.9,R.6 W; a group of fourteen in the neighborhood of Mr. Smith's, in the third tier of sections of T. 12, R. 8 W., not far from Myersville. Mr. Smith's house was on one of the latter and there were four other mounds within 150 feet of the house.

Clarence B. Moore[1] mentions but does not describe a fine group of mounds near Mayersville (presumably the group noticed by Dr. Smith), and one or more mounds near Chotard, in the southern part of the same county.

At Hardee, Issaquena Co., east of the railroad and in plain view from the train, is a large mound upon which stands a big barn. There is also a small mound about fifty yards from the large one.

From Issaquena Co. came the fine rattlesnake tablet illustrated in figures 182 and 183, and described in the accompanying text.

On Deer Creek below Cary in Sharkey Co. are two small mounds which I partially excavated in May, 1921. The first of these lies about five miles south-west of Cary, and is much spread by cultivation, being now not more than 1.5 to 2 feet high. Mr. J. H. Moore, on whose property the mound stands, began the excavation, and had removed 20 skulls before notifying me. With the assistance of Mr. Moore and Mr. Powers I took out about 25 more. Nearly half of the mound was excavated, beginning on the north and taking a strip two feet wide at a time. The skulls were packed very closely along with other human bones in great quantities, and were poorly preserved. Apparently there was no special orienta-

---

[1]Moore: Some Aborig. Sites on Miss. River, Philadelphia, 1911, pp. 368, 369.

tion of the skulls or bones; some of the skulls faced up, some down, some lay on the side.

The second mound is about a mile nearer Cary, and about 350 yards from Mr. Robert Flannagin's residence. It is about 3.5 to 4 feet high and in cultivation. Beginning on the east side, about one-fifth of the mound was excavated, yielding 20 skulls. Here the same crowded method of burial was observed as in the preceding smaller mound.

Relatively few artifacts were found in these two mounds: a few pots were taken from each, some right side up, one at least inverted. Most of the ware was black or gray, one piece was red. Mr. J. H. Moore retains a pretty vessel only 2 inches high and 2.5 inches in diameter, with a decoration of three parallel incised lines. Another vessel, entirely plain, is 7 inches high and 7.3 in diameter, with opening 4.5 inches. A beautiful piece, unfortunately in fragments, was found on the surface of the larger mound, unusual in that the opening was not circular but elliptical, with axes 2.4 by 1.6 inches. It is described at length in the chapter on pottery.

Two knob-like objects of clay were found, each with a perforation in the smaller end for suspension. A few stone implements were found on the surface; these were of good workmanship.

Just south-west of Cary, Sharkey Co., is a group of four mounds, two large rectangular mounds and two small conical ones.

Mound A, the tallest, is about 22 feet high, rectangular, the lines running with the semi-cardinal points, measuring north-east by south-west 80 feet on top, in the other direction 74 feet on top. It is much worn by rain and the trampling of stock. The original approach seems to have been on the north-east end. There are a number of intrusion burials.

Mound B stands about 200 yards east of A and near the

railroad. It is rectangular, with the sides running with the semi-cardinal directions, being 114 feet on top north-east by south-west, and 100 feet in the other direction. The height is about 18 feet. The embankments thrown up on top of the mound during the Civil War still exist.

Mound C is about 100 yards south-east of A; it is of the flat conical type and has been long under cultivation, at present it is about 5.5 feet high and 75 feet in diameter. Much of the northern side has been hauled away.

Mound D is several hundred yards south of the others, between the railroad and Deer Creek. This cultivated mound is conical in form and now 3.5 feet high. The probe met no resistance in this tumulus. Scattered about are fragments of pottery, some of it shell-tempered; fragments of flint are scarce.

There are said to be other mounds a mile further south.

Near the railroad a mile south of Rolling Fork, Sharkey Co., is a group of three mounds on the property of Mr. F. B. Graft, whose residence is on the one furthest to the west, the middle-sized one. The group is just east of Deer Creek.

Mound A, the tallest, standing to the east, is 38 feet high, and is nearly square on top, being 85 by 95 feet. It has suffered much from erosion of rain and the trampling of cattle. A slight elevation runs out from the base of it toward the west.

Mound B to the west, on which Mr. Graft's house stands, is at present (1921) 20 feet high; Mr. Graft expects to lower it by nearly half.

Mound C south of A is near the barn; it has been worked over and is now about 1.5 feet high. Mr. Graft reports that nothing of consequence was found in it except burnt earth.

He knows of no artifacts found about here. I saw a few fragments of pottery. Dr. Chaney told me in 1916 of a remarkable stone pipe which was found in the vicinity in earlier days and taken to Arkansas.

At Mt. Helena, Sharkey Co., two or three miles northeast of Rolling Fork, there is a large mound, on which is located the home of Mr. George C. Harris, plainly visible from the railroad (fig. 14). Mr. Harris, in a letter of January 23, 1917, gives the following data:

FIG. 14. Mount Helena, near Rolling Fork, Sharkey Co. Residence of Mr. George C. Harris.

The mound is rectangular in form, the longer axis being north and south. The present dimensions in feet are:

North and south at bottom 270, at top 168;

East and west at bottom 210, at top 150;

Height about 25, tho somewhat greater in the rear.

The mound was cut down 10 feet in grading for the residence and most of the dirt put at the north and south ends. No relics were found in this mound, tho it was cut down 10 feet and a cellar 7 feet deep was dug in it.

There are two smaller mounds nearby, one standing north-east about 300 feet, the other south-east about 900 feet. The one to the north-east is very low, having been in cultivation for many years. It has yielded numerous relics, such as broken pottery and stone implements, including a black stone hatchet about 2 inches by 1 inch, highly polished skin-cleaners, and one small arrow-head. This material was sent to the Smithsonian Institution. The other small mound has yielded no artifacts, nor have Indian graves been found in that vicinity, within the knowledge of Mr. Harris.

Near Anguilla, Sharkey Co., is a mound of considerable size, standing west of the railroad and easily seen from the train. It stands near a residence and has what seems to be a cistern-house upon it. A letter from Mr. Fields gives the height as about 18 feet after leveling on top, very little having been cut away; the periphery at base is 480 feet, at top 200 feet.

At Panther Burn, near the north-west corner of Sharkey Co., I saw from the train what seemed to be a low Indian mound standing east of the railroad. Mr. J. W. Johnson writes me that back of this mound about a mile farther east there is a group of four mounds. Mound A, the largest stands to the north, is 20 or 25 feet high, and has a spur or apron about 10 feet high extending toward the east; mound B to the east is about 12 feet high; mound C to the south is the lowest, being only 6 feet high; mound D to the west is about 10 feet high. From A to C is about 450 feet, from A to D about 180 feet.

IN WASHINGTON COUNTY.

A mile and a half or two miles south of Arcola, Washington Co., the railroad passes thru a group of six aboriginal mounds. The railway here runs almost due north and south; mounds A, B, C, and D are west of the railroad, mounds E and F and two ponds are east of it. The three largest mounds are rectangular.

Mound A farthest north is a conical mound, now in cultivation, and 5 feet high. Pieces of burnt clay with cane impressions are found here, and fragments of pottery and other artifacts seem more abundant than about the other mounds.

Mound B is the great dominant mound, standing 27 feet above the plain and commanding a magnificent view. It is rectangular in form, with steep sides; a gentler approach leads up from the east.

Mound C is a small conical mound in cultivation and no doubt much spread; the present height is 3 feet. It stands a short distance south-west of B and north-west of D.

Mound D is 14 feet high, rectangular in form, with lines following the cardinal directions. This is the most southern of the group. It has been used for modern burials.

The rectangular mound E faces B across the railroad. It is 12 feet high, and is at present in pasture.

Mound F is small and stands still farther to the east or somewhat to the south of east.

There are two depressions with water east of the railroad. Pond 1 extends irregularly around the north and east sides of mound E. Pond 2 is a little circular pool farther to the north. The creek is farther east.

There are mounds in the triangle made by the three railroads connecting Leland, Stoneville, and Elizabeth, in Washington County. Just west of the railroad between Leland and Elizabeth may be seen from the train two mounds, one of which is quite tall, the other about half as high. These form part of the so-called Avondale mounds, described and figured by the Bureau of Ethnology, 1890-91.

According to the Bureau account the tallest was 30 feet high, nearly 200 feet long, and about 175 feet broad, and was used as a graveyard for white people; the second in size was 15 feet high and used as a graveyard for negroes. West of the largest mound was a depression of about three acres from which the material was probably taken to build the mound. Many fragments of pottery and pieces of burnt clay with impressions of cane and grass were found near the surface of the small mounds. According to the illustration given (fig. 161; fig. 15 in this book), there were seven

FIG. 15. The Leland Mounds (Avondale Mounds), Washington Co., reduced from 12th Ann. Rept. of Bu. of Am. Ethn., 1890-91, p. 260, fig. 161.

mounds in the group. One of the smaller mounds was opened but no human bones or evidences of burial were discovered.

Just north of the railway between Leland and Stoneville on the Sherwood place there is a medium-sized mound with tombstones on it.

A few miles to the east, on the Dunleith plantation in Washington County, there is a group of mounds. They stand south-west of Dr. Alfred H. Stone's residence and near the bayou. The largest is 14.5 feet high, is approximately square, and has an area of one-eighth of an acre on top. Two others are situated nearby toward the south-east, the nearer small, the remoter considerably larger. To the north-east are three more elevations quite irregular in outline; whether natural or artificial, I did not determine. There are very few potsherds and flint fragments lying about, and no shells, tho the bayou is large and deep. Nevertheless a number of relics have been found on the plantation.

There is also an isolated mound of medium size on another part of the Dunleith plantation perhaps a mile south of the station.

One of the finest group of mounds in the state is the Winterville group (fig. 16), situated about a mile south of Winterville, Washington County, and five or six miles north of Greenville. This group is about two miles from Black Bayou and but little farther from Point Chicot on the Mississippi River. These mounds are also called the Blum mounds and the Hunt mounds.

A group of mounds described and plotted in 1879 from notes by James Hough[1] would seem to be the Winterville group. The position seems to correspond closely with the Winterville group, tho the plot of the mounds is not accurate for that group. The height of the great central mound is given as 55 feet.

In 1907 Mr. Clarence B. Moore made a very careful and detailed study of the prehistoric site at Winterville and in 1908 published his findings. The following description is condensed directly from Mr. Moore's publication[2] and the map is reduced from Mr. Moore's map.

The group on a plantation belonging to A. Blum, Esq., consists of a great central mound, marked A, 55 feet high,

---
[1]Annual Report of the Smithsonian Institution for 1879, pp. 383, 384.
[2]Moore: Certain Mounds of Ark. and of Miss., Part III: The Blum Mounds, Philadelphia, 1908, pp. 593-600.

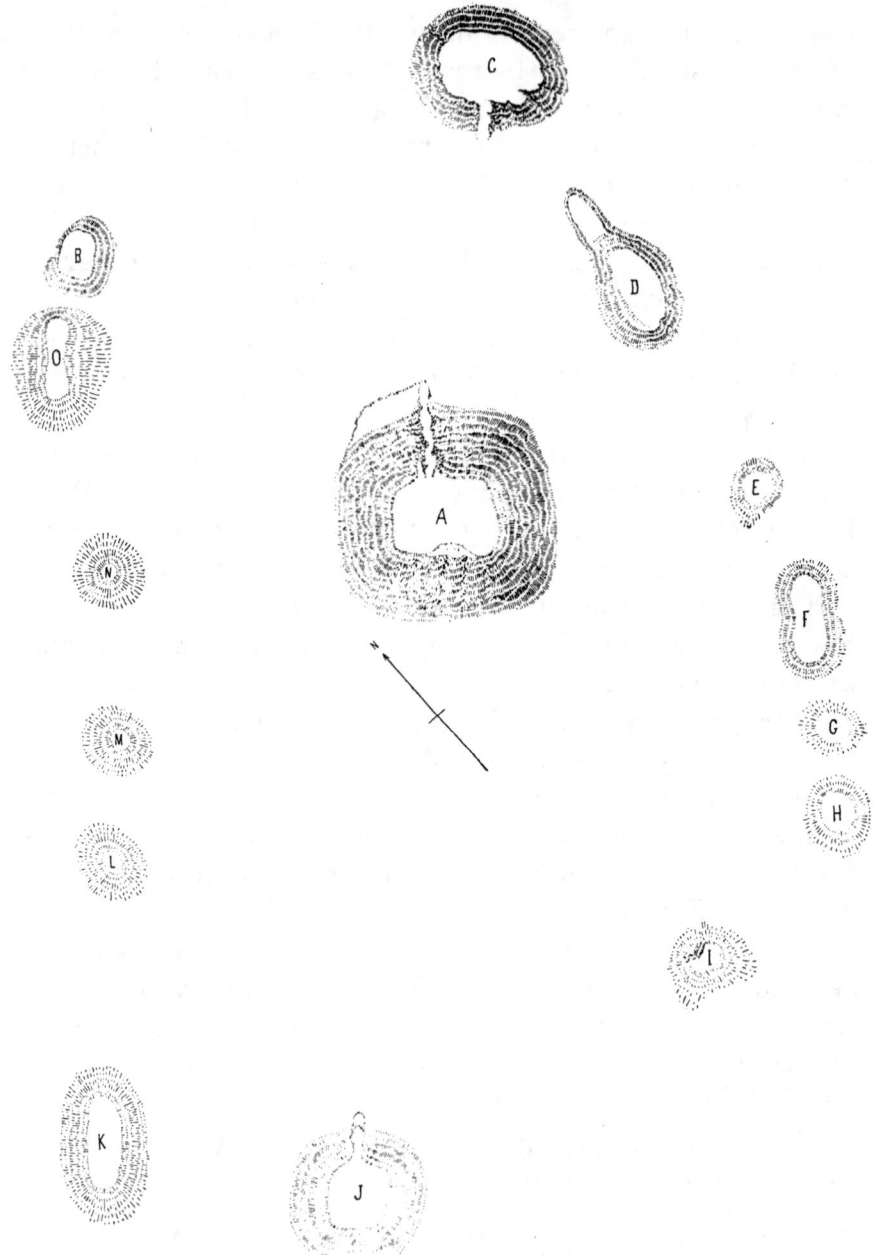

Fig. 16. The Winterville Mounds, Washington Co. Scale 1 inch to 250 feet. Reduced from Moore, page 595.

surrounded by fourteen other mounds, marked B to O inclusive, forming an irregular ellipse. The axes of this ellipse are about 1600 feet north-east and south-west and 1000 north-west and south-east.

These mounds on the river plain and consequently on land subject to overflow are not however exposed to wash of water in time of flood, it is said, the distance from the river being such that the current has no influence. The summits of the more important mounds of the group, so far as known, have never been submerged, the usual rise of water, about the mounds when there is a flood being, it is said, from 3 to 5 feet.

The irregularity of outline of some of the mounds is probably due to long-continued cultivation, to the constant tread of cattle and mules, to the deep and extensive rooting of hogs, and to the wash of rain.

Mounds A and J have approaches from the north-east; mound C has an approach from the south-west. They thus have their approaches from within the enclosure. Mound D has an apron or platform toward the north.

The height of a mound often depends on the side from which the measurement is made. The subjoined list gives the altitudes of the Winterville mounds, as taken from within the enclosure, together with other descriptive matter:

Mound A—55 feet; summit 100 by 132 feet.
Mound B—13 feet 2 inches; summit 44 by 60 feet.
Mound C—19 feet 6 inches; summit 90 by 136 feet.
Mound D—17 feet 6 inches; summit 60 by 112 feet.
Mound E— 6 feet 7 inches; partly cut away for a road.
Mound F— 9 feet 7 inches; oblong.
Mound G— 4 feet; nearly circular.
Mound H— 7 feet 7 inches; slightly elliptical.
Mound I— 9 feet; irregular outline.
Mound J—30 feet 10 inches; summit 76 by 80 feet.

Mound K—12 feet 5 inches; oblong.
Mound L— 7 feet 6 inches; slightly elliptical.
Mound M— 7 feet 3 inches; circular.
Mound N— 8 feet; circular.
Mound O—10 feet 10 inches; oblong.

Certain small elevations outside and inside the ellipse, probably dwelling-sites, have not been indicated in the plan.

The Winterville mounds and surrounding territory have comparatively no history as to the discovery of artifacts or of human remains. No human bones were seen by us on the surface, though extensive ditching had been done, and much of the level ground and a number of the mounds are regularly plowed over; and only a limited number of fragments of earthen-ware lay around—all this lack of signs of former occupancy being in marked contrast with our experience at the great group of mounds at Moundville, Alabama.

We commenced to investigate the Winterville group of mounds by sinking trial-holes in the summit-plateaus of the mounds, and in the level ground where appearances indicated the possible presence of a cemetery, with the intention, should burials be discovered, of prosecuting the search in a more thoro way. The trial-holes in the Blum mounds were intended to be 6 feet long by 3 feet wide and 4 feet deep, but as the material of which the mounds were made was, as a rule, a tenacious alluvial deposit, dried comparatively hard and in places still further hardened by fire, the dimensions given were not always adhered to exactly. Sometimes when ground unmistakably undisturbed was reached, the holes were not carried to a full depth of 4 feet.

Mounds A, C, E, H, I (previously opened), M, N, and O, yielded nothing.

Mound B contained recent burials. Mound D yielded an isolated skull badly decayed, and fragments of another skull. Mound F yielded a small oblate-spheroidal vessel of coarse ware from near the surface.

Mound G gave nine double-pointed fish-scales, identified by Mr. H. W. Fowler as probably belonging to the alligator-gar *(Lepisosteus tristoechus)*, a fish abundant in the lower Mississippi River. The scales of this fish, which Du Pratz calls *poisson-armé,* are said by him sometime to have served as points for the arrows of aborigines of the lower Mississippi region.

Mound J afforded the skeleton of an adult, at full length on the back, two and a half feet below the surface.

Mound K contained a number of fish-scales, one overlapping the other as if a portion of the fish had been present originally; and also five small pots and a fragment of excellent yellow ware.

Mound L had the skeleton of an infant about two feet below the surface.

In the level ground a large number of trial-holes were also dug.

Thruout the digging, sherds were rarely met with. Such as were found in the trial-holes, and those encountered on the surface, were mainly of common ware, though a few, including one we have already described, were of excellent material—one fragment of black ware having an especially high polish on both sides. Decoration, when present, almost invariably consisted of simple designs rudely incised. Decoration with red paint was several times found.

On the surface were a small chisel wrought from a pebble of chert, and a disk of pottery which had been given its form before baking and had not been cut from a fragment of an earthen-ware vessel.

From the trial-holes came mussel-shells which have been identified by Dr. H. A. Pilsbry as *Quadrula perplicata; Q. heros; Lampsilis anodontoides.*

We are at a loss to account for our limited success in finding burials and artifacts in the neighborhood of the Winterville mounds. We know that domiciliary mounds, such as those forming this group probably were, are often without burials in their summit-plateaus, but one would expect to find cemeteries in the surrounding level ground. Did such cemeteries still exist in the neighborhood of the mounds, it is strange that we failed to find them—for one rarely digs to any extent among skeletons without encountering some of them. If cemeteries underlie the cultivated fields (and practically all the territory near the mounds has been under cultivation for a long time) one would look for numerous accounts of the finding of bones and artifacts in post-holes, in trenching, and in cultivation; but such accounts, as we have seen, are not forthcoming.

I need not add anything further to Mr. Moore's account than to say that on the occasion of my visit to these mounds in August, 1916, there were very many fragments of pottery and flint on and about mound D, which was exposed to the trampling of stock.

The group of mounds at Shadyside Landing, Washington Co., was investigated by Moore in 1911 and a report[1] published the same year, which is here condensed:

Near Shadyside Landing are three mounds which would be in full view from the Mississippi River but for the presence of trees. Near these mounds are various small ridges and flat elevations, which evidently were aboriginal dwelling-sites, tho apparently much of their superficial parts had disappeared.

The mound nearest the Landing is of irregularly circular outline, with basal diameter of 166 feet, and height of about 13 feet. Trial-holes yielded no return.

---

[1]Moore: Some Aborig. Sites on Miss. River, Philadelphia, 1911, pp. 388 and fol.

In full view from this mound is another somewhat larger but much spread, and evidently considerably reduced in height thru wash of rain and trampling of feet. In fact a house built upon the mound, resting on supports, has beneath it a part of the mound about 2 feet higher than the rest of its surface. In fig. 13 [of Moore] is shown this house under which may be seen the ground rising as described.

Within a few feet of this mound is the third one, having a circular base about 95 feet across, and a height of 7.5 feet. Our digging in this mound was not rewarded.

A short distance in a north-westerly direction from the mound nearest the river is a small flat rise in the ground, on which were some fragments of pottery and other debris. This area was fairly riddled with our trial-holes, which showed that burials had been put down from a higher level, but that most of them were near the surface owing to the amount of material which had been ploughed and washed from that part of the site. There were found here fifteen burials, including a bunched burial containing the bones of four persons. With the bunched burial were the crumbling remains of a small earthen-ware vessel.

A few feet east of the ridge which we have described was another or perhaps an extension of the mound. The surface of this ridge was covered with fragments of pottery and bits of human bone were plentiful on it. This ridge or extension was thoroly investigated, but it became evident that nearly all the made ground which had formed during aboriginal occupancy had been worked or washed away, as but two burials were found, one a bunch burial having a single adult skull, the other a burial of the same class with ten skulls. The upper part of the burial was visible on the surface, while none of it lay more than one foot deep.

With the latter burial were three vessels of earthen-ware: one of medium size, having a body with four lobes, without decoration; another badly crushed, on which were two encircling incised lines; a third (fig. 14, Moore; fig. 326, Brown) having a round opening and a square, flat base on which were a number of concentric, incised squares. The body of the vessel has incised encircling lines, containing diagonal ones. With this burial also were part of a small celt of fine-grained sandstone, and near the surface a fine pipe of limestone (plate xxix, Moore; figs. 216, 217, Brown), representing a human figure on hands and knees.

On the surface, near this burial, was a small barbed arrow-head of white flint. Scattered in the soil were found also: two small rude celts; a pebble shaped to resemble somewhat a celt; a pebble grooved to form a pendant; a pebble with an artificial semi-perforation; part of an antler 5.5 inches long; a number of small chisels chipped from flint pebbles.

All other ridges and rises at this interesting place were carefully dug into by us, but while it was evident that they were of artificial origin, it was also apparent that the parts in which burials probably had existed, had washed or worn away.

IN BOLIVAR AND OTHER COUNTIES.

On the Virginia plantation belonging to the heirs of Mr. Charles Scott, between Rosedale and the southern part of Bolivar Co., are a large mound and a small low one near each other, and two other mounds at some distance. Moore's[1] account of his work here is condensed in the following paragraphs:

About two miles in a north-east by east direction from Neblett Landing there is on the old Neblett place, now known as Virginia plantation, the property of Mr. Charles Scott of Rosedale, Miss., a mound about 7 feet high. It is nearly

---

[1] Moore: Some Aborig. Sites on Miss. River, Philadelphia, 1911, pp. 391-400.

square and has a summit-plateau. The entire mound has been under cultivation that has rounded its corners and extended its diameter, which, at the time of our visit, was about 125 feet. Trees on the side of this mound show it to have suffered extensive wash of rain, the roots of one tree being exposed for 2.5 feet above the present surface. The mound presumably has suffered more extensively on the sides than on the level top, tho it was evident that the plateau also had suffered to a considerable extent. Some burials were found partly uncovered by the plow, and presumably many more had been totally destroyed.

In shape this mound has every appearance of having been a domiciliary one, and our digging in it, which lasted two and one-half days, with seven men, confirmed this view, for while the mound contained many burials in the summit-plateau and part-way down the sides, it was evident that these had not been made during the building of the mound, but had been sunk from the surface after its completion. The mound was composed largely of raw clay material, with more or less sand. The graves, none deeper than three feet, had been dug into this material, which had a distinctive color, making it easy to define the limits of the graves. Presumably, then, a domiciliary mound had been utilized superficially as a place of burial.

Sixty-five burials came from this mound, of which forty-four were bunched burials. Three of these latter were noteworthy in that, instead of having the long-bones in layers or in piles horizontally, they were arranged almost vertically in the ground. Of the bunched burials, some contained seven, eight, and even twelve skulls. The bones at this place were badly decayed, none being in a condition for preservation.

In connection with eight burials—five bunched burials and three extended ones—bark was present, usually below the burial, but exceptionally, above it. Presumably, however, other burials in the mound had been accompanied with bark, which had disappeared through decay.

The only objects, except earthen-ware vessels, found in the soil apart from burials, were a pebble-hammer and a piercing implement of bone. Singularly few artifacts, except earthen-ware, had been placed with burials in this mound. Ninety-one vessels of earthen-ware lay with burials in this mound and six vessels were found apart from them. Of the ninety-seven vessels, twenty-four were unbroken or nearly so, most of the remainder being badly crushed.

The bunched burials at this place had their full share of earthen-ware vessels, the deposits with some of the larger burials being greater than those with smaller ones.

Burial no. 17, consisting of six skulls of adults and one of a child, lay upon bark, and had with it thirteen vessels, an interesting feature being that some of these are diminutive and evidently had been placed with the burial on account of the child included with it.

Burial no. 33, in which were eight skulls, two of them having belonged to children, was accompanied with eight vessels, and here again toy vessels intended for children were present.

The pottery from this mound is not of the best, and no vessel shows a polished surface. Decoration is a marked feature of the ware, consisting in the main of line-work, engraved, incised, or trailed, with much repetition of design. Decoration in color is present on but two vessels, a design in red and white in each instance. Moore gives ten illustrations of this pottery, figures 15 to 24, seven of which are reproduced in the chapter on pottery in this book, figures 319 to 325, to which the reader is referred for full descriptions.

In sight of the mound just described is a considerably larger mound, the surface of which apparently has not been under cultivation. It is said that this mound has been used largely for burial purposes in recent times. A number of trial-holes sunk in the summit-plateau were unproductive.

Between the two mounds was level ground which had been long under cultivation. On the surface were scattered some debris from aboriginal sites and a few fragments of human bones. A considerable number of trial-holes in this ground came upon three burials, with one of which was an inferior vessel of earthen-ware.

There was described and illustrated by Squier and Davis[1] a circular enclosure with mounds situated in the southern part of Bolivar Co., near William's Bayou in the Choctaw bend, one mile and a half from the Mississippi River. These works are plotted in figure 22 of their book and described as follows:

They consist of two truncated pyramidal mounds, accompanied by two small conical mounds, the whole surrounded by a circular embankment of earth 2300 feet in circumference and 4 feet high, there being no ditch. A gateway opens into the enclosure from the east.

Mound A is 150 feet square at the base, 75 feet square on top, and 20 feet high, with a graded ascent from the east. Mound B is 135 feet square at the base, 50 feet at top, and 15 feet high, with ascent from the north. The two small conical mounds are about 30 feet in diameter and 5 feet high. The sides of the pyramidal structures do not vary two degrees from the cardinal points.

Apparently the same group was described and illustrated thirty years later from notes by James Hough[2]. The group is said to be on the plantation of Mr. William P. Perkins. The dimensions correspond closely, but the directions appear to be confused. If the Hough drawing be turned ninety degrees and viewed thru the paper it corres-

[1]Squier and Davis: Ancient Monuments, Washington, 1848, p. 116.
[2]Smithsonian Ann. Report for 1879, p. 385.

ponds very closely to that of Squier and Davis. Hough notes an additional mound outside the enclosure near the river. I have not seen this group.

Mr. W. G. Trimble of Gunnison furnishes data of a group of five mounds, near Gunnison, Bolivar Co., on the land of his sister, Mrs. A. R. Blanchard. The mounds are now nearly obliterated by the processes of occupation and cultivation. One seems to have been a burial mound.

A short distance south of Alligator, Bolivar Co., is a group of mounds which was investigated by Dr. Charles Peabody in the summer of 1918. The first elevation examined was either a mound or a refuse-heap; from it were obtained many potsherds and small stone pieces and some excellent bone awls, but no whole pots or other artifacts of striking interest. At the time of my visit Dr. Peabody was just beginning the excavation of the second mound, a relatively small one with height of about 5.75 feet. There are also three other mounds in the group, the largest a rectangular domiciliary mound about 17 feet high. Dr. Peabody's report on this work has not been published.

There is a small mound west of the railroad at Shelby, Bolivar Co.

The Twelfth Annual Report of the Bureau of Ethnology (page 258) describes briefly a mound in Sunflower County near the shoals of Sunflower River which was about 125 feet long, 100 feet wide, and 25 feet high to the summit of the cone near the eastern end. On it was a white oak 6 feet in diameter. In it were found human bones, burnt clay, and clay vessels, including the interesting shell-shaped piece pictured on page 259 of the report.

Malmaison, the old home of Greenwood Leflore, stands a short distance north of the railroad in Carroll Co., between Greenwood and Carrollton. The grave of the old chief is in the family cemetery nearby. A mound is reported three or four miles to the south, about two miles from Valley Hill.

Seven miles east of Sidon, in Carroll Co., there is a group of mounds near the iron bridge over Abiaca Creek. I visited them in 1906 but made no survey. I was told that bones and skulls are sometimes plowed up in the adjacent field. Here I found the diminutive celt shown in figure 78.

The town of Shellmound, Leflore Co., took its name from a large Indian mound with abundance of shells on its surface.

Three-fourths of a mile west of the railroad bridge at Philipp, Leflore Co., there is a series of mounds or fortifications along the river and between two sloughs which lead into it. A chain of irregular mounds or earth-works runs parallel with the river; at its highest point near the west end it is perhaps 24 feet high on the river side; the east end is much lower. The public road divides and runs on each side of this line of earth-works. The photograph (fig. 17) shows the west end as it was in the summer of 1916. There are several mounds and remains of mounds in the cultivated field to the south. The group deserves more extended study. Mr. R. C. Townes reports that he has dug into two of these elevations, uncovering skeletons and crude pottery.

In the town of Charleston, Tallahatchie Co., south-west of the public square, there stands a conical mound of considerable size, which has been in cultivation. On the top there is abundance of burnt clay with straw impressions. In the field nearby are various fragments, most abundant about 75 yards from the mound in the direction of town.

On the Buford place one mile north of Sumner, Tallahatchie Co., there stands on the west bank of the bayou a much worn mound perhaps 22 to 25 feet high.

Under one of the stores in Tutwiler, Tallahatchie Co., is part of an old mound about 3 feet high, from which I saw bones protruding. Mounds are reported between Sumner and Vance.

At Marks, Quitman Co., on the bank of Coldwater River, are refuse-heaps, containing many shells, fragments of pottery, and some bones. Mr. W. R. Wallis reports eight

FIG. 17. West end of Indian fort or mound at Philipp, Leflore Co., looking east, Aug. 24, 1916. C. S. B.

mounds in the vicinity of Marks. The massive frog pipe shown in figure 211 came from this vicinity.

IN CLARKSDALE AND COAHOMA COUNTY.

Clarksdale and the territory immediately about it were formerly rich in mounds and earth-works; many of these have been destroyed in the building of the city and the development of the country. In this vicinity Mr. Charles W. Clark collected much valuable material, which is still in his private collection in Clarksdale.

When I first visited Clarksdale, there stood on the east bank of Sunflower River just north of the railroad bridge a large mound partly cut away for a street and other purposes. I estimated the height in 1912 at 13 or 14 feet and the length parallel with the river as 220 feet. There was a large area on top apparently undisturbed. In 1918 this mound appeared to be entirely removed. From it Mr. Henry Davis obtained a handsome earthen-ware bottle 10 inches high and 7 inches in diameter, decorated with four sets of concentric circles in color. This was no doubt the great rectangular mound illustrated and described by the Bureau of Ethnology in 1890-91[1].

The plan of the Clarksdale earth-works is given in figure 158 of the Bureau report by Col. P. W. Norris. According to this plan and the accompanying description, which Mr. Charles W. Clark of Clarksdale considers hurried and inaccurate, the group consisted of a rectangular mound and three conical mounds enclosed by an earth-wall, an excavation at one end of the wall, and further away two other conical mounds, a cemetery, and a number of house-sites. The description, condensed, follows:

There is a semicircular inclosure fronting the river, the surrounding earthen wall being partially obliterated by the plow, tho sufficient remains to trace satisfactorily the line. The length following the curve, as ascertained by pacing, is 2004 feet; the height where least disturbed is from 3 to 5 feet.

The largest and most interesting of the mounds is situated within the inclosure and directly on the bank of the river, so that the slope of the west side of the mound is continuous with the slope of the bank. It is rectangular in form, consisting first of a platform 5 feet high, which forms the base, projecting as a narrow terrace on all sides except that

[1] Twelfth Annual Rept. of Bu. of Am. Ethn., 1890-91, Washington, 1894, pp. 256-8.

next the river. Above this rises the mound proper, 20 feet high, 153 feet long at the base, and nearly 100 feet wide. The top is flat and level and on it now stands the village church, but formerly there stood on it a little conical mound 5 feet high and 25 feet in diameter, consisting as is stated almost wholly of burnt clay, charcoal, ashes, and fragments of pottery, beneath which were found a fine scallop-edged, double-eared pot and a skeleton.

The other mounds are small and of the ordinary conical form; the most northerly one, a cemetery mound, is but slightly elevated and scarcely deserves to be called a mound. The main portion of this low, dark-colored mound or slightly elevated space was covered by a residence and small garden, but along a few feet of its vacant northern edge some excavations were made. The skeletons were nearly 3 feet below the surface in a single tier, lying horizontally, but without uniformity as to direction. The pottery, of which only two entire vessels were obtained, like that from Dickerson's mound, is lighter-colored and thinner than usual.

Human bones having been found in grading a roadway thru the low gravelly banks of a washout between the burial mound and the river, trenches were cut in both banks. Human bones, so hard as to be cut with difficulty by the spade, were found thruout the 50 feet in length of the trench, both above and below the road, but the heaviest deposit was above the road on the north side, where they formed nearly a solid layer of skeletons scarcely a foot below the surface. So many entire skeletons were traceable that it is evident it was not a deposit of bones from scaffolds, but a burial of bodies en masse with little regard for regularity. No weapons, charcoal, ashes, or pottery were found with them, and, altho tradition gives us no information in regard to them, it is probable that the burials were comparatively modern.

Still farther north where the ancient bayou joins the

river valley, was found an extensive line of house-sites marked by patches of burnt clay. In the excavations made among these house sites a small stone mortar, a rude celt, and two very fine ones, also many fragments of pottery, a number of fleshers and scrapers were obtained; also a coarse clay pipe, donated by Mr. John Clark.

The largest excavation at this place is situated at the south-west corner of the inclosure. From this, in all probability, was obtained the material for building the large mound.

The position of some of the mounds in Clarksdale, as sketched for me by Mr. Charles W. Clark, differs considerably from that indicated in the Bureau report. I give in this paragraph the substance of Mr. Clark's sketch. The great mound extended along the east bank of the river all the way from Third Street to the Y. & M. V. Railroad. The next largest mound stood in the Y of the Tallahatchie branch of the railroad, south of the main Y. & M. V. line, just about in the line of Sharkey Avenue. It was about 15 feet high. No burials or artifacts were found in it. Another small mound stood between the great mound and Delta Avenue near the present railroad; another in the courthouse yard. In the latter were found Mr. Clark's twin vase and two copper hatchets. Remains of two mounds, one of which stood west of the railroad hotel between Yazoo and Delta Avenue and south of Third Street, the other at the extreme north end of Yazoo Avenue, may still be seen. The latter was near the side entrance to the old Clark home, now the main entrance to the Cutrer residence. There were also two mounds near the place where the continuation of Delta Avenue strikes the old channel in the northern part of town, one east of the road, one west. The earth-wall enclosed much more ground than indicated in the report of the Bureau of Ethnology.

In 1901 Dr. Charles Peabody and Mr. William C. Farabee under the auspices of the Peabody Museum of Harvard University opened a mound on the plantation of Mr. Elleston L. Dorr, Jr., at Clarksdale, Coahoma County. The following account of this work is taken from Dr. Peabody's detailed report[1]:

The mound was a rectangular one, measuring north and south 90 feet, east and west 60 feet; the height above the surrounding field was 9.5 feet. Near the top was a transverse trench one foot and two inches deep, probably the result of tentative excavations previously made by the owners.

The remains of fifty prehistoric burials were found. The burials lay scattered through the mound with a greater number in the south-west quadrant. Their depth below the surface varied from one foot to eight feet. As a whole they lay deeper than the surface burials of the Edwards Mound. Six were full-length burials, two were bundle burials, and eight had the knees doubled up, most of the latter skeletons lying on the side. Besides these prehistoric burials there were fifteen modern burials in the mound.

There were found in the mound also projectile points, fragments of pottery, charcoal in small bits, a bead of galena, a tall bowl with triangular base, and a few shells.

The excavation of the mound was carried on from the north, east, and south, and a parallelogram 80 feet from north to south and 52 feet from east to west was dug through down to the level of the surrounding field. The soil varied from heavy sandy loam to the very heavy alluvial soil called "buckshot." No soil foreign to the district was noted.

With horses and a scraper the mound was restored on May 18th nearly to its original appearance, and cotton was immediately planted upon it.

[1]Peabody: Exploration of Mounds, Coahoma Co., Miss., Cambridge, Mass., 1904.

Four small mounds in the neighboring field vary from two to five feet in height.

The mounds at Oliver, Coahoma County, were investigated in 1901 and 1902 by the same archeologists. The account which follows is condensed from Dr. Peabody's detailed description in the publication just cited.

This group (fig. 18) is situated sixteen miles south of Clarksdale on the land of Mr. P. M. Edwards. At least three mounds are north of the Sunflower River; twenty are south of it. The large central mound stands a short distance south of the river near a small depression; it measures 190 feet from north to south and 180 feet from east to west, and has a vertical height of 26 feet. The other mounds are small; the third from the east, called the cemetery mound, is 5.4 feet high; the two nearest the great mound to the northeast are somewhat over 3 feet high; the one farthest south is 2.5 feet high; the rest under two feet high.

The long irregular depressions in the surrounding fields may have been formed originally by taking the soil for building; rain and ploughing having since lowered these hollows till their significance has vanished. Search in the fields and woods near by failed to reveal large pits, such as are in evidence near the Carson group of mounds in the same county.

Surface specimens were abundant and good. Flint points and knives of fine workmanship were scattered about by the hundreds, and knives, celts, and other stone implements, disks, and sherds of pottery were picked up in great numbers.

The principal investigation was made in the great central Oliver mound. Of the total surface of 36,000 square feet of this mound, more than 11,000 square feet were excavated. Excavations on a small and informal scale were made in mound 3, the cemetery mound, by Mr. Farabee, and tentative diggings were tried elsewhere.

Shells were numerous in the north-eastern portion of

102 ARCHEOLOGY OF MISSISSIPPI.

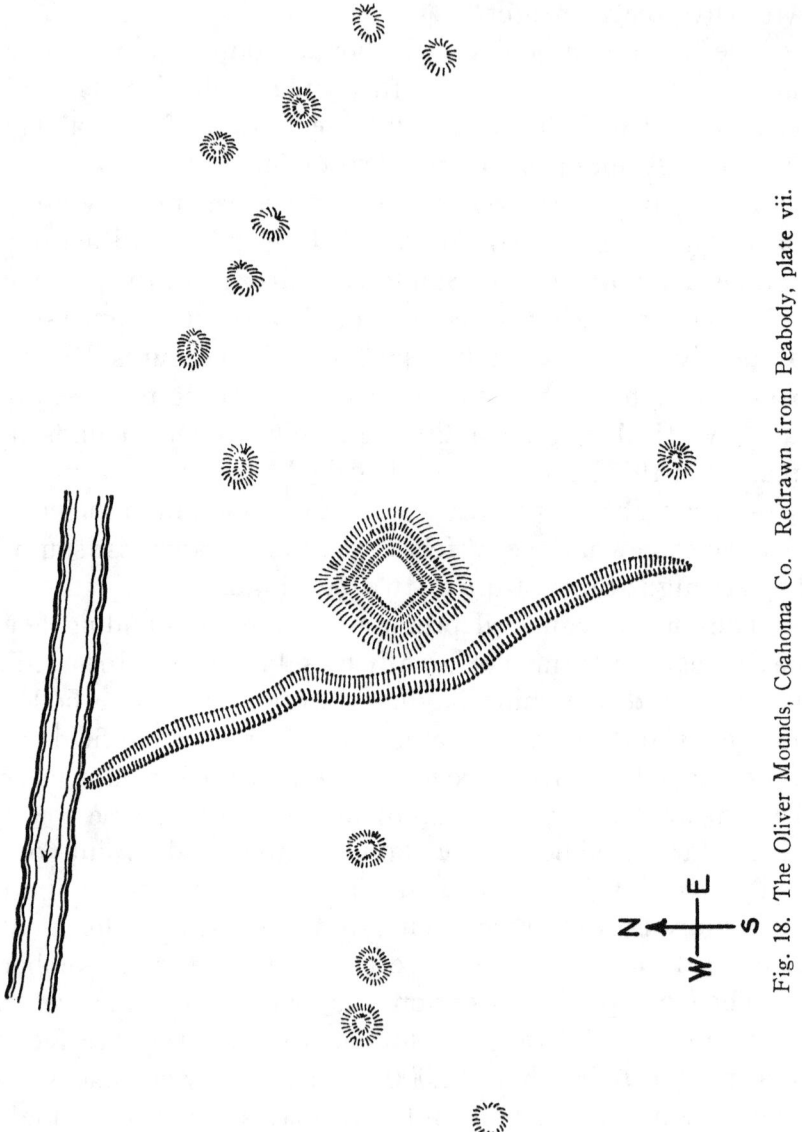

Fig. 18. The Oliver Mounds, Coahoma Co. Redrawn from Peabody, plate vii.

the central mound. Burnt clay in strata or nuggets was abundant thruout, especially near the surface. Pottery fragments and animal bones were more numerous in the upper part of the mound than in the lower part, and in the eastern half of the mound than in the western. Burials and unbroken pottery were more frequent on the western slope, and holes in the eastern half.

A characteristic feature of the Oliver mound was the holes that occurred in great numbers, one hundred and ninety-one of these being found and measured during the two years' work. They were usually vertical; otherwise the base trended indifferently to the north, east, south, or west. The great majority of them were empty or with an accumulation of soft soil at the bottom. Many contained charcoal; several charred wood; one a charred post; several contained ashes; one wide shallow hole contained corn in considerable quantity. Seventy-three of these holes had their tops at or near a level about one-third the height of the mound; one hundred and six holes had their tops at or near a level a little higher. The 73 holes of the lower level when plotted suggested a rude circle.

In the Oliver mound were discovered and noted 158 burials. In many cases the skull when taken out was found not worth preserving. The weight of the damp earth often crushed and broke the bones. Otherwise the larger and stronger bones were in a better state of preservation than at Clarksdale. Burials were very numerous on the western slope of the mound. No regularity as to their position in the mound was observed, nor any reason for their greater frequency towards the south and west.

There were 119 bundle burials, 35 full-length burials, and 4 irregular burials. Heads were found toward all the cardinal points, and a few toward a semi-cardinal point: most bodies were on the back, three on the face, one on the side.

Burial no. 14 (plate x in Peabody; figure 19 in this book) was "scissors-shaped," with the legs folded at full length on top of the body, and accompanied by a brass bell. Burial no. 49 was in a sitting posture. Burial 35 had no skull and was accompanied by five arrow-points, one in the right pelvis, one by the back bone, two among the ribs, and one between

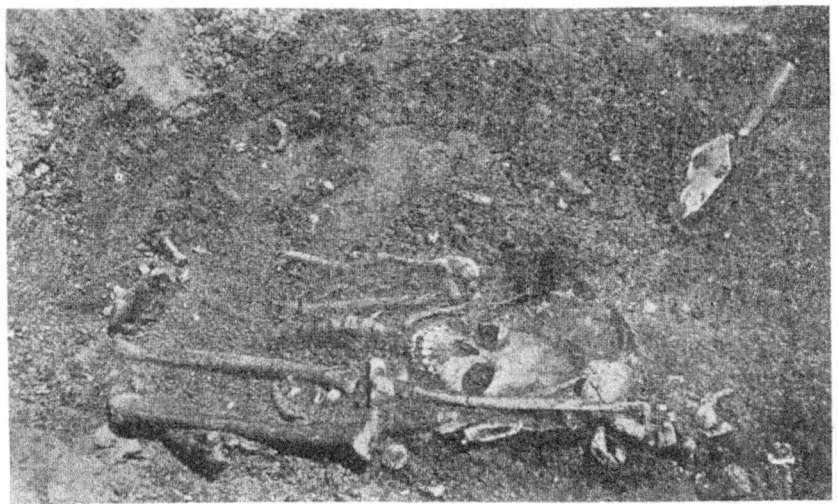

FIG. 19. "Scissors-shape" burial, no. 14, Oliver mound. Reduced from Peabody, plate x.

the spines of the back bone. Vases or pottery were found with 41 burials.

Artifacts were abundant both on the surface and in the mound; among those found in the large Oliver mound may be mentioned: a large variety of earthen-ware vessels (some shown in figures 315 to 317), clay disks, clay pipes, burnt clay with cane impressions; stone implements including projectile points, perforators, scrapers, celts both polished and chipped, hammer-stones, stone disks, perforated pendants, a rough plummet; stone beads; shell beads, perforated shells; glass beads; brass bells, brass points; bone perforators and projectile points (figures 256 to 260); and more than a hundred turquoise beads.

The greatest depth recorded at which articles possibly of white man's manufacture were found was a little more than three feet. There is no reason to believe, from the evidence of the articles found, that the lower part of the Oliver mound was constructed or disturbed after white contact.

The following animals were identified from bones found during the exploration of the Oliver and Dorr mounds:

>Deer *(Cariacus virginianus)*.
>Bear *(Ursus americanus)*.
>Raccoon *(Procyon lotor)*.
>Opossum *(Didelphys virginiana)*.
>Beaver *(Castor canadensis)*.
>Wildcat *(Lynx rufus)*.
>Rabbit *(Lepus aquaticus)*.
>Squirrel *(Sciurus carolinensis)*.
>Dog *(Canis familiaris)*.
>Turkey *(Meleagris gallopavo americana)*.
>Sheepshead *(Aplodinotus grunniens)*.
>Alligator Gar *(Lepidosteus tristoechus)*.

Dr. Peabody sums up his conclusions as follows:

"The Edwards mound may be considered as a typical Indian mound of a later period placed within a typical village site. The characteristic features are first, the division of the mound into an upper and lower part separated by strata A and B, and second, the variety and richness of the articles found at or near the surface of the surrounding field.

"Below the 'critical level' were the greater number of full length burials; above it the greater number of bundle burials. Below the 'critical level' were found but five of the sixty-eight vases, and very few manufactured articles of any kind, while above it they were frequent. These facts, coupled with the amount of ashes in stratum B and with the rude ring of holes above referred to, induce to the opinion, that the mound has been built in two periods: that the lower portion was gradually built and used as a burial place, that a stockade of posts was set up about a centre to the east of a later apex; that, after a period of occupancy, this stockade was burnt down, and another population continued to build the mound to a conical apex some ten feet higher. Further we conclude that the latter people buried their dead from time to time, generally intrusively in the bundle fashion and deposited pottery, and necklaces and strings of stone, shell, and glass beads with the bones; further that the latter people were undoubtedly post-Columbian and were well skilled in working stone and had some acquaintance with white people and other tribes, at least by trade. . . .

"The most striking characteristic of the specimens found is the consummately good workmanship bestowed on the smaller flint implements, particularly the scraper, in comparison with the rudeness and the infrequency of the larger forms belonging to the stone age. The specimens, except the turquoise, are what would be expected from the civilization of the Arkansas-lower-Mississippi district. In connection with this a paucity of worked shells is to be noted."

There are three small mounds west of Bobo in the southern part of Coahoma Co.

Three miles north-west of Clarksdale up the river on the Oak Ridge road there are one or two small mounds. Five miles out the same road at the Rufus Davis place there is a large mound with a house upon it. About 150 yards from this mound back from the river is a smaller mound with large trees upon it. In front of the large mound on the river bank by the road are found many potsherds.

About Coahoma and Friar's Point in Coahoma Co. there are a number of mounds.

Two and a half miles north-east of the town of Coahoma there is a group of mounds consisting of two large mounds and several small ones. There are recent burials on the tallest. The group has not yet been surveyed and studied.

A mound is reported on the Roselle place two miles southwest of Coahoma.

The present writer has never examined the Dickerson mounds located a few miles east of the Mississippi River in northern Coahoma County. They were visited about 1883 or 1884 by Col. P. W. Norris and described in the Twelfth Annual Report of the Bureau of Ethnology as follows:

"On the Dickerson farm, 4 miles east of Friar's Point, is another interesting group of mounds. These are situated on the dry, gravelly bank of the Sunflower River. There is no inclosure, but several fields of the farm are literally strewn with stone chips and fragments of ancient pottery, and upon long oval hillocks are found numerous fragments of human bones.

"The Sunflower is here scarcely a creek during low water and its gravelly banks are high above the floods; yet the mounds are mostly oblong or oval and flat on top, like those found on the bottoms subject to overflows. They are built as usual of the material from adjacent ground, which, being gravel instead of clay or mud, rendered the outlines of the beds of burned clay distributed through them more distinct than usual. Most of them seem to have been the sites of dwellings, the same as those upon the bottoms; yet on the intermediate areas are saucer-shaped depressions, indicating that the earth lodge so common farther north had been in use here.

"Of the numerous mounds explored only one was found to be a true cemetery of the ancient inhabitants. This was, as usual, one of the least conspicuous of the group. The first tier of skeletons was barely covered and the vessels, which are usually a little higher than the skeletons, were broken into fragments, only one whole one being found in this tier. The next tier was about 2 feet below the first and the bones more decayed. Relatively fewer vessels were found and these so badly broken that but two bowls were obtained entire. The third tier was 2 feet below the second, or 5 feet from the top, and slightly below the original surface of the ground.

"As less than a hundred skeletons were found here, there are doubtless other burying places in this group, but there are so many modern burials in these mounds that it was impossible to sink a pit without disturbing the skeletons of whites and negroes."

Near Stovall Station in western Coahoma County is a large group of mounds and an earth-wall enclosure. This section was visited about 1884 by Col. P. W. Norris and later by Mr. W. H. Holmes, whose investigations are published by Mr. Cyrus Thomas in a report of the Bureau of Ethnology[1]. This report is summarized in the following paragraphs:

Along the eastern bank of an old channel, on the plantation of the Carson brothers, 6 miles south of Friar's Point, is an interesting group of mounds and earth-works. The general plan of these works is shown in pl. xi [figure 20 in this book]. In the north-west is an enclosure surrounded by an earthen wall and a ditch. Nos. *a* to *f* are mounds. There are also several excavations. The area embraced in the plat is about 1 mile east and west and something over half a mile north and south.

The inclosure fronts west for a distance of 738 feet on a cypress swamp. It is in the form of a parallelogram, the wall on three sides measuring 1173 feet long, and embracing an area of about 5 acres. This wall is from 15 to 30 feet wide at the base, and from 3 to 5 feet high. A ditch is distinctly traceable along the whole length of the outside, but it is not exhibited on the plate.

Within this area, a little north-west [south-west?] of the

---
[1] Twelfth Ann. Rept. of the Bu. of Ethn., 1890-91, Washington, 1894, pages 253-5.

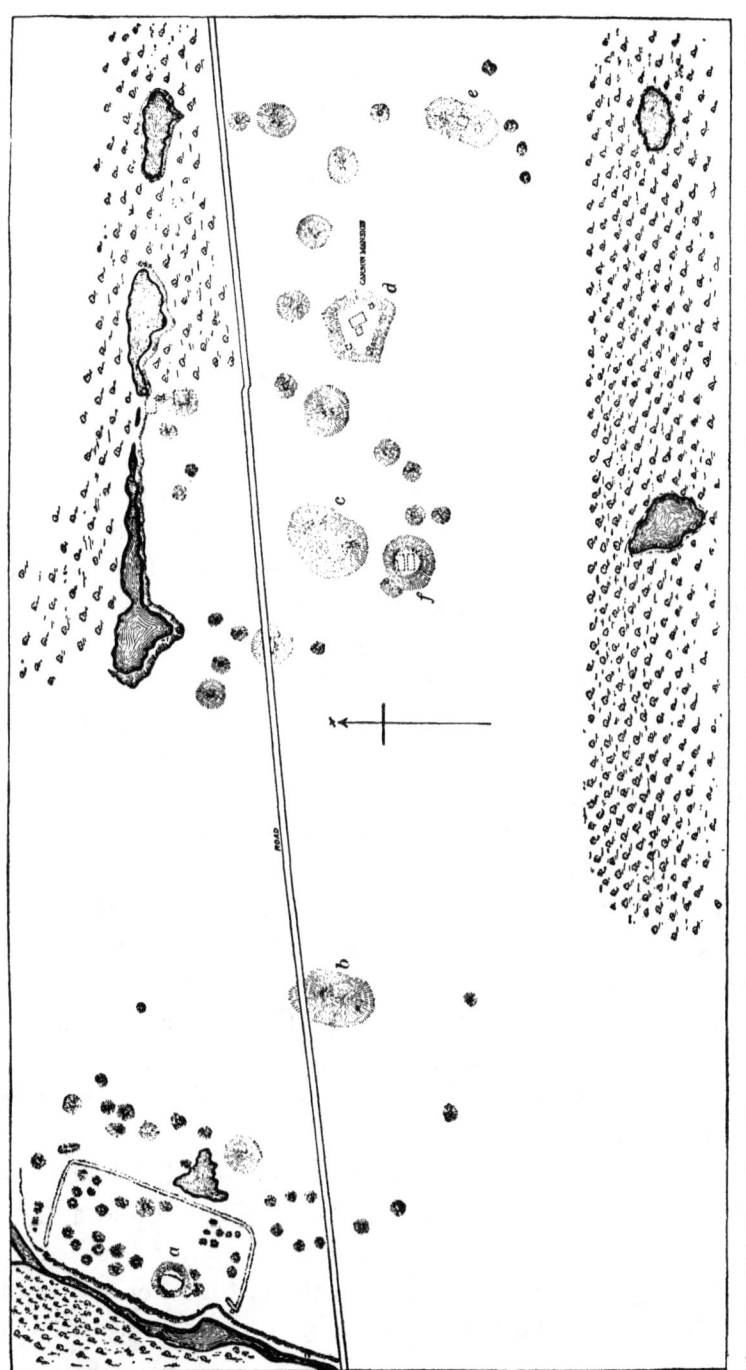

Fig. 20. The Stovall or Carson mounds and earth-works, Coahoma Co., length about one mile. Reduced from 12th Ann. Rept. of Bu. of Am. Ethnology, pl. xi.

center, is a circular mound *a,* 192 feet in diameter at the base, 15 feet high, and 66 feet across the nearly flat top. There appears to have been originally a platform some 5 or 6 feet high, on which the mound proper was built. Several excavations made in the top and on the sides showed that it was composed of earth from the bottom land, probably obtained from the excavation near the south-east corner of the inclosure. A number of fire-beds of burnt clay were found near the summit and at different elevations thruout the mound. Charcoal, ashes, and fragments of pottery and stone were also discovered, but no bones. It is probable, therefore, that these spots mark the sites of houses.

Just outside of the south-west [south-east?] corner is an artificial excavation about 100 feet in diameter, but now partially filled and converted into a bog.

Mound *b,* shown in photograph in pl. xii, is double. There are at the bottom indications of an oval platform, probably 10 feet high, with a length of 240 feet at the base. On this, two truncated cones, which occupy the entire length, but not the entire width of the platform, rise jointly for 18 feet, and above the union rise separately 8 feet higher. The entire height of the mound is therefore 36 feet [Mr. Holmes's estimate is 25 feet]. The cones are level on top, the one being 42 feet in diameter at this point and the other 48. On this mound, near the top of the northern cone, stands a thrifty black oak, 5 feet in diameter. Little excavating was done in this mound and nothing of interest found, except the ever-present fire-beds of burnt clay, stone chips, and fragments of pottery.

Mound *c* is oval and rounded on top, 210 feet long, 150 broad at the base, and 16 feet high. This mound and several smaller ones near it are so nearly masses of fire-beds, burnt clay, fragments of stone and pottery, together with more or less charcoal and ashes, as to indicate clearly that they are the sites of ancient dwellings thus elevated by accumulation of material during long continued occupancy.

Mound *d,* pl. xiii [fig. 21 in this book], the finest of the group, is roughly pentangular and very symmetrical, level on the top, 25 feet high (including the platform), 310 feet in diameter at the base, and 210 feet across the top. Besides the broad, sloping platform, 5 feet high, on which the mound rests, there is near by, almost adjoining, a small mound which

FIG. 21. Mound *d,* Carson Group, Coahoma Co., from the 12th Ann. Rept. of Bu. of Am. Ethn., pl. xiii.

forms a kind of appendage to the large one. This is about 100 feet long, 75 feet wide, and 8 feet high, rounded on top. Not only are beds of hard burned clay (the fragments of which show the casts of cane and grass) abundant upon the surface and sides of the mound, but are also found in the wells and cisterns and in other excavations made in digging cellars and for the foundations of buildings. It is evident from this that it was used as a dwelling-place or as a location for a temple or some other public building.

Mound *e* [fig. 22 in this book] is double and similar in almost every respect to *b*. The platform is 5 feet high and 120 by 80 feet on top. Near the top of one cone is a red oak tree, four feet in diameter, and near the top of the other a black oak, 6 feet in diameter. In the depression between the two cones a partially decayed skeleton was found in digging a grave for a person now interred there. This skeleton

FIG. 22. Twin mound *e*, Carson Group, Coahoma Co. Photograph by author.

was under a bed of burnt clay, and other similar beds are found near the surface of the sides and summit.

Mound *f* is oval, rounded on top, 150 feet long by 75 feet wide and between 5 and 6 feet high. A thoro examination of this mound revealed the fact that from base to summit it was composed of burnt clay, mud, or alluvial earth in irregular layers formed of lumps or little masses burned to a brick red or actually melted into slag. Much of the top of this mound is a deposit resembling mud or clay plastering, from which the sustaining canes and timbers have been burned out, leaving their casts. It seems evident, therefore, that mud-walled and perhaps partitioned dwellings stood here which were destroyed by fire.

The places from which a part at least of the dirt was taken that was used to form the mounds are shown by the unevenness of the surface of the ground immediately around them. But there are several excavations which must have furnished a large portion of the material for this purpose. They are still so deep as to form swamps, bogs, or open ponds, some of the last being well stocked with fishes.

During all the excavations made and digging done by the present proprietors, who have made all the improvements there are on the plantation, but few skeletons have been unearthed, and no whole vessels of pottery found. Still, it is possible that more extensive explorations of the small mounds may reveal these.

IN PANOLA, TUNICA, AND DE SOTO COUNTIES.

The Batesville mounds (fig. 23) are somewhat unusual in that the principal conical mound C is so much taller than the principal pyramidal mounds A and B. This group of earth-works is situated about three miles north-east of Batesville, Panola Co., just south-west of the crossing of the Illinois Central Railroad and the Sardis public road, between the two, and in sight of both.

Mound A, farthest north of the large mounds, is an irregular rectangle with the sides 120 to 130 feet in length and a maximum height of 7 feet. It has suffered much from cultivation, particularly on the east and west sides toward the south, so that now both the surface and the outlines are irregular. When I first visited the mounds in 1906 this one was better preserved than now, as I remember it, tho I then noted its irregularity. Only part of it is now (1918) in cultivation.

Mound B is slightly larger and higher and has suffered

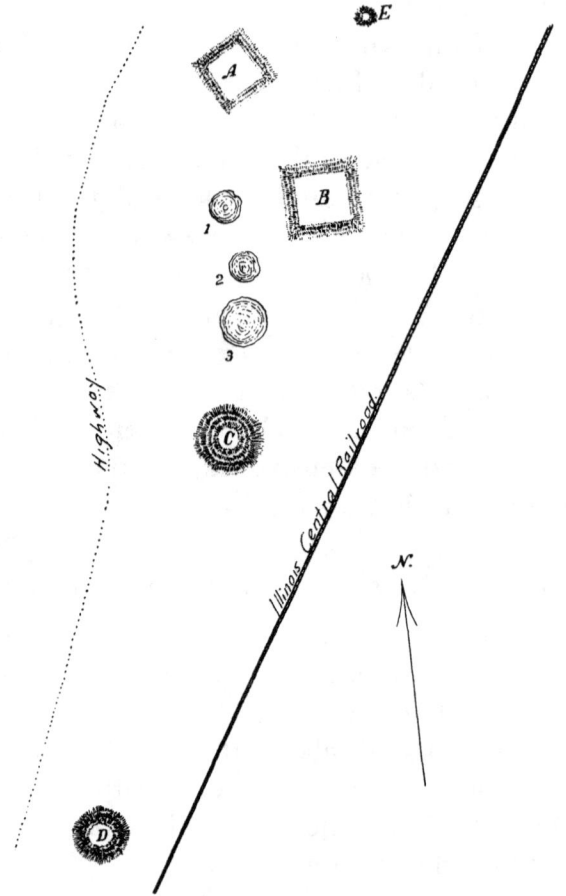

FIG. 23. The Batesville Mounds, Panola Co., scale 1 to 400.

less from the ravages of time and cultivation. It is comparatively regular in outline and level on top.

Mound C is a fine conical mound 434 feet in circumference, hence 138 feet in diameter at the base, and 20 to 21 feet high. The top is slightly flattened or truncated. It is very uniform in outline and well preserved. At present it is covered with a thick growth of saplings.

Mound D is at considerable distance south by south-west from the others and differs from the three just described in that it is a very low flat conical mound. No doubt it has been very much spread and hence lowered by cultivation; in fact a little clump of bushes which has warded off the plow for some years stands a foot and a half higher than the rest of the mound, which is in cultivation. The barrow seems somewhat elongated in its east and west axis, also probably a result of plowing. The present height is 6.5 feet, except under the little cluster of bushes, where it is 8 feet.

Mound E to the extreme north-east is quite low and flat, being now not more than a foot and a half or two feet high. No doubt it has been much modified by cultivation.

The following are the distances from centre to centre of the mounds: A to B 318 feet; B to C 524 feet; C to D 860 feet.

An interesting feature of this group is the three pits or holes west and south-west from mound B, the two northerly ones of which are quite deep for their size, perhaps the deepest that I have seen. Earth was no doubt taken from these for the construction of the mound or mounds; it is also possible that they were used for reservoirs or swimming-pools, tho the Tallahatchie River is not far away. South of mound D there is a depression trending east and west which may have been an excavation for building material for that mound or may have been a moat, but is most probably a natural formation.

About these mounds fragments of flint abound and a perfect arrow-head may be found occasionally. Fragments of pottery are still seen, tho they are not so numerous as the flint fragments.

This is no doubt the group mentioned in the *Ancient*

Monuments by Squier and Davis[1] as situated three miles east of Panola, that being the old name of a village which stood on the river near the site of the present town of Batesville.

A few miles south-east of Delta, Panola Co., according to Squier and Davis[1] there is a square enclosure of some 20 acres. It contains several mounds, one of which is 40 feet high, truncated, and ascended by a graded way. Within this enclosure there is also a square excavation 15 feet deep and 100 feet in diameter. It is surrounded by a low embankment of earth 3 feet high. I know nothing of this group.

At Dundee, Tunica Co., there is a group of four large mounds in approximately semi-circular arrangement and several smaller ones. They are in a cultivated field and have been altered by the plow. There is an abundance of pottery fragments and burnt clay.

Mound A is 10 to 20 feet high, the ground on which it stands being quite irregular.

Mound B is still higher. From it I dug a badly disintegrated skeleton which was partially exposed; this was apparently aboriginal, tho possibly an intrusion burial. A large elm stands on top. The west side is very precipitous, Bear Lake lying just back of it.

Mound C is 14 to 16 feet high and more symmetrical than A and B.

Mound D is flat and broad and has an altitude of 4 or 4.5 feet. Medium sized trees stand on it.

A mound two miles north-west of Dundee was reported to me but not visited.

At Evansville, Tunica Co., there are four or more mounds. The largest mound stands just at the west end of the main street of the town. It has been badly abused by cultivation and erosion; it now measures on top approximately east and

---
[1]Squier and Davis: Ancient Monuments, Washington, 1848, p. 113.

west 95 feet, north and south 55 feet. The height is from 14 to 18 feet, the west end being higher than the east.

North-west of the large mound is a smaller one with a school-house upon it. South-west of the great mound about 225 feet is a small mound in cultivation.

South of town half a mile, overlooking Beaver Lake, is another large mound, lower on the east and higher on the west, the major axis being twice the minor. The trees on it are but little more than a foot in diameter and apparently the mound has been cultivated in former times. A few white people have been buried in this mound. It is said that Dr. Southworth took some pottery and other artifacts from this mound about 1880.

Between the town mounds and this one, especially in the first quarter of a mile from town, there are quantities of pottery fragments, some of them quite large, indicating that they are still being plowed up. This was probably a burial-ground. There are two places on the public road where I observed quantities of burnt clay with cane impressions, one near town, the other about 400 feet north of the southern mound.

There are depressions north to east of each of the large mounds, from which earth may have been taken for the construction of these tumuli.

A mound is reported on Walnut Lake about six miles from Dubbs, larger than the great Evansville mound.

Just south of Hollywood, Tunica County, at the railway mile-post marked N. O. 420 is a mound about 14 feet high with a negro burying-ground on top of it. The railway comes close up to the mound on the east and the highway is but a short distance to the west of it. Scattered about are many fragments of burnt clay, fewer potsherds, and still fewer flint chips.

Clarence B. Moore[1] in his explorations along the Mississippi River investigated two mounds in Tunica County, one on the Johnson place near Mhoon Landing, the other near Commerce. His report is condensed in the following paragraphs:

About two miles east by north from Mhoon Landing, Tunica Co., is a mound in a cultivated field which forms part of the plantation of Mr. W. M. Johnson. This mound, about 13 feet high and 120 and 150 feet in diameter of base, has been spread by the long-continued cultivation, doubtless with considerable impairment of height. A number of trial-holes sunk into this mound soon came upon raw clay where there was no likelihood of encountering a burial.

Surrounding the mound is a considerable aboriginal dwelling-site, part of which on a slope has been subjected to much wash of rain, judging from the quantity of fragments of human bones on the surface. Superficially on this site, on which lay considerable debris, were gathered by us: a flint drill; a barbed arrow-head of flint; a pebble on which a cutting edge had been ground; numerous fragments of pottery colored red, and some showing stripes of white and red; a modeled earthen-ware head of some animal, colored red in places, and having protruding eyes coated with white pigment. Apart from human remains, in the soil was a pipe of earthen-ware, having a flat base protruding slightly beyond the bowl.

Unfortunately at this place, which has long been under cultivation, most of the burials, in all probability, had been ploughed and washed away. Diligent work over all parts of the site came upon four burials, one the bones of a young child. With the child's burial was a small vase coated with red pigment, and many fragments of another vessel. No artifacts lay with the other burials.

---

[1]Moore: Some Aborig. Sites on Miss. River, Philadelphia, 1911, pages 411,412.

Commerce, Tunica Co., is a small town on a great plantation belonging to Mr. R. F. Abbey. About three-quarters of a mile in a southerly direction from the landing is a mound on cultivated ground, which has been very symmetrical and is still imposing in appearance, though the corners are somewhat rounded. This mound has been extensively used for burials in recent times. Its height is slightly more than 20 feet. Its sides face the cardinal points, approximately, measuring north and south 193 feet, east and west 173; the summit-plateau in the same directions measuring 114 feet and 83 feet.

Near this mound is a limited area of artificially made high ground, on which lay some fragments of pottery, a few flint pebbles, and much baked clay, remains of aboriginal fireplaces, broadly scattered by the plow.

Two and one-half working days were devoted by us to the dwelling-sites at this place. The twenty-nine burials found were rather widely scattered; some were near the surface and had been disturbed by the plow, the land having been long in cultivation; it is likely that many burials have been ploughed away in the past. Fragments of human bones lay in all directions over the sites.

But little successful work could be done with the sounding rod at this place owing to the number of fire-places below the surface, whose hardened clay impeded the passage of the rod. Consequently, trial-holes were practically our only means of discovering burials. A number of burials were found, including one cremation. The cremated bones, in rather small fragments, formed a mass about 20 inches long, 14 inches wide, with a maximum thickness of 2 inches.

Twelve vessels were found by us at this place. These vessels consist of eleven bowls of moderate size and one flat bowl or platter. All are without decoration of any kind, with the exception of one vessel covered with rude punctate marks and of another vessel with a fillet-like decoration around the margin of the opening.

The sole burial having with it any object other than pottery was that of a child about four years of age, which lay at a depth greater than did any other burial found by us at this site, namely 3 feet 8 inches. No pottery lay with this interment, but on the chest was a face-shaped gorget about 5 inches long made from the body whorl of the conch *(Fulgur perversum)*. This ornament has two holes for suspension at the top, or broader end. The decoration consists of a scallop-like carving on the lower ends of both lateral margins, and traces of workmanship intended to represent a nose and mouth on one flat side.

At the left side of the pelvis of this burial, where the left hand rested, was a ceremonial axe of a silicious conglomerate, of the hoe-shaped class, 4 inches in length and 3 inches in maximum breadth of blade. The perforation usually found on axes of this kind is absent. The size of this little axe, much smaller than is usual with axes of this kind, marks it as a toy and quite in keeping with the age of the child to whom it belonged.

Near the two groups just described from Moore is a third and more interesting group which Moore seems not to have visited or mentioned. This group, which the author examined in September, 1923, is situated on Mr. G. D. Perry's land, and is two or three miles west of Bowdre and about the same distance north of Hollywood, standing just west of Mound Bayou and about three-eighths of a mile north of the section-line road.

The group (fig. 24) consists of a large central mound with a rectangular embankment or series of small mounds surrounding it. The accompanying sketch is merely approximate; no measurements were taken of the outlying works because of the heavy cotton. The measurements of the mound are as follows:

side	at base	at top
south side	200 feet	128 feet
east side	180 feet	106 feet
north side	160 feet	100 feet
west side	160 feet	90 feet

The corners have been so worn and rounded by cultivation and the weeds and cotton were so tall that accurate

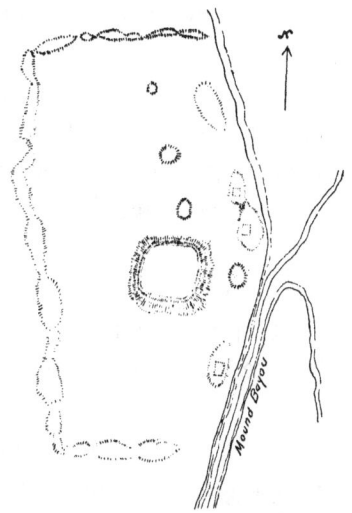

FIG. 24. Bowdre Mounds, Tunica Co.
C. A. B.

measurements were impossible. The height is 22 feet. The top of the mound has been cultivated, tho it was not in cultivation in 1923.

The surrounding earth-works are not a uniform earth-wall, but a series of mounds or elevations more or less elongated and sometimes connected by lower elevations. These mounds are higher on the east and west, reaching in some cases six or eight feet; less prominent on the north and south. All were in cotton in 1923 except those on the east along the bayou. Two of those on the east hold tenant houses and one a barn. Some of the tumuli on the west are burial mounds, as evidenced by the human bones and pottery fragments.

Within the enclosure, north of the big mound, are at least three small mounds or elevations.

Among the surface finds were several small smooth stone disks, two chipped and partially polished stone implements about three inches long similar to those from Walls, and an unfinished bead made of a clear quartz crystal 1.75 inches long.

Mr. Charles A. Barton calls these the De Be Voise mounds from the former owner of the land and gives the location as the south-west quarter of Sec. 33, T. 3 S., R. 11 W. Mr. Barton enumerates several other small mounds in this vicinity.

Walls, in DeSoto Co., a short distance south of the Tennessee line, has proved to be a most interesting archeological field. In the vicinity are numerous mounds and extensive burial-grounds.

About a mile and a half west of the station is a group of mounds on the largest of which stands the residence of Mr. Richard Cheatham. This mound has been slightly cut down and leveled to a height of about 5.5 feet. Nothing was found in the great mound. Circling this large mound were a number of small ones, several of which may still be seen to the south of the dwelling. From one of the small mounds to the west in the lot were taken several clay vessels, some of them prettily decorated with incised lines.

Farther on, four or five miles west by north-west from the station and in sight of the levee, almost in the very north-west corner of the state, is a large cemetery from which much pottery and many other artifacts have been taken. The surface of the field is somewhat uneven. Many bones, flakes of flint, and potsherds lie scattered about, and beds of ashes are frequently encountered. The bodies lie from one and a half to two feet beneath the surface. No particular orientation seems to have been observed in placing the bodies;

FIG. 25. Mound near Walls, De Soto Co., 1917. C. S. B.

heads lie toward every point of the compass. The pottery is generally found near the head of the skeleton.

An old log house stands upon the first mound. Farther on toward the levee is a mound (fig. 25) probably 20 feet high with an apron or platform of about half that height extending off toward the west. Large trees stand upon the mound. Half a mile farther on just across the Tennessee line at Blue Goose is another large mound.

The culture of the Walls people would seem to be entirely old; so far as I know no post-Columbian material has been found there. In the chapter on pottery I give many illustrations of the earthen-ware of this culture, and in other chapters additional examples of artifacts. Fig. 26 shows some skulls.

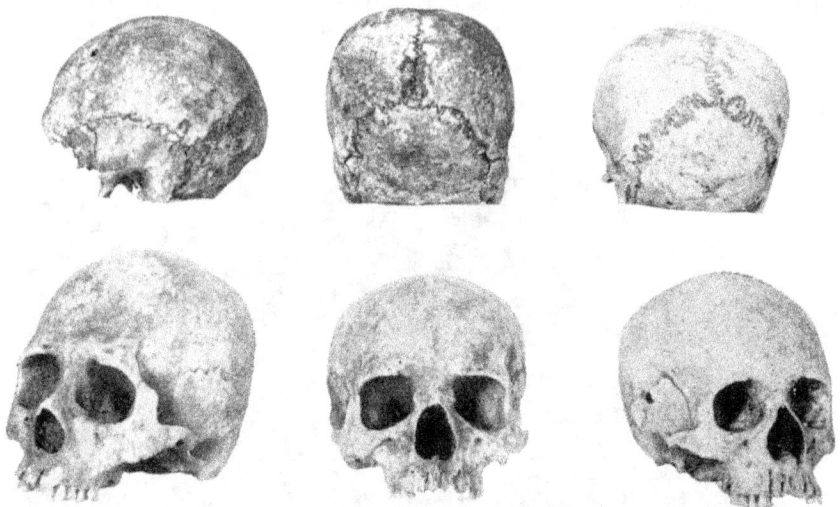

FIG. 26. Skulls from graves at Walls, De Soto Co.

About five miles south of the Walls field and about a mile north-east of Lake Cormorant in the same county is a rise of ground along the railroad, in which the fine massive pipe illustrated in figure 210 was found. Five or six mounds are reported about Lake Cormorant.

CHAPTER II.

ARROW-HEADS, SPEAR-HEADS, AND PERFORATORS.

The small flint points usually called Indian arrow-heads together with the accompanying flint chips are the most numerous of the prehistoric remains to be found in this country. There is hardly a section of the state in which some of these flaked points have not been found. The implements of wood, the leather, and the woven fabrics of prehistoric man have generally disappeared; metal, with the exception of copper in very small quantity, was scarcely known; the pottery has for the most part been broken and the fragments are passed by unobserved. Hence of all the artifacts of the Amerind stone implements and weapons are by far the most numerous, and as there were undoubtedly more of the small flint implements than of the large stone axes and celts, these small projectile-points are now the commonest remains of the red man to be found.

They exist in great variety of form and size, ranging from small bird-points half an inch long to immense spear-heads eight inches long and longer. The point illustrated in figure 30 is 7.25 inches long; the flint knife from Haynes Bluff illustrated in figure 59 is 8.25 inches long. As to form, the variety is almost infinite, hardly any two being exactly alike. Some are broad and triangular, others are long and slender; many are sharp-pointed, others blunt or rounded; some are notched near the base, others are without notches and neck. Yet with all the seeming variety most of the forms may be derived from a few elemental types. Mr. Gerard Fowke[1] gives four simple forms from which all the small flint

---

[1]Fowke: Prehistoric Objects Classified and Described, Bull. I, Mo. Hist. Soc., St. Louis, 1913.

implements may be fashioned with a few touches of the flaking implement.

Flint points are found on the surface, in the Indian graves, and in the mounds; there is no difference in type in regard to these three methods of occurrence; those in the mounds and in the graves differ in no respect from those scattered upon the surface of the fields and woods.

The commonest materials of which arrow-points are made are flint, chert, and jasper, while poorer stones are occasionally employed. Relatively few white quartz points are found in the state. Obsidian, so commonly used in the West and in Mexico, is seldom if ever found; the present writer has never found an obsidian point from Mississippi. Arrowheads of bone and fish-scale were sometimes used. After the coming of the white man metal points and glass points were used to some extent.

Many of these stone arrow-points are of excellent quality and workmanship, others are crude; sometimes the crudeness is due to the poor quality of the stone and sometimes to unskilled flint-chipping. Some of the jasper and better flint points, however, are of very artistic workmanship.

The choice of material for making projectile points depended largely upon the stone available. In many parts of the state good material was scarce, in other parts more abundant. The commonest material used in the western and central part of the state was the pebbles or gravels found all along the bluff which runs north and south thru the western part of the state paralleling the Mississippi River. These pebbles vary in size from that of a small shot or pea to four or five inches in length and even longer, and are composed of flint which breaks with a good conchoidal fracture, thus affording excellent material for chipped implements. Not infrequently an arrow-head is found that shows part of the original surface of the pebble from which it was flaked. In the north-eastern part of the state also there is an abundance of good quarry material in the chert pebbles that are found in great quantities. No doubt also some of the material came from beyond the limits of the state, as we know to have been the case in regard to the larger stone implements. Often the Amerind showed considerable taste in the choice of the stone which he used for points. Variegated or party-colored stones often appealed to his fancy. Many points of beautiful jasper are found. The banded triangular flint on the extreme right in figure 44 might be called an agate.

Not only are the completed stone points found, but flakes and chips which were struck off in the manufacture of the points also occur in quantities in old Indian fields and open-air workshops; also cores and rejected pieces are frequently seen. Occasionally arrow-heads are found which have been re-worked after being broken; these usually have rather blunt points. Specimens of points may be found in all stages of development from the scarcely touched pebble to the completed arrow-point. The flaking was probably done for the most part by percussion and pressure, stone hammers being used for breaking off the larger pieces and small implements of stone or bone being used for pressing off the smaller flakes. No hard metal was used in the earlier times for this purpose.

The smaller lighter points are usually considered arrow-heads, the larger heavier ones spear-heads or knives. Some archeologists consider that only those pieces two inches or less in length could be used as arrow-points, the heavier specimens being used as spear-heads, daggers, and knives[1]. The arrow-points were fastened upon shafts of wood and cane, which have long since disappeared. The larger spear-heads were fastened upon long pikes, and were probably

---

[1]Fowke: Prehistoric Objects Classified and Described, Bull. I, Mo. Hist. Soc., St. Louis, 1913, p. 22.
Holmes: Handbook of Am. Indians, Bull. 30, Pt. I, Bu. of Am. Ethn., page 90.

used both for hurling and for thrusting. Other pieces were probably mounted with short handles of wood or stag-horn for use in the hand as knives and daggers. Some of the pieces commonly called arrow-heads are probably scrapers, perforators, graving tools, or reamers, and there are many of peculiar or special shapes whose use is hard to determine.

The injury that it was possible to inflict with one of these stone projectiles may be inferred from figure 27. This skull

FIG. 27. Human skull with embedded arrow-point, Natchez, Rhodes collection, now in Chamberlin collection, Torresdale, Pa.

of a child with a flint point embedded in it was found by Bert Barton near Natchez, Miss., after a freshet, and obtained by W. B. Rhodes. Mr. Rhodes afterward sold his entire collection to Mr. B. Chamberlin of Torresdale, Pennsylvania. I have not seen this specimen, but others who have seen it, including Mr. Christopher Wren of the Wilkesbarre museum, consider it genuine. Similar illustrations may be seen in the *Handbook of American Indians,* page 90, and in Moorehead's *Stone Age in North America,* page 102. On the preceding page of the latter book is shown a buffalo skull with an arrow-point embedded in it. Mr. C. B. Moore in his

Aboriginal Sites of Green River, Kentucky, page 478, pictures a human vertebra transfixed by a spear-point of antler; the specimen is from "the India Knoll," Ohio Co., Ky. Other examples are cited in the books just mentioned. Mr. George C. Heye in his *Artifacts from San Miguel Island, California,* shows a plate (72) with four different examples of human bones with embedded arrow-points.

Figure 28 is a group of thirty-four flint points of a great variety of shapes. The top row contains small triangular pieces without notches, some of which are no doubt scrapers. The fourth one is pointed after the manner of a perforator. The fifth in the second row has a very long neck without pronounced tangs. The middle specimen in the third row and the first one in the fifth row are leaf-shaped and have the neck and stem continuous without tangs; they may be compared with the piece in figure 30 and the last piece in figure 34. The sixth specimen in the third row has very prominent barbs or shoulders, so that it is nearly as broad as long. The last specimen in the third row is a gracefully formed piece with concave or in-curving base. The third specimen in the fourth row, no. 68, is an unusually fine point with a long thin stem. The last one in the fourth row and the second in the fifth row have concave bases and are unnotched.

Two especially fine lance-heads are shown in figures 29 and 30. The former from Lowndes County is 7 inches long; the latter from Union County in the vicinity of New Albany is 7.25 inches long.

Figure 31 is a group of five long flints of varying types from the north-eastern part of the state. The longest is 5.5 inches; the first and fourth are rather broad; the second is lance-shaped with rounded base, the third is very narrow in proportion to its length and somewhat irregular on its edges. All are more or less notched but none have prominent tangs.

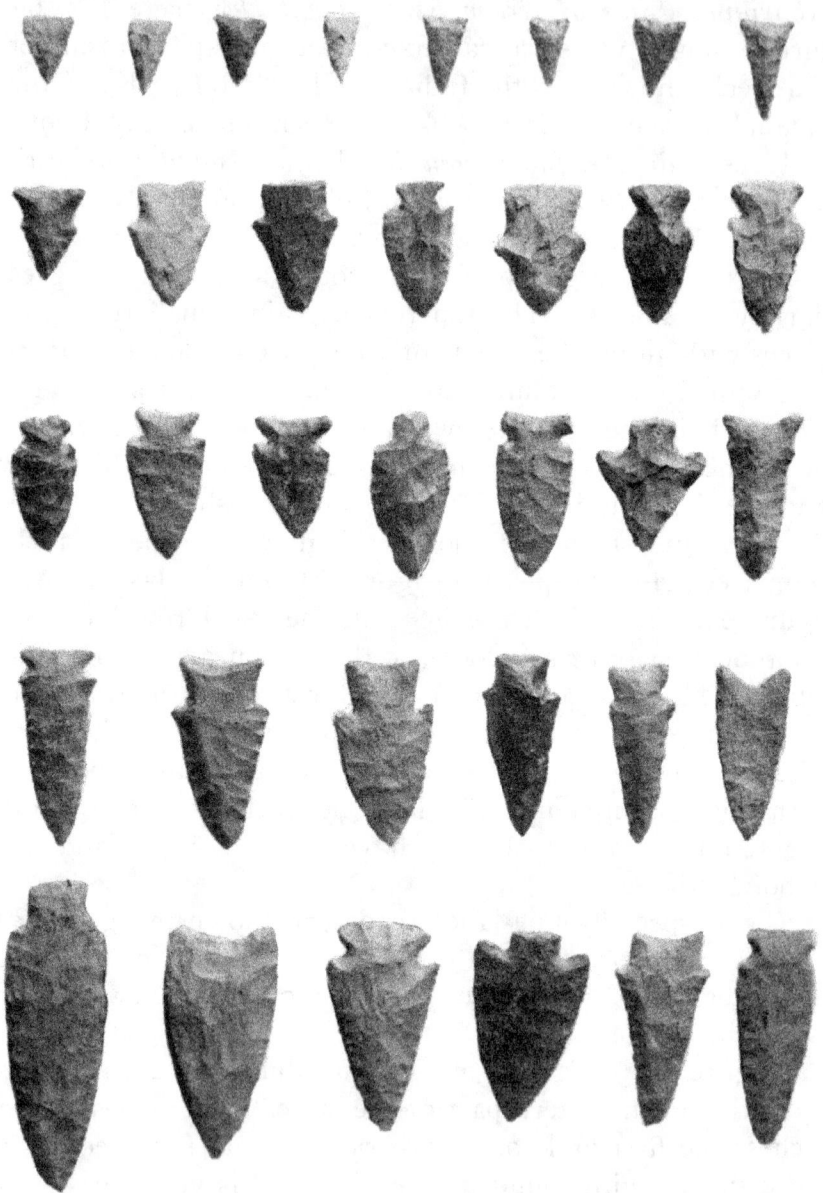

Fig. 28. Arrow-points, spear-heads, etc., about ⅓ size, author's collection.

ARROW-HEADS, SPEAR-HEADS, AND DRILLS. 131

FIG. 29. Spear-head from near Columbus, 7 inches long, Chapman collection.

FIG. 30. Spear-head from near New Albany, 7.25 inches long, Ticer col.

Figure 32 is a group of twenty beautiful red jasper points from the vicinity of Columbus, Lowndes County. They are all less than one inch in length; most of them are triangular in form, a few have concave bases, and a few are leaf-shaped. The first and last in the second row are specially worthy of notice. These are from the collection of Mr. W. A. Love, who has many more of them. Somewhat similar points from Lafayette County are in the author's collection at the University.

FIG. 31. Five spear-heads from Corinth and New Albany, longest 5.5 inches, Gift and Ticer collections.

Figure 33 represents a group of arrow-points of the Coldwater type. This type is common in the vicinity of the town of Coldwater near the Coldwater River in Tate County. The bases curve inward slightly, the gracefully-curving edges swell somewhat towards the middle and then come to a point of medium bluntness at the forward end. Instead of being notched they are but slightly constricted about the neck, in some cases this constriction being only apparent. It is on the whole a rather graceful type. A shortened form of the Coldwater type is seen in the last piece in figure 45.

ARROW-HEADS, SPEAR-HEADS, AND DRILLS. 133

A handsome flint from Coldwater 3.8 inches long (author's collection) has the general form of a lance-head but it is unnotched and has the base brought to an edge after

FIG. 32. Twenty red points, Columbus, natural size, property of W. A. Love.

the manner of a chipped chisel. A similar piece from the same locality is only 1.6 inches long and has the two edges more convex. The form of these is very similar in outline to Moorehead's figure 58, on page 73 of the *Stone Age in North America,* Vol. I.

Some interesting types are photographed in figure 34.

FIG. 33. Arrow-heads of the Coldwater type, Coldwater, ½ size, author's collection.

The first two flints are of a peculiar hooked form; the first is slightly more, the second slightly less, than two inches in

FIG. 34. Flaked implements, north Miss., slightly more than one-third size; two hooked flints, Walls, Schubach collection; four scrapers, author's collection; two curved knives, Walls, Schubach collection, and Iuka, Geol. Survey museum; four spear-heads, Corinth, three in author's collection, fourth in Gift collection.

length; they were found near Walls. The next four pieces are of the more or less triangular form usually called scrapers; they are sharp-pointed at one end and chisel-shaped at the other.

In the second line we see two interesting curved knives; the first 4.2 inches long is from Walls, the second 3.7 inches long is from Iuka. They are sharp on both edges. Next follows a group of four flints from Corinth; the first is a well-formed spear-head; the second is nicely serrated; the third has a peculiar zigzag form somewhat suggesting the conventional lightning design of modern artists; and the fourth has the neck and stem united into a rounded head.

A narrow chert scraper over 4 inches long from Corinth (author's collection) suggests by its shape adaptation to a

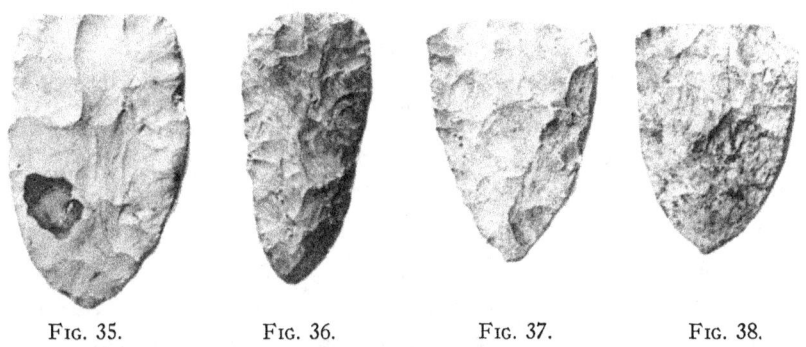

FIG. 35.   FIG. 36.   FIG. 37.   FIG. 38.
    Flint blades from north Miss., slightly more than one-third size:
      FIG. 35, from Corinth, Gift collection.
      FIG. 36, from Corinth, author's collection.
      FIGS. 37, 38, from New Albany, Geol. Survey museum.

left-handed person. In the Ballard collection there is a little chipped stone disk (no. 285) only one inch in diameter, figure 49; it is brought to a blunt edge all round the circumference with equal bevel on each face. Circular scrapers have been pictured by the archeologists, but there is doubt as to whether this piece should be called a scraper.

In figures 35 to 38 are shown four unnotched pieces of the broad knife type. All have rather blunt points and chisel edges and come from the north-eastern part of the state. These should be compared with some of the pieces illustrated under agriculture, as for instance figures 159 to 162.

An interesting flint from Mr. Gift's collection at Corinth is 1.9 inches wide and only 2.2 long; it is of a beautiful white or cream-colored stone; it is deeply notched and has the thickness of its body overcome by a rather sudden sharpening near the forward end and on one face; it may therefore be a re-worked piece, and is probably a scraper.

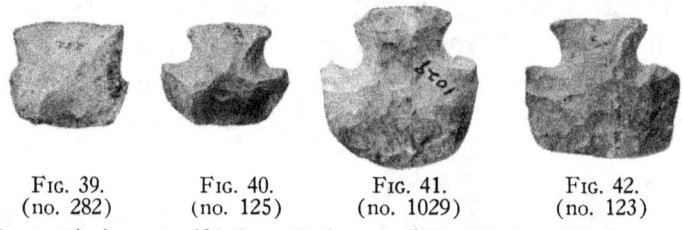

FIG. 39. (no. 282) FIG. 40. (no. 125) FIG. 41. (no. 1029) FIG. 42. (no. 123)

Bunts ½ size; no. 282 from Lafayette Co., author's collection; nos. 125, 1029, 123 from Montgomery Co., Ballard collection.

A somewhat similar piece is no. 1029 (fig. 41) of the Ballard collection; it is dubbed off on both faces, slightly more on one face than on the other, and has the forward end almost semicircular. There are several other interesting bunts or blunt arrow-points in the Ballard collection; as nos. 125 (figure 40) and 1017 which are relatively thick and evidently re-worked on both faces, no. 56 which is dubbed off quite bluntly and unevenly on only one face and no. 123 (figure 42) which has the forward end almost a straight line. No. 282 in the author's collection (figure 39) is a good illustration of this type; it is dubbed off quite bluntly in a straight line. No. 293 ends in a very flat Gothic arch. It has been suggested that arrow-heads with the forward end rounded or squared instead of pointed were used for obtaining birds or small animals without injuring the plumage or fur.

FIG. 43. Curved arrow-heads; ½ size; first, author's col.; second, Survey museum.

A handsome white or cream-colored flint from Corinth in the author's collection is lanceolate in shape, being but slightly narrower at one end than at the other; it is 2.3 inches long and only .7 inch wide. A similarly shaped piece in brown flint, no. 717 of the Ballard collection (figure 48), is notched in the middle of both edges.

In figure 43 are shown two curved flints viewed edgewise. The first from Coldwater measures 3.15 inches long and 1.3 inches wide; the second from Monroe County is 3.2 inches long and 1.5 inches wide and has a still deeper curvature than the first. Both are of a yellowish brown color. Number 287 in the author's collection is also curved, having been made in

FIG. 44. Chipped flints, scale 1 to 1.6, author's collection.

all probability from a large flake. Number 464 in the Ballard collection, figure 52, is curved as to the edges rather than as to the face. It is probable that in many of the curved arrow-heads the curvature is due to the conchoidal fracture of a flake utilized in the making rather than to any desire on the part of the flint-workers to produce a curved piece.

In figure 44 we have two flints of a lozenge or diamond shape, the second apparently having had a point broken from the longer end; two pieces of the arrow-head type with the point sharpened into the drill or perforator type; and a fifth piece (no. 255 in the author's collection) of banded agate, triangular in form. The fourth piece, from the vicinity of Aberdeen, is of a beautiful rose or wine-color showing on the back some of the weathered surface of the original pebble from which it was made. The point resembles the usual perforator point, and in this case seems to be considerably worn.

Figure 45 shows still other types; the first three are long and slender, the first being broken at the base, the third at the point; the fifth in the upper line has rather blunt edges and is deeply fluted on both faces; it may be compared with no. 139 of Thruston's *Antiquities of Tennessee;* the sixth is a handsome double-notched point from Vicksburg with rather

FIG. 45. Flints of various types, from various parts of the state, scale 1 to 2.2, Brown, Barringer, and Clark collections.

long neck; the fourth in the second line is of an unusual paddle shape; with it should be compared no. 116 of the Ballard collection, figure 51, which is somewhat similar; the fifth (author's collection no. 50) is a broad-necked sharp-pointed flint with lateral arms; it comes from the Yocona River bottom near Delay, Lafayette County. The type, while it can scarcely be called rare, is not very common. In some examples the point is that of an arrow-head rather than of a drill or perforator, as in a small one from Aberdeen which is 1.2 by 1.2 inches; another from the same locality is broader than it is long. The last piece on the plate is a modified form of the Coldwater type, being shorter in proportion to its width than those illustrated in figure 33.

In figure 46 is shown a triple-notched arrow-head 2.2 inches long from the Columbus territory. It is slightly adze-shaped or curved, the convexity being toward the camera.

Beveled arrow-heads are not unusual though certainly not very common. The bevels are always on opposite faces, and if the point were used as a projectile they would serve to

Fig. 46. Triple-notched arrow-head, from vicinity of Columbus, nat. size; Chapman col.

Fig. 47. Beveled arrow-heads from Coldwater and Winona, half size, author's collection.

give a rotary motion while in progress, thus producing the same effect as the rifles in a modern gun-barrel. Gerard Fowke calls attention to the fact that such points are nearly always thick and thinks that these implements should more properly be called skinning-knives.[1] It has also been suggested that they were used as reamers. In an example from Aberdeen in the author's collection the bevels are so completely developed that it gives to the flint the appearance of being warped, the blade being quite thin and sitting at a considerable angle with the plane of the stem.

---

[1] Fowke: Prehistoric Objects Classified and Described, Bull. I, St. Louis, 1913, p. 24; and Arch. Hist. of Ohio, Columbus, 1902, p. 675.

Figure 47 shows three beveled arrow-heads from the author's collection; the first from Coldwater, the second and third from Winona. The bevel for all of these is to the left when the flint lies before the observer with the point forward,

| Fig. 48 | Fig. 49 | Fig. 50 | Fig. 51 | Fig. 52 |
| (no. 717) | (no. 285) | (no. ?) | (no. 116) | (no. 464) |

Flaked flints from Montgomery Co., ½ size, Ballard collection.

and this seems to be the general rule. This method of beveling would give a rotation contrary to the motion of the hands of a clock if the point should be used as a projectile.

Fig. 53. Perforators, etc., one-third size, author's collection.

Unusual flaked specimens are shown in figures 48 to 52 from Montgomery County; figure 49 is mentioned in an earlier paragraph among scrapers; figure 50 is an unusual heart-shaped flint.

Figure 53 represents a group of flints of drill or perforator type. The first and second pieces (numbers 74 and 85 of the author's collection) are probably arrow-heads, spear-heads, or perforators, tho they are of a type suggesting daggers, assuming that a part of the handle has been broken off. So-called daggers have been found in Tennessee and Alabama. The third is a long broad-headed perforator or drill from Aberdeen. The fourth and sixth have very prominent barbs but no tangs. The fifth is a handsome wine-

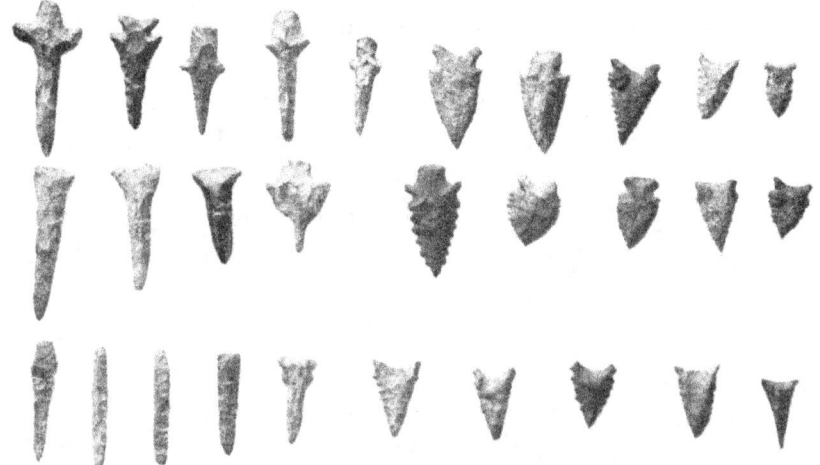

FIG. 54. Perforators and arrow-heads, Montgomery Co., 2/7 size, Ballard collection.

colored flint from Aberdeen, having the tangs and shoulders extending out to about the same distance and separated from each other by rather deep notches, the base coming to an edge. The remaining pieces are various types of perforators, drills, and bars. The first piece in the second line (catalog no. 42, Lafayette Co.) is bluntly pointed at each end; the fifth, from the vicinity of Winona, has a chisel-edge of about three-tenths of an inch at each end. It should be said that while some perforators show signs of wear at the point many do not.

Figure 54 is a group of chipped flints from the Ballard

collection, formerly at Winona, now at the University. The first piece is quite similar to the first two in the preceding illustration. There are several good pieces with saw-toothed edges, as for instance the middle piece, which is an unusually fine one. There are several good serrated arrow-heads in the collection which do not appear in the illustration. A number of drills and perforators are also shown, including one with a very broad handle. No. 1031 of this collection, not shown in the illustration, is nearly an equilateral triangle, and has each of the three edges hollowed out in about the same curve.

Figure 55 is a large drill with broad unshaped head from Iuka, in the north-east corner of the state. It is a chert of a soft gold color. A drill in the Ballard collection (no. 92) has a beautiful leaf-shaped head with short stem.

Fig. 55. Perforator from Iuka, natural size, author's collection no. 342.

In the north-eastern part of the state about A b e r d e e n, Amory, and Nettleton are frequently found chipped flints roughly rectangular in f o r m. Figure 56 shows three of these from the vicinity of Amory in M o n r o e County. They are slightly less than two inches in l e n g t h, the illustration being somewhat undersize. The first piece in this illustration shows part of the original surface of the pebble. Several small pieces of the rectangular type w e r e taken from a grave near Nettleton and are now in the museum of the Geological Survey at the University. The purpose of such pieces is not positively known to me; they may have been used as scrapers.

 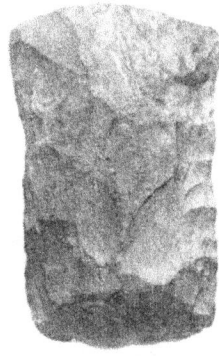 

Fig. 56. Rectangular flints, Amory type, slightly under size, State Geol. Survey museum nos. 452, 448, and 450, gift of Mrs. Fears.

Figure 57 is a group of flint points from Wilkinson County in the south-western part of the state; they are all except one in the collection of Mr. A. W. Harris of Natchez.

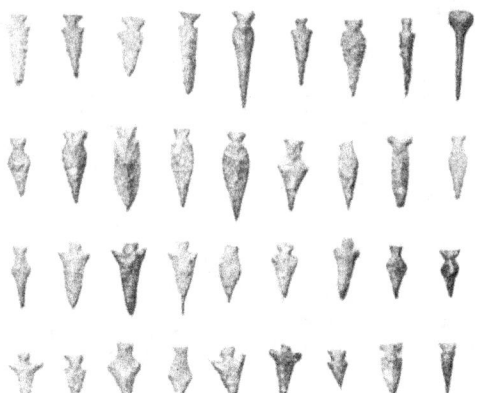

Fig. 57. Thirty-six arrow-heads from Wilkinson Co., one-fourth size, Harris collection (except upper right hand awl).

Several of them are long, thin, delicate, and graceful, such as the middle one in the first and the second rows. Others have the base in-curving and the tangs projecting in a way almost suggesting an insect form. The upper right-hand piece is a very fine keen awl, two inches long, the property of Dr. Carter. Mr. Harris has brought together from Wilkin-

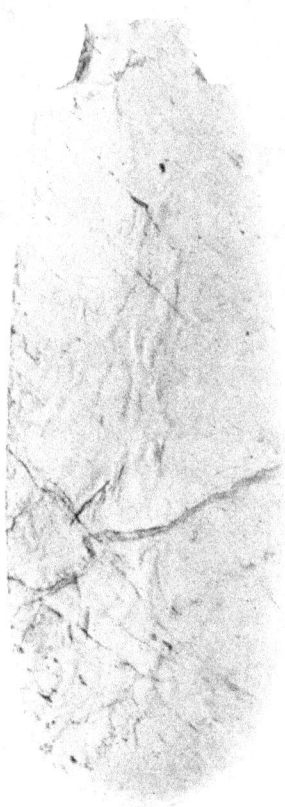

Fig. 58. Chert knife, Pontotoc Co., natural size, Barringer collection.

Fig. 59. White flint knife, Haynes Bluff, ½ size, museum of Davenport Acad. no. 8157. Photo. from museum.

son County a good collection of archeological material including about sixty celts, a number of disks and round stones, a longitudinally grooved sinker, figure 123, many arrow-heads, and much other material.

A peculiar knife blade from Pontotoc County is shown in

figure 58. It is slightly over four inches long and 1.15 inches in the widest part of the blade proper. Both the edges are sharp. The arrangement of notch and projections at the base is unusual.

A very fine knife or spatula-shaped flint is the white one shown in figure 59. It is three inches wide and over eight inches long, and is a handsome example of the flint-chipper's art. It was found in the large mound on the Yazoo River about a mile above Haynes Bluff, and is in the museum of the Davenport Academy of Sciences.

CHAPTER III.

AXES AND CELTS.

A large variety of stone axes and celts is found within the state. They are usually of polished stone, whereas the flint implements are usually flaked or chipped. Of this class of polished stone implements the grooved ones are usually called axes, the smooth or ungrooved ones celts. Figures 60 and 61 give a good idea of two of the grooved types; the first one of these has a groove extending completely around the implement, and is unusual in that the bottom comes to a point rather than to a blade; the second specimen has the groove extending along two faces and across the back while the front of the ax has a shallow vertical groove. The accounts of early travellers as well as the form of the axes themselves indicate that these grooved axes were hafted with wooden handles. Further evidence of the manner of hafting is furnished by a few unusual monolithic axes found in neighboring states. Dr. Joseph Jones describes a fine stone ax with handle, poll, and blade, all cut from one stone; it is 13.5 inches long, and was exhumed from a mound on the bank of the Cumberland River opposite Nashville, Tennessee.[1] Mr. Clarence B. Moore pictures a beautiful monolithic ax 11.6 inches long from Moundville, Alabama[2].

The manner of hafting these grooved axes varied, no doubt. In some cases forked sticks or branches of trees, in other cases, split wooden handles were employed, leather

---
[1] For an illustration of this ax see Jones, Antiquities in Tenn., page 46; Thruston, Antiq. of Tenn., page 259; and Jones, Antiq. of the Southern Indians, pl. 12.
[2] Moore: Certain Aborig. Rem. of Bl. War. River, Phila., 1905, p. 135, fig. 6.
Moorehead: Stone Age in N. Am., Vol. I., Boston and N. Y., 1910, p. 327.

thongs being used to bind the implement securely in place; in other instances, a living branch or small tree was split and after the ax had been inserted was allowed to grow firmly around it. Axes with a vertical groove on one edge and a horizontal groove the rest of the way around, such as

FIG. 60. Grooved implement, near Columbus, ⅔ size, Chapman col.

FIG. 61. Grooved ax, near Columbus, ⅔ size, Chapman collection.

the one shown in figure 61, were mounted with the vertical groove pressing firmly against the wood of the handle and the thongs around the horizontal groove.

Figures 62 and 63 show axes in the author's collection having the groove extended all the way around the poll or head of the ax. Figure 62 is 7.25 inches long by 3.5 inches wide and has a very shallow broad groove. The inequalities of the stone are not completely worked away and it is not highly polished except near the edge. It is from Tremont, Itawamba County. Figure 63 is much broader in proportion to its length and has a wide groove as the former has, altho a deeper groove. The blade is highly polished, the poll less highly finished. It is 6.25 by 4.5 inches and is from Lowndes County near Columbus, the gift of Mr. W. L. McCullough.

In the author's collection is a thick reddish-brown ax (no.

 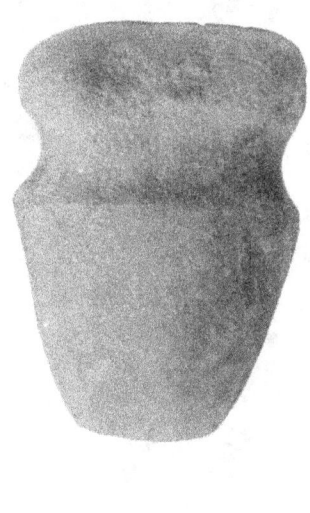

FIG. 62. Grooved ax from Itawamba Co., slightly over ⅓ size, author's col. no. 63.

FIG. 63. Grooved ax from Lowndes Co., slightly over ⅓ size, author's col. no. 249.

346) of elliptical cross-section; the groove is relatively deep, goes completely around the ax, and is very near the poll. The length is 4.9 inches, the width 3.8 inches; it has seen hard service, and the length given does not quite represent the full original length. It was found on the Markette place about eight miles south of Oxford.

There is an interesting toy ax from Montgomery County

in the Ballard collection (no. 47) which is only 1.55 inches long and only three-quarters of an inch wide; it is grooved in the middle all the way around and has the groove re-enforced by a parallel ridge or projecting band on each side,

FIG. 64. Grooved stone ax from Aberdeen, natural size, author's collection no. 333. Aberdeen type.

rising above the general surface of the ax. One end of the ax comes to an edge, the other almost to a point.

Other axes from the north-eastern part of the state have not only the horizontal groove around the poll of the ax, but also an additional groove running vertically over the poll. A thong of leather or a withe of wood, passing over the back of the ax in this groove, would serve to hold it in place and keep it from being driven from its setting in its handle when used for chopping or bruising. Such an ax is shown in full size in figure 64 (author's collection no. 333). It is from the vicinity of Aberdeen, Monroe County. The material is a heavy

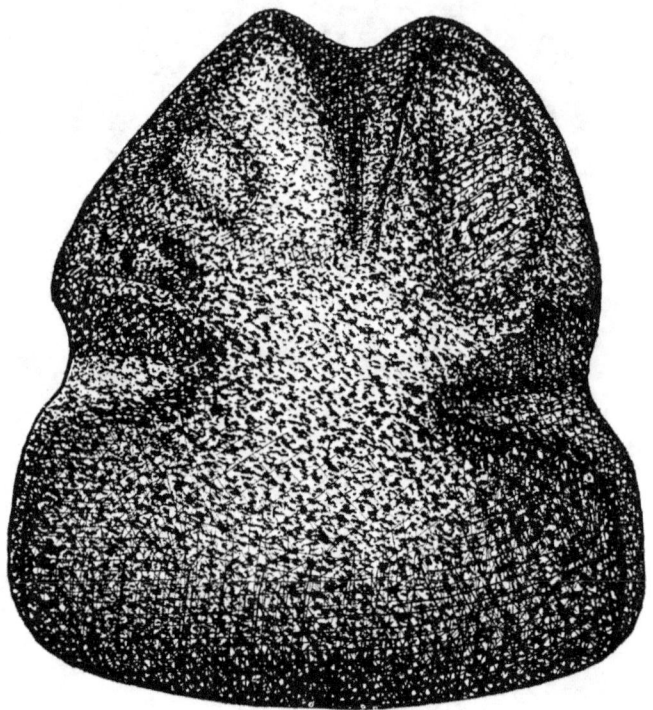

FIG. 65. Stone ax, Pontotoc Co., natural size, Barringer col.

dark ferruginous sandstone. It is roughly polished everywhere except in the grooves, which have the appearance of having been pecked in at a later date. The vertical groove extends slightly below the horizontal groove on both faces. Number 334 of the author's collection is a very similar piece in every respect, except that the grooves do not appear to differ in finish from the rest of the ax, and the vertical groove does not extend below the horizontal groove. Number 335 is considerably larger than these two and may have had the poll broken, and undergone slight re-working, altho

Fig. 66. Grooved ax of conglomerate, Lowndes Co., 3.7" by 3.2", Chapman collection.

that is by no means certain; at any rate the groove is quite near the back of the ax. The groove on the faces is very shallow and over the back consists merely of two notches. These three are all from the same vicinity and in the same material and have the appearance of great age, tho that appearance may be due to the character of the stone of which they are made. Mr. Ben H. McFarland has given to the Geological Survey a good grooved ax of this type from the same territory. A specimen from the Columbus territory in the collection of Mr. Felix M. Chapman has the poll considerably flared in its broader dimension and a well-defined vertical groove.

Figure 65 is a beautiful chocolate-colored ax from Pontotoc County. It has grooves across the two edges and

No. 189   No. 259

FIG. 67. Crude implements, Lafayette Co., ⅓ size, author's collection.

across the top, but these grooves do not come together on the face of the ax. The edge of the blade is quite broad in proportion to the rest of the ax.

Number 468 of the author's collection, found near Oxford, has a slight vertical groove over the middle of the poll and crude re-worked notches in the two sides.

Figure 66 is a rough ax made of conglomerate or pudding-stone; it is from the collection of Mr. Felix M. Chapman, and comes from Lowndes County or from that vicinity.

The groove runs all the way around and the top of the ax is broadly concave.

Grooved axes are found in limited numbers in the northeastern part of the state; few if any are found in the southwestern part or in the low country between the Bluffs and the Mississippi River known as the Delta.

The crude implements in figure 67 are intermediate in

No. 187   No. 325   No. 296

FIG. 68. Three crude celts, Lafayette Co., ⅓ size, author's collection.

form between axes and celts. They are both from Lafayette County and are made of rough shale. As the material is rather soft and brittle, they could not have been very serviceable for hard chopping or pounding. Both are roughly chipped around the edges and are only partially polished. The first is considerably flared on one side of the blade, the second is nearly triangular in form. No. 15 in the author's collection, likewise from Lafayette County and of the same material, is brought to a good keen edge, and has the rest of the body crudely formed. There is a rough shallow notch in each lateral edge and in the back, doing duty for grooves. This implement is slightly curved after the manner of an adze.

The fact should not be forgotten that a large part of the Indian material found is very crude. In illustrated books authors are inclined for the most part to select the better

FIG. 69. Celts from Pontotoc Co., ½ size, Barringer collection.

pieces of Indian material, and readers are hence in danger of getting exaggerated ideas of the beauty and perfection of Amerindian art as a whole. Some of the cruder work is illustrated here in order that the reader may get a fair idea of the usual level of Indian art. The pieces just described and those in figure 68 are examples of the cruder every-day workmanship. The three celts in the latter group are made of coarse sandstone and are of very ordinary execution. The first one (no. 187), 4.75 inches long, is polished only about the edges. The second (no. 325), 6.5 inches long, has more polished surface and is slightly curved or adze-shaped; it is not easy to determine whether the inner curvature is original or due to some later influence; tho it is probably original. The

Fig. 70. Celt from Yazoo Co., ⅓ size, Butler col. no. 1683.

Fig. 71. Celt from Yazoo Co., ⅓ size, Butler col. no. 156.

third (no. 296) is not polished even on the edge and is considerably lopsided; the blade is very blunt.

Figure 69 shows two celts from Pontotoc County more highly polished; the first 4.7 inches long is of the broad rectangular type; the second 5.6 inches long, which in the illustration is turned edgewise toward the observer, is rather thick in proportion to its width. In the collection of Mr.

Charles W. Clark at Clarksdale there are two thick celts with unequal faces, one face being flattened after the manner of a gouge but not fluted. A red stone celt from Walls (Schu-

FIG. 72. Celt from Columbus, ⅓ size, Archives museum no. 328L.

FIG. 73. Celt from Tunica Co., ⅓ size, Archives museum no. 327A.

bach collection) 5.25 inches long and similar in form to the first one in figure 69 has engraved upon one face a figure somewhat between a U-shape and a V-shape.

A few of the celts are quite large and heavy. The longest celt in the Clark collections is 9.5 inches; the longest

AXES AND CELTS.

in the Ballard collection is 11.6 inches. Figures 70 and 71 show two handsome specimens from the Brevoort Butler collection; they are both from Yazoo County. Figure 70, number 1683, is of the rectangular type and is 10.3 inches long; it was found in a mound in 1896. Figure 71, number 156, has a semicircular cutting edge and is peculiar in having a slight groove running up each lateral edge; this groove may be seen on the left edge in the photograph. The celt is 10.4 inches long and is 4.5 inches wide.

Next are shown two fine celts belonging to the Department of Archives and History at Jackson. Figure 72, number 328L, the longer of the two, is from the vicinity of Columbus and was presented to the museum by Mr. W. A. Love; it is 11.5 inches long. Figure 73, number 327A, is from Tunica County, and was presented by Mr. R. S. Alexander; it is 11 inches long. An eight-inch celt from Copiah County (Barringer collection) is handsomely flared at the blade.

A fine example of the stone polisher's art is seen in figure 74. This is a very beautiful gray celt mottled with green, 10.3 inches long, found June 15, 1917, on one of the small burial mounds at the Mound Place on George Lake, near the Sunflower River, a short distance from Holly Bluff. It is peculiar in that the planes of the two ends are not parallel with each

FIG. 74. Celt from Holly Bluff, ½ size, Geol. Survey museum no. 334.

other, but make an angle of about eight degrees; this gives to the celt a slightly warped appearance (Geol. Survey museum no. 334).

The next celt, figure 75 (Butler collection no. 817), is likewise from the George Lake region; it was found in 1905 in a plowed field near Brevoort. It is only 4.75 inches long. A peculiar feature of it is that it is sharpened at both ends.

FIG. 75. Double-edged celt, Yazoo Co., ½ size, Butler col. no. 817.   FIG. 76. Celt of petrified wood, ½ size, Butler col. no. 1671.   FIG. 77. Celt of coal, Yazoo Co., about ½ size, Butler col. no. 834.

In the south-western part of the state are found many celts of dark green stone, of medium size and rather uniform pattern. Mr. W. A. Harris has forty or fifty from Wilkinson County and other collectors about Natchez have a number from Adams County. Two of Mr. Harris's small celts are perforated near the top and thus converted into pendants (figure 124). More than fifty celts of various types are catalogued from this part of Mississippi in the Dickeson collection[1]. Of these, nine are less than two inches long;

---
[1] Culin: Dickeson Collection of Am. Antiquities, Philadelphia, 1900.

seven are over seven inches long; several are of jasper; one is of jasperized wood; one is perforated. A slate gouge 6.25 inches long (no. 14,509) was obtained at Ellis Cliffs in the southern part of Adams County; the groove is .38 of an inch deep, quite broad at the blade end, and tapers toward the smaller end. Celts seem to replace grooved axes almost entirely in this part of the state.

There are two celts of petrified wood in the Butler collection. One of these, no. 1671, is shown in figure 76; it is from Yazoo County and is 5.5 inches long. Other examples of artifacts in silicified wood are occasionally found, and fragments of this material are not infrequently scattered about village-sites and mounds.

The celt pictured in number 77 could have had no practical use, for it is made of cannel coal. It is in the Butler collection (no. 834), now at Jackson, and according to the catalog was plowed up at the base of the big mound at Mound Place. It has a length of 5.5 inches and a maximum width of 2.5 inches, and is perforated slightly above the middle.

The little triangular celt shown in figure 78 was found June 19, 1906, near the mounds at the iron bridge over Abiaca Creek, Carroll County, seven miles from Sidon. It is quite small, being only 1.75 by 1.25 inches (author's collection no. 130). One might ask whether such small celts were of any practical use or whether they were only playthings.

FIG. 78. Small celt, Carroll Co., natural size, author's col. no. 130.

Figure 79 is a group of celts or chisels from Walls in the north-western part of the state. They are all flaked yellow jasper, only partially polished, and hence represent a stage intermediate between the chipped implements and the polished implements. Many such pieces have been found near Walls by Mr. Schubach and Dr. Davies. The polish on some of these is quite high but it has in none of them gone deep enough to remove all the marks of chipping.

FIG. 79. Chipped celts partly polished, Walls, ⅖ size, Schubach collection.

Elongated pebbles are found with one end chipped or sharpened, the rest of the stone being scarcely altered. Many of these crude pieces were collected in 1918 by Dr. Charles Peabody during his excavations near Alligator in Bolivar County. Such pieces are found also at Walls.

A copper celt from Lafayette County is represented in the chapter on *Shell, Bone, and Copper* further on in this book (fig. 261).

CHAPTER IV.

ORNAMENTAL, CEREMONIAL, AND PROBLEMATIC STONES.

DISCOIDAL STONES.

The name discoidal stone is given to a large variety of circular stones, some of which are concave on both faces, some of which are convex on both faces, some of which are plano-convex; some of which are variously modified. They are popularly called chunkey stones (also spelled chunky, chunkee, and chungke). The name bicave is also sometimes used for discoidal stones, but it can properly be applied only to those with two concave faces. The game of chunkey in which such stones are supposed to have been used is described by several of the early travellers and writers and seems to have existed in various forms. Adair says[1]:

"The warriors have another favorite game called chungke, which, with propriety of language, may be called 'running hard labor.' They have near their state-house a square piece of ground well cleaned, and fine sand is carefully strewed over it, when requisite, to promote a swifter motion to what they throw along the surface. Only one or two on a side play at this ancient game. They have a stone about two fingers broad at the edge, and two spans round; each party has a pole of about eight feet long, smooth and tapering at each end, the points flat. They set off abreast of each other at six yards from the end of the play-ground; then one of them hurls the stone on its edge, in as direct a line as he can, a considerable distance toward the middle of the other end of the square; when they have ran a few yards, each darts his pole anointed with bear's oil, with a proper

---

[1] Adair: History of American Indians, London, 1775, page 401.

force, as near as he can guess in proportion to the motion of the stone, that the end may lie close to the stone; when this is the case, the person counts two of the game, and, in proportion to the nearness of the poles to the mark, one is counted, unless by measuring both are found to be at an equal distance from the stone. In this manner the players will keep running most part of the day, at half speed, under the violent heat of the

FIG. 80. Discoidal stone from Vicksburg, ⅔ size, Birchett collection.

sun, staking their silver ornaments, their nose, finger, and earrings; their breast, arm, and wrist-plates; and even all their wearing apparel, except that which barely covers their middle. All the American Indians are much addicted to this game, which to us appears to be a task of stupid drudgery; it seems, however, to be of early origin, when their forefathers used diversions as simple as their manners. The hurling-stones they use at present were, time immemorial, rubbed smooth on the rocks, and with prodigious labor; they are kept with the strictest religious care from one generation to another, and are exempted from being buried with the dead. They belong to the town where they are used, and are carefully preserved."

Figure 80 will serve as an example of the discoidal stones of the usual type. It is a rather large specimen, coming from the vicinity of Vicksburg. The two faces are similar and the concavity begins some distance back from the cir-

FIG. 81. Perforated discoidal stone from Pontotoc Co., ⅔ size, Barringer col.

FIG. 82. Discoidal stone from Pontotoc Co., ⅔ size, Barringer col.

cumference of the stone; there is formed therefore a considerable ridge around the margin on each face. This particular specimen of light-colored sandstone is rather thicker than usual, being 1.8 inches in thickness. The circumference of the stone is uniformly shaped on each side and it could well be used as a rolling stone, so far as balance is concerned. Many of the circular stones however are not so formed, but have one face smaller than the other so that if used as rolling stones they would not move in a direct line but in a curve. This is true of a number of the plano-convex discoidal stones. Three good specimens in the Barringer collection are of this type. It has been suggested that these stones were used as paint cups or mortars for the mixing of paints, and this may have been the purpose in many cases. That could hardly be true however of a stone like figure 81, from Pontotoc County, which is perforated by a hole half an inch in diameter in the center of the disk. This hole is not the result of wearing by long use; the perforation is intentionally made. In this specimen the concavity begins very near the circumfer-

FIG. 83. Discoidal stone from Lee Co., natural size, author's collection no. 10.

ence and a maximum depression is thus obtained. The diameter is 3.4 inches; the thickness somewhat more than one inch. The piece shown in figure 82, likewise from Pontotoc County, is smaller but thicker than the preceding and has rather deep concavities extending out nearly to the margin. It is made of light-colored close-grained material.

Figure 83 is slightly larger than figure 82 but is much thinner and of darker stone. It has on the face presented to the observer two rather crude diamond-shaped figures with a little pit marking the middle of each. On the reverse side is a larger diamond with the middle pit corresponding with the center of the circle. These diamonds may be of a later date. The diameter of the stone is 2.85 inches; the thickness about three quarters of an inch. This discoidal stone is from Cross Roads in Lee County.

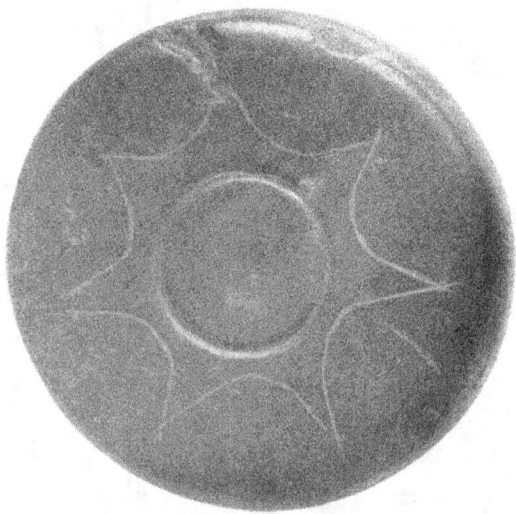

Fig. 84. Discoidal stone from Bryant, Yalobusha Co., natural size, Geol. Survey museum.

The four discoidal stones just described are all symmetrical, that is, they have the two faces alike in form. Such is not the case with the handsome specimen shown in figure 84, from a grave near Bryant, a short distance from Coffeeville, in Yalobusha County. The front side of this discoidal stone is plain or flat and figured as seen in the illustration; in the center is a slight depression; this is surrounded by a rather deep-cut circle; and outside of this is a lightly inscribed seven-pointed star with the lines connecting the points hanging in festoon fashion. The back face which is slightly smaller than the front is convex. The stone is rather highly polished thruout all of its surface, and seems to be siderite or carbonate of iron, oxidized on the outside to a thin layer of limonite or brown hematite.

A very similar piece in the collection of Mr. Barringer comes from Copiah County or that vicinity; the shape and

FIG. 85. Discoidal stone from Lafayette Co., natural size, author's collection no. 506.

size are nearly identical with the Bryant stone. The thickness of the coating in the Copiah County stone can be very plainly seen at several places where the outer covering of limonite has been broken away. This latter piece is undecorated except by a small cross in the center of the plain face, the two lines of which make angles of about 100 degrees and 80 degrees instead of right angles.

A specimen in the Geological Survey museum found by

Dr. Peabody at Alligator, Bolivar Co. (no. 61,067), and other specimens have much of the outer layer of limonite peeled off. Compare the stone tube shown in figure 142.

An excellent piece from Lafayette Co. (fig. 85) apparently has had the limonite layer cracked in various directions and these cracks re-cemented (author's collection no. 506).

The plano-convex type of circular stone, the type with one face plain and the other face more or less convex, is not

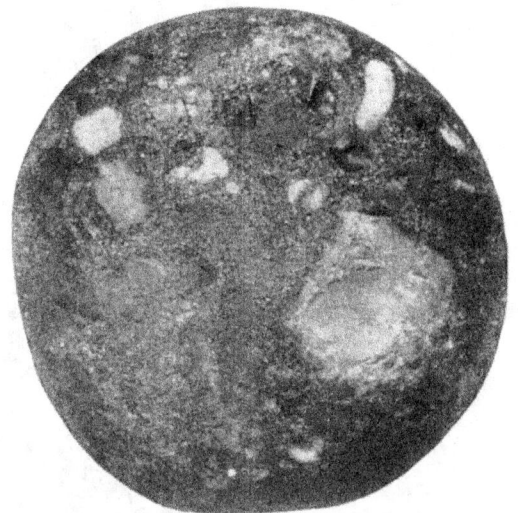

FIG. 86. Discoidal stone of conglomerate from Walls, natural size, Davies collection.

uncommon. These could not, of course, be used in games in which it was the purpose to roll them in right lines; indeed very few of the more highly finished discoidal stones show rough usage that would indicate that they had been used in rough games. They were well kept and were apparently precious objects.

The next piece illustrated, figure 86, is a rather crude one made from a pudding stone or conglomerate, a stone with pebbles set in an iron matrix. It is double-convex. The outline is not perfectly circular and the finish is rough. It comes from Walls, which is quite near the Bluffs, where an abundance of conglomerate may be found.

A much finer piece made from a conglomerate is shown in the next illustration, figure 87. This is a very beautiful and very highly polished stone; the photograph falls far short

Fig. 87. Beautiful polished conglomerate discoidal stone from Yazoo Co., natural size, Butler collection.

of doing it justice. It was found in 1885 in a mound on Silver Creek in Yazoo County and belongs to the Butler collection. This piece is 3.6 inches in diameter and 1.6 inches in thickness. A fragment of a beautiful polished conglomerate round stone 1.4 inches thick was found at the Commerce mound, Tunica Co., in 1923.

In the museum of the Geological Survey there is a roughly

blocked disk of stone approximately two and a quarter inches in diameter which is apparently a discoidal stone in the process of making; the rough blocking-out had been finished and the process of polishing had not yet been begun when the work was finally interrupted. The piece is from Nettleton, and is instructive in so far as it throws light upon the process of manufacture.

Fig. 88. Granite discoidal stone from Copiah Co., natural size, Barringer collection.

Under the head of stone plates in the chapter on agricultural and domestic implements mention will be made of much larger stone disks ranging from 7 to 12.5 inches in diameter and relatively thin. They may be thought of as the extreme limit of discoidal or circular stones. Moore considers the large disks from Alabama to be paint palettes.

In some examples of discoidal stones both faces are convex. A granite specimen from Copiah County (figure 88) modifies this type by having the faces in turn pitted to the extent of nearly half the diameter; so that they are convex on their outer margin and concave about the center.

It will be seen from the accompanying descriptions and illustrations and from many examples not here described that there is an almost endless variety of discoidal stones, such as bicave, double-convex, plano-convex, convex-concave on the same surface, symmetrical and asymmetrical, perforate and imperforate, inscribed and unfigured. Some have a secondary depression in the middle, others do not. In their different forms they merge into mullers and pestles, mortars, hammer-stones, stone disks, and palettes. Many of them show very excellent workmanship, and they are far more numerous than boat-stones and spuds. As to their use various types have been variously considered as gaming-stones, paint-cups, and spindle-whorls. It may be surmised that many were ceremonial or ornamental; certainly many have not been subject to hard usage.

SPUDS.

Among the many interesting problematic forms are the spuds, or spade-shaped stones, sometimes called also hoe-shaped implements and spatulate forms. They are of rather wide distribution, tho nowhere numerous; their use was probably ceremonial. I here describe four spuds from this state and illustrate them on a scale of one half.

The first one, figure 89, is 7.5 inches long and over 6 inches wide. It is of gray quartzite polished over its entire surface, which is however somewhat uneven. The shoulders are broad; the edges of the handle are not so nearly parallel as in the other three. It was presented to the U. S. National Museum by Mr. A. J. Gholson of Round Lake, Miss., but the provenience is not indicated.

Figure 90, the smallest of the four, is only 4.8 inches long, and its greatest thickness is only half an inch. It is of dark gray sandstone and its semicircular edge is sharp enough to have been used as a digging or scraping implement. It shows no signs of such use, tho there is a small piece broken from this edge. It is from the Grubb Place in Quitman County.

The third piece, figure 91, is a fine heavy stone an inch thick and weighing more than a pound and a half; the semi-

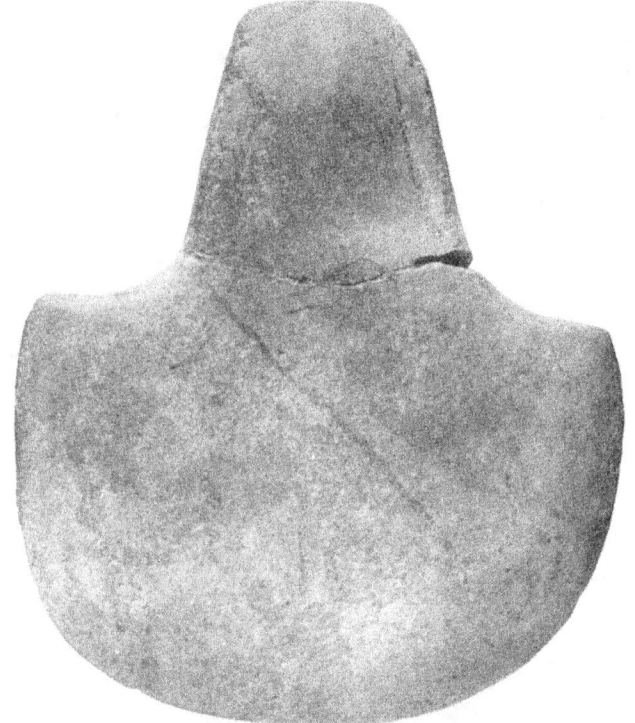

FIG. 89. Spud from Miss., ½ size, U. S. Nat. Mus. no. 209,720.
Photograph by U. S. N. M.

circular edge is too thick and blunt to have been used for any cutting or scraping purposes, and shows no indications of such use. The handle has a slight shoulder on both faces and has the appearance of having been hafted; it is probably a ceremonial ax. It comes from a grave near Walls in the north-western corner of the state.

The fourth specimen, figure 92, differs from the other

172 ARCHEOLOGY OF MISSISSIPPI.

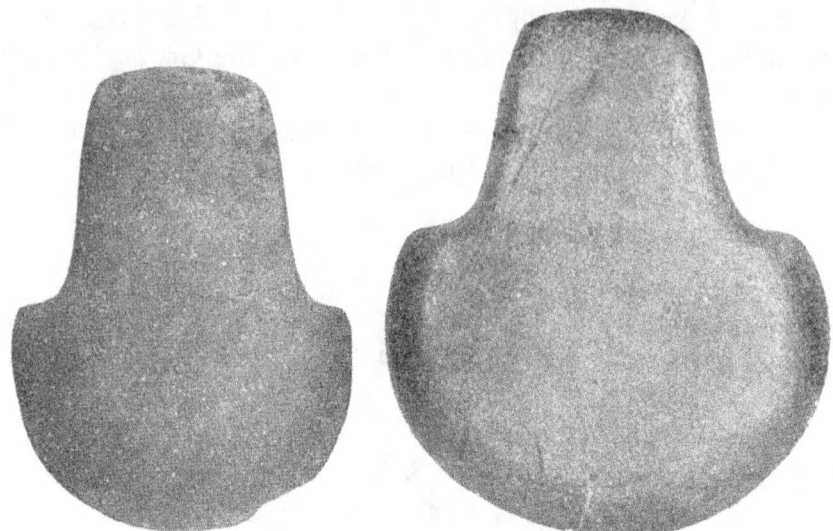

Fig. 90. Spud from Quitman Co., ½ size, Clark collection.

Fig. 91. Spud from Walls, ½ size, Davies collection.

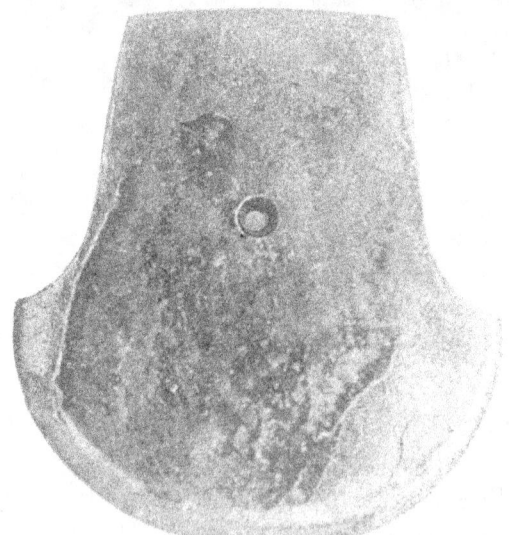

Fig. 92. Spud from Natchez, ½ size, Learned col.

three in being perforated in the vertical axis somewhat above the line of the shoulders. The handle is also wider in proportion than on the other three and the end of the handle is nearly a straight line. It is in the collection of Mr. Rufus Learned at Natchez. Mr. Shaw of Natchez has a similar but narrower piece from across the river in Louisiana. Another perforated Mississippi spud is shown in Squier and Davis's *Ancient Monuments,* page 218, figure 114, number 6.

BOAT-STONES.

The name boat-stone approximately defines another type of problematic artifact relatively infrequent of occurrence. Boat-stones vary greatly in their shape and character, but they all preserve something of the canoe or trough shape;

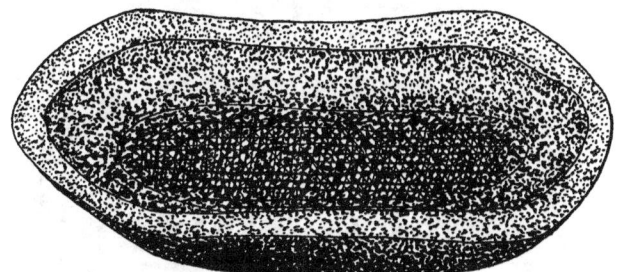

FIG. 93. Boat-stone from Clarksdale, natural size, Clark col.

some are perforated with two holes thru the bottom of the boat, some have no perforations. It has been conjectured that the imperforate ones are paint containers, but the fact that so many perforated ones are found would seem to indicate that the general purpose was something else. They may have been ceremonial or ornamental; certain it is that it required much labor to make the better ones. Some found in other states have a groove connecting the two holes on the outside, as if for the passage of a string or cord. Five boat-stones from Mississippi are illustrated here, all in natural size, three from drawings by Prof. Raymond Mathews and two from photographs by the Heye Museum.

Figure 93 shows a rather flat type of boat-stone; it is

completely hollowed out, has the sides slightly compressed, and is without perforations. It is from Clarksdale.

Figure 94 presents two views of a red boat-stone with two perforations in the bottom. The keel is flat and relatively broad. The piece was collected by Dr. Birdsong in Copiah County, or that vicinity, and is now in the collection of Mr. Victor C. Barringer at Monroe, Louisiana.

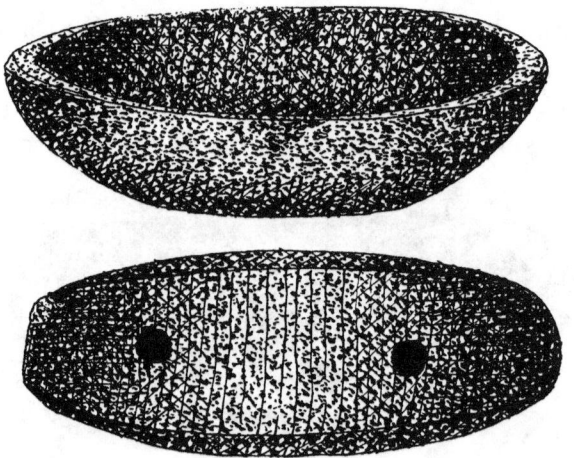

FIG. 94. Two views of red boat-stone from Copiah Co., natural size, Barringer collection.

Figure 95 is a remarkably fine boat-stone cut from dark green material with great accuracy and finished with great care. It is 5.4 inches long and only nine-tenths of an inch wide at its widest; the outside depth is 1.4, the inside depth three-quarters of an inch. The keel is one-fourth of an inch wide and very uniform thruout except that it shows a slight narrowing and rounding at one end. The boat is so well balanced that it can stand on its narrow keel. There are no perforations, but there is a slight notch in each end, which is clearly represented in the drawing. This excellent specimen is from Ballground, Warren County, north-east of Vicksburg and a short distance from Haynes Bluff.

ORNAMENTAL STONES. 175

Figure 96, a brown jasper boat-stone from Columbus, is a valuable specimen in that it seems to show the method of hollowing out the boat. The two small end holes have been put thru, and a large hole has been bored in the middle of the boat which does not go entirely thru the stone. It would seem that the piece is therefore an unfinished boat-stone and that it remained for the artisan to cut away the portion between the holes and give the final finish to this little piece when his work was interrupted. With this boat-stone should be compared those represented in figures 50 (Ohio) and 53 (Pennsylvania) of Moorehead's *Stone Ornaments of the American Indian*.

Another specimen from the same locality and of the same material, figure 97, may represent a less advanced stage in the process of boat-making; here the two smaller holes have been drilled thru but the larger central one has not yet been begun. These two interesting pieces formerly belonged to the Joseph Jones collection and are now in the Museum of the American Indian, Heye Foundation, New York.

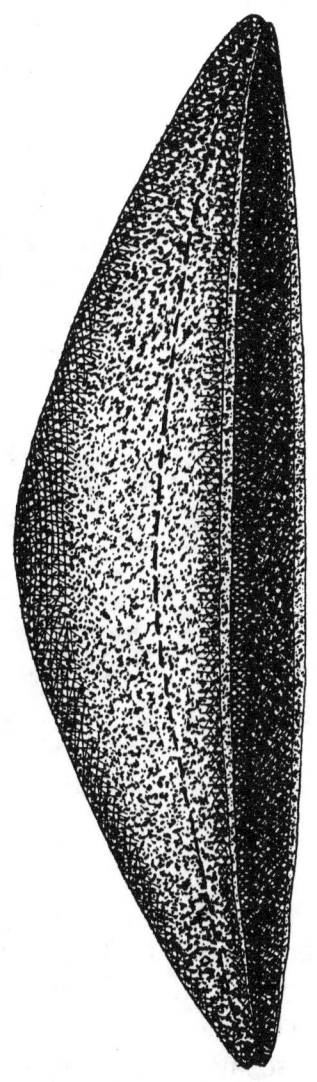

FIG. 95. Slender boat-stone, from Ballground, Warren Co., natural size, Birchett collection.

Other boat-stones have been found in the state, for

instance those of Miss Rebecca Miller at Selma near Natchez, and those in the Dickeson collection at Philadelphia, Pa.

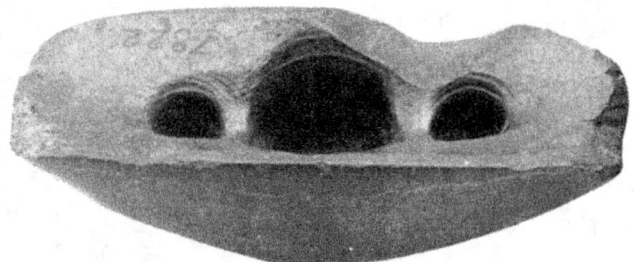

Fig. 96. Jasper boat-stone from Columbus, natural size, Heye museum no. 7822.

Fig. 97. Jasper boat-stone from Columbus, natural size, Heye museum no. 7823.

GORGETS.

The word gorget signifies etymologically something worn about the throat; archeologically the term is used to name certain plates of stone, shell, and copper, with one or more perforations, generally two. Some of the various forms of these interesting objects may be seen in the accompanying illustrations.

Figure 98 shows two plain stone gorgets from the Ballard collection, of the usual elliptical form and of ordinary workmanship and finish; each has two eyes.

ORNAMENTAL STONES.   177

Figure 99 is similar to those just described but has the ends more nearly straight; it is of banded brown sandstone

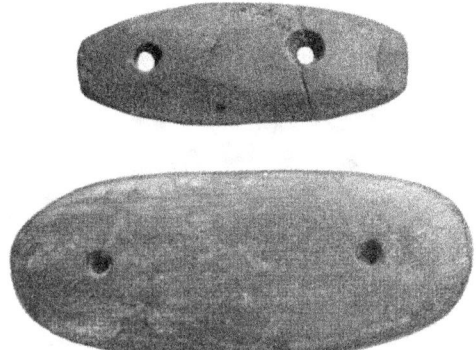

FIG. 98. Stone gorgets from Winona, slightly over half size, Ballard collection.

and comes from Lodi, Montgomery County. It is 2.75 inches long and half an inch thick.

In figure 100, number 944 of the Butler collection, we see

FIG. 99. Sandstone gorget from Lodi, Montgomery Co., slightly under size, U. S. Nat. Mus. no. 146,316. Photograph by U. S. Nat. Mus.

illustrated the economy of the Amerind; a gorget which had the misfortune to be broken was re-perforated and its use continued. In the Butler collection there is a gorget from another state which has two holes at each end; the inner holes were evidently drilled after one of the outer holes had been broken out, the extra hole at the unbroken end being neces-

FIG. 100. Broken stone gorget from Yazoo Co., ½ size, Butler collection no. 944.

sary to maintain the proper balance of the stone. Re-worked implements of various kinds are not uncommon.

In figure 101 is shown a small spindle-shaped form of stone gorget with the eyes nearer the middle of the piece

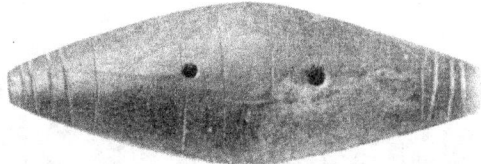

FIG. 101. Stone gorget from vicinity of Aberdeen, ½ size, Geol. Survey collection.

than is usual. This gorget is ornamented with several incised lines at each end, running at right angles to the main axis, and several others in the middle or broader part of the stone.

An unusually fine gorget is represented in figure 102. It has four bands at each end, the third one in each case passing thru the middle of the eye. Both the ends and the sides of the gorget are notched. In the central field of the stone there is a rather elaborate incised drawing, which I have been unable to interpret in terms of any animal figure. The whole stone suggests somewhat a beetle form, but nothing definite can be made of it. This very fine gorget was found in 1896.

Two types of gorgets are represented in figures 103-108. In the second column are three pieces of the general type just described, in which the under side is flat and the upper side somewhat rounded, while the general outline is elliptical. In all three of these the eyes are near the end. In the first column are represented three gorgets in which the upper and lower faces are both alike and flat or nearly so, and the longer sides are concave instead of convex, as in the right hand group.

Figure 103 is from Pontotoc County and has not only the two longer sides concave but also the two ends. The eyes are

FIG. 102. Stone gorget, natural size, Butler collection no. 1698.

coned on both sides, the left one being drilled at a considerable angle, as can be seen from the reproduction of the photograph. The faces are flat. Figure 105 is concave on the

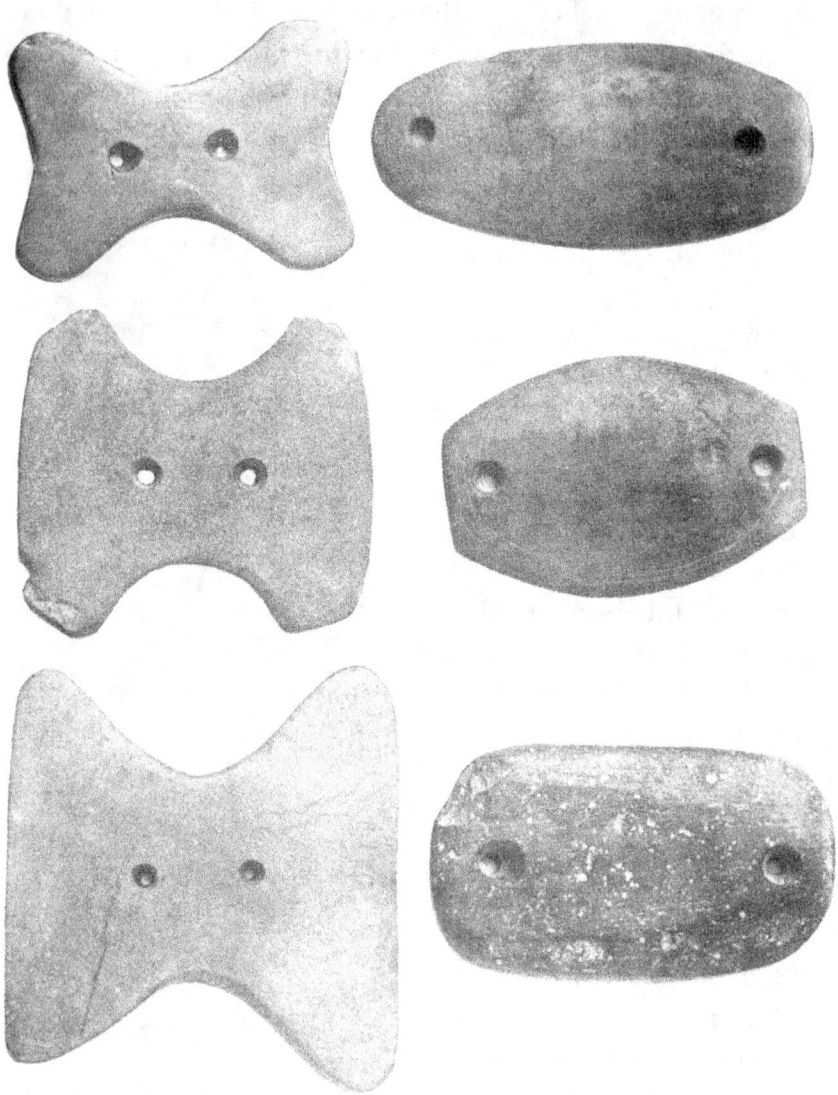

Fig. 103. Pontotoc Co., Barringer col.
Fig. 105. Lafayette Co., Brown col.
Fig. 107. Walls, Davies collection.
Fig. 104. Pontotoc Co., Barringer col.
Fig. 106. Clarksdale, Clark collection.
Fig. 108. Copiah Co., Barringer col.

Two types of stone gorgets, scale 6/10.

ORNAMENTAL STONES. 181

two longer sides almost to the extent of semicircles, while the two ends are slightly convex. The piece is somewhat injured. The eyes are coned entirely from the side next to the observer. The gorget is slightly thicker in the middle and feathers out toward the ends and sides. Figure 107 is a very fine specimen, tho not quite symmetrical. There are deep recesses on the two sides whereas the two ends are right lines; the form is therefore intermediate between the two preceding forms. The holes are drilled almost entirely on the side exposed to the observer with very slight reaming on the reverse side. The two faces are similar with a slight increase in thickness in the middle of the stone. This type of gorget with concave sides is much less frequent than the type with convex sides.

Figure 104 is a very plain gorget of the elliptical type. The coning of the eyes is mostly from the flat or back side and the holes are rather large and near the ends. Figure 106 is not distinct in the reproduction; the cutting of the stone brings out a series of bands on the upper surface, and in addition there are two incised lines parallel with the margin passing outside the eyes and a row of hatches passing entirely around the stone on the margin. The ends are cut off rather squarely and the swelling of the sides is rather greater than usual. The eyes are large and drilled from both sides. Figure 108 is a plain undecorated gorget with ends terminating rather abruptly. The eyes are coned from both sides, the left eye being drilled at a considerable slant on the upper surface tho vertically on the lower surface.

In figure 109 is shown a stone somewhat similar to the usual elliptical gorget type except that it is thicker and has only one perforation, that being in the middle of the stone. The specimen is from Coldwater, De Soto County. Below it in figure 110 is shown a similarly-shaped stone, flat on the lower surface and rounded on the upper surface, but having no perforation. This may be an unfinished piece lacking the central perforation, but is more probably a finished piece of the polishing-stone or rubber type.

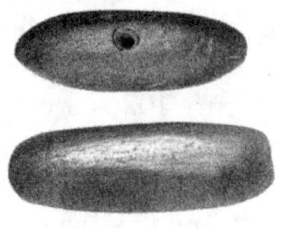

FIG. 109. Perforated stone from Coldwater, ½ size, Mr. A. B. Presley.

FIG. 110. Stone bar from Alcorn Co., ½ size, author's collection no. 339.

The Smithsonian Institution possesses a handsome banded slate pendant with only one eye or hole (figure 111). It comes from a mound in Mississippi, but the exact location is not given.

The Museum of the American Indian, Heye Foundation, has an interesting five-sided limonite pendant from Pontotoc, the gift of Harmon W. Hendricks (fig. 112).

An unusual form is shown in figure 113; here the end containing the eye is much broader than the other end. The eye has the appearance of being much worn by a string passing to the right in front of the stone and to the left behind the stone, or else it was drilled from both faces and the two holes failed to center upon each other. The upper broad end is not highly finished on the edge and seems to be broken; it contains segments of two small holes. The gorget is made of a greenish stone worked quite thin, and has a length of 4 inches. These two latter specimens bear considerable resemblance to a slate gorget from Page County, Virginia, illustrated by Fowke[1]. Warren K. Moorehead[2] illustrates two similar forms.

A fine shell gorget is described in the chapter on shell and bone objects (fig. 248).

---

[1] Fowke: Arch. Invest. in James and Potomac Valleys, Bu. of Am. Ethn., Washington, 1894, fig. 10.
[2] Moorehead: The Stone Age, vol. I, page 336; Stone Ornaments, page 21.

ORNAMENTAL STONES. 183

Fig. 111. Banded slate pendant from a mound, natural size, Smith. Inst. no. 6630. Photograph by Smith. Inst.

Fig. 112. Limonite pendant from Pontotoc, ½ size, Heye museum no. 6-1560.

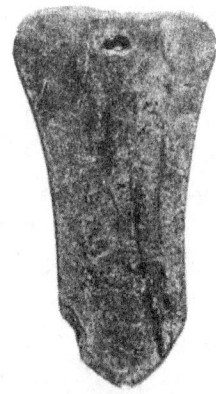

Fig. 113. Stone gorget or pendant from Copiah Co., ½ size, Barringer collection.

PLUMMETS AND SINKERS.

In all parts of Mississippi but perhaps most abundantly in the Natchez territory are found stone objects of the plummet, sinker, and pendant type. Under the heading of gorgets several flat thin pendants have been shown; in the present subdivision are shown objects of the plummet and sinker types. The purpose of these objects is problematic; it has

FIG. 114. Stone plummet, New Albany, natural size, Ticer collection.

FIG. 115. Limestone pendant, Haynes Bluff, nat. size. From C. B. Moore.

been variously surmised that such artifacts were personal ornaments, ceremonial objects, charms or amulets, sinkers, and actual plummets. Many are made of hematite and other hard stone and are carefully wrought; others are made of limestone and have less labor expended upon them; still others are made from natural pebbles and have no further alteration than a constriction or groove around one end. One of the latter class was found by the author on the surface of a mound near Alligator during Dr. Charles Peabody's investigations there in August, 1918.

ORNAMENTAL STONES. 185

Some of the better types of plummets are shown in figures 114 to 118. Figure 114 is a common type. Figure 116 is an unusually interesting piece; it has a perforation thru the flattened small end and four grooves lower down around the neck, the first and last being quite shallow, the other two being deeper; the stone is highly magnetic. The specimen is

FIG. 116. Magnetite plummet from Walls, nat. size, Davies col., Geol. Survey museum.

FIG. 117. Hematite plummet, Vicksburg territory, nat. size, Birchett collection.

from Walls in the north-west corner of the state. Figure 117 is slightly larger and has a deep constriction about the smaller end; it is of limonite or brown hematite and comes from the Vicksburg territory.

Some plummets are relatively thick for their length and thus have an egg-like appearance; such are figure 115, a limestone specimen obtained by Mr. C. B. Moore at Haynes Bluff in Warren County, above Vicksburg, and a similar but larger one in the collection of Dr. Birchett. Others are long and slender, such as the interesting specimen with one flat side shown in figure 118 and one in the Learned collection at Natchez. Dr. Birchett has a unique pestle-shaped implement of beautiful yellowish flint or jasper, in which a boring has just been begun near the small end (fig. 119). The large

FIG. 118. Plummet with one flat side, nat. size, Heye museum no. 7755.

FIG. 119. Plummet (?) with perforation just begun, Vicksburg territory, nat. size, Birchett collection.

end of this piece is scarcely shaped like a pestle, tho it shows slight wear, not more however than might result from accidental contact with other stones.

Two plummets of the cruder type are illustrated by Dr. Charles Peabody in his report on explorations of mounds in

ORNAMENTAL STONES.

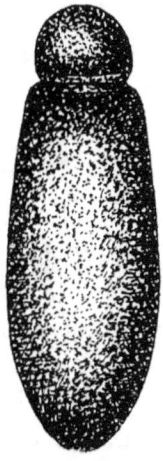

FIG. 120. Slightly flattened stone plummet, Clarksdale, natural size, Clark collection.

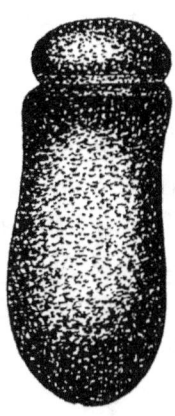

FIG. 121. Greatly flattened stone plummet, Columbus territory, natural size, Chapman collection.

FIG. 122. Stone plummet or sinker, from Corinth, natural size, Gift col.

FIG. 123. Stone sinker or plummet, from Wilkinson Co., natural size, Harris collection.

Coahoma County[1], one from the surface and one from the Edwards mound; both are pear-shaped and have a groove about the smaller end.

---

[1]Peabody: Explor. of Mounds, Coahoma Co., Miss., Cambridge, Mass, 1904, pl. 16.

In figures 120 and 121 are pictured two plummets which are flattened in cross-section, the former slightly, the latter greatly. Very probably the stone-worker took advantage of natural forms in the making of many such pieces.

Well wrought tho not highly polished pieces of the sinker form are shown in figures 122 and 123; both are grooved longitudinally; the former is rectangular in general outline, the latter is a prolate spheroid and resembles a large nut in general appearance; they are from opposite corners of the state.

 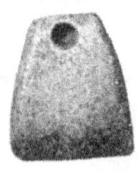

Fig. 124. Perforated celts, Wilkinson Co., ½ size, Harris collection, Natchez.

There are still other types of pendant objects. In figure 124 are pictured two small celts perforated for suspension; one is relatively long, the other relatively broad; both are from the south-western part of the state, and with the exception of the perforation resemble the many small dark celts or "thunderbolts" found in the Natchez region.

A pretty pendant of red banded stone from the Dunleith plantation is shown at the bottom of figure 128 among the flat circular beads.

BEADS.

Among the most beautiful of the pendant objects are the beads. Since they were used as personal ornaments they were often buried with the dead, and hence are often found in excavation of the graves, sometimes in large quantities. The material used was stone, shell, bone, teeth, clay, rolled copper, and in later times glass. Illustrations of shell beads are shown in the chapter on bone and shell objects (figs. 238-240) and of trade beads in the chapter on modern material (fig. 346).

Mississippi soil has yielded many fine examples of jasper

and other handsome stone beads. The workmanship is often excellent and the perforations rather remarkable for length, delicacy, and accuracy. In some however the perforation is incomplete. One from Lafayette County in the author's collection (no. 60) is one and a quarter inches long and has a boring one inch deep in one end and a boring well begun in the other end, yet the two do not quite come together.

Charles Rau[1] describes and partially illustrates a remarkable find of jasper ornaments mostly unfinished, in Lawrence County, Mississippi. Of the 449 pieces which came into the possession of the National Museum there were: 295 beads of cylindrical shape from one-fourth of an inch to three inches in length and from one-fourth of an inch to one inch in thickness, polished, but rarely perfectly cylindrical in form, ten showing the beginnings of holes; 101 round beads of a more compressed or discoidal shape, length one-eighth to five-eighths, diameter one-fourth to three-fourths, polished, five showing incipient holes; 2 small animal-shaped objects; 29 chipped or polished pieces; 22 jasper pebbles showing no work. Twenty objects were not sent to the National Museum; there were therefore in all 469 pieces in this deposit, by far the greater number of them being beads.

Dr. Robert B. Fulton[2] describes a collection of 30 jasper pieces in his possession found on the summit of a hill in Lincoln County, four miles west of Wesson and about twenty-five miles west of the locality where the Lawrence County specimens were discovered. In this collection were 13 polished perforated beads of cylindrical form, 5 perforated beads of nearly spherical form, 1 carved deer, and several bird forms. On one of the long beads a separate ring of the same material was firmly fixed.

---
[1] Rau: The Stock in Trade of an Aboriginal Lapidary (Mississippi), Ann. Rept. of the Smith. Inst., 1877, p. 291.
[2] Fulton: Prehistoric Jasper Ornaments in Miss., Pub. Miss. Hist. Soc., Oxford, Miss., 1898, vol. I, p. 91.

Excellently finished beads have been found in the vicinity of Winona, Montgomery County, which may be seen in the Ballard collection.

Some good stone beads of cylindrical type are shown in figure 125, the longest is nearly three inches long.

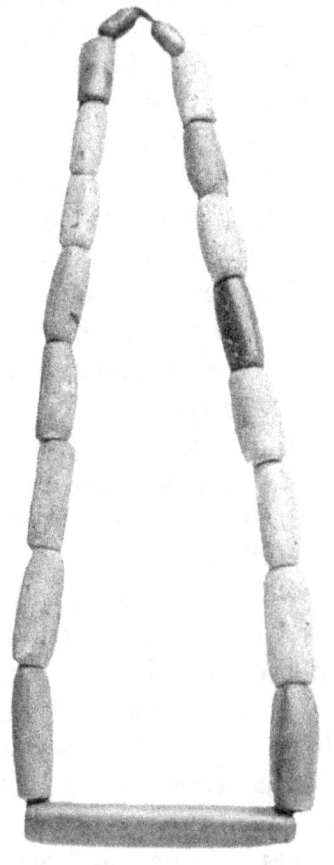
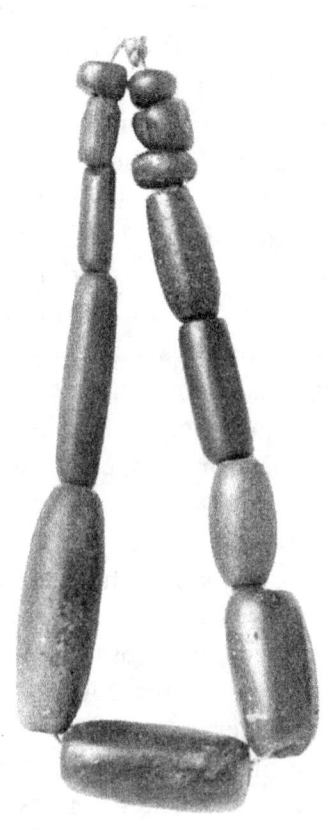

FIG. 125. Stone beads, ½ size, Barringer collection.

FIG. 126. Jasper beads from mound at Melrose, Yazoo Co., ½ size, Butler collection.

In figures 126 and 127 are shown some beautiful jasper beads found in 1892 by Brevoort Butler in a mound on the Yazoo River at Melrose, Yazoo County. Those shown half size in figure 126 are of the red and brown shades, the longest being 2.6 inches; those shown full size in figure 127 are of a greenish mottled appearance, the longest being 2.2 inches.

FIG. 127. Jasper beads from mound at Melrose, Yazoo Co., natural size, Butler collection.

The beads of this mound show a high character of craftsmanship.

A unique transparent quartz bead (no. 2210) was found by the author in 1923 at the Bowdre mounds in Tunica County. It is made of the ordinary six-sided quartz prism, probably from Hot Springs, Arkansas, and has a length of 1.75 inches. The perforation was never finished; it extends

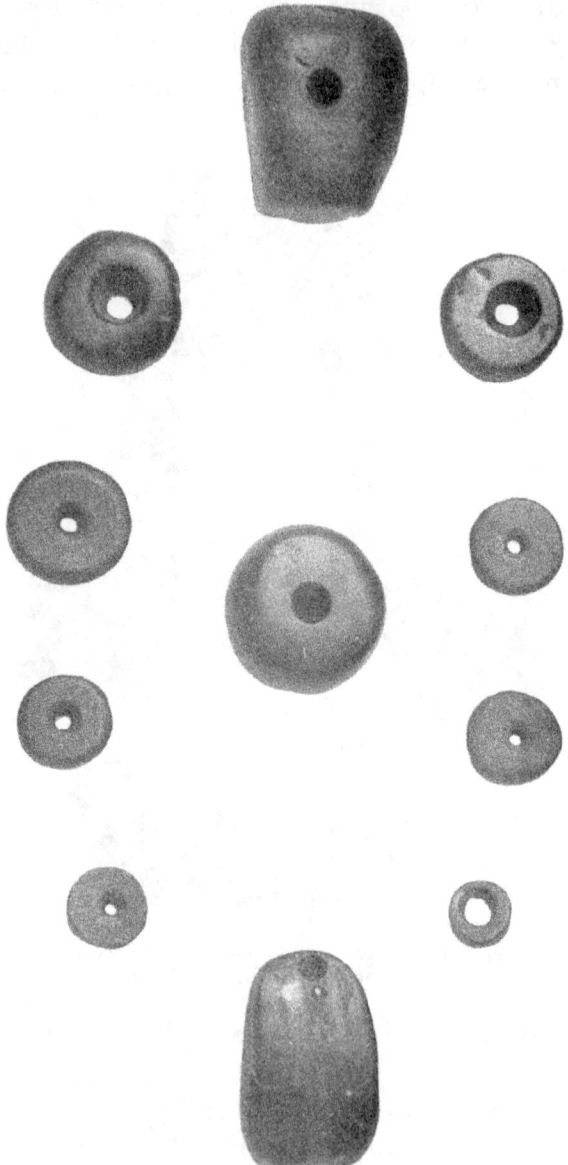

FIG. 128. Jasper and red stone beads from various parts of the state, natural size.

0.45 of an inch into one end and is only well begun on the other.

Stone beads of the disk type are also frequently found, sometimes of fine finish. In figure 128 the top piece and the bottom piece are of irregular outline, the remaining pieces are good examples of the flatter type of circular beads. The perforated pebble at the top of the page is from the vicinity of Columbus and belongs to Mr. E. R. Hopkins of that city; the reddish banded pendant at the bottom was found on the plantation of Dr. Alfred H. Stone at Dunleith and is kept in his home; the handsome large central bead of red jasper is from Monroe County and is in the museum of the State Geological Survey at the University; the two upper circular beads, left and right, are from Montgomery County and are preserved in the Ballard collection (nos. 140 and 138); the remaining six circular beads are from the vicinity of Columbus and are the property of Mr. Felix M. Chapman.

BANNER-STONES.

The banner-stones form another interesting group of problematic artifacts, relatively numerous in Mississippi, tho often broken. A typical form is photographed in figure 129. The main axis is represented by a perforation, in this particular case extending only half way through the stone; on each side is an expanding semicircular wing which is worked down at the circumference to a relatively thin tho not sharp blade. The form shown in figure 129 is sometimes called a butterfly-stone. There are many variations in the forms of the wings or projecting parts of banner-stones, tho the two wings of any one piece are usually symmetrical.

The purpose of such stones can only be conjectured. The name "banner-stone" was given on the supposition that they were mounted on a rod or staff by means of the perforation. The fact that in many specimens the perforation extends only a part of the way thru the piece lends some weight to this theory. Three have been found in North Carolina with stone staffs[1]. It has been suggested that they were used as a balance or auxiliary on spear-shafts. Moorehead[2] says that whether they were so used or not, many broken specimens clearly show that they were fractured by being driven forcibly upon their spindles. A broken specimen in the author's collection (no. 231) would seem to indicate that the fracture

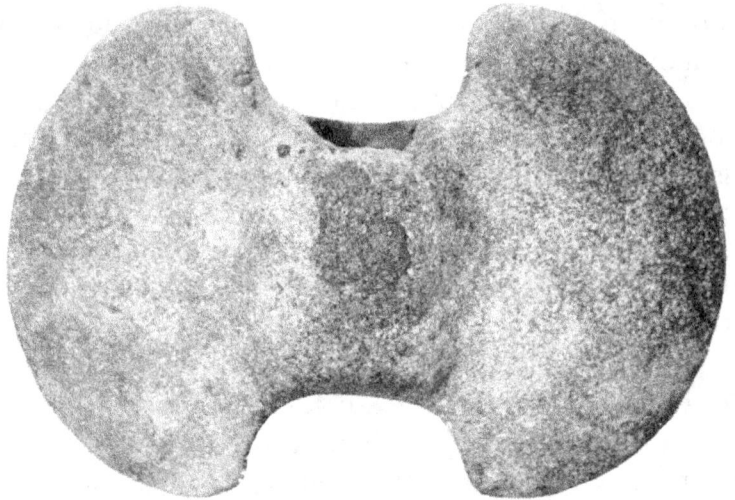

FIG. 129. Banner-stone, natural size, Barringer collection.

was due to pressure from within. The fracture begins in the hole but soon passes out into the thicker stone leaving most of the hole intact. It is difficult, however, to be positive on this point. In this specimen, which is of the butter-fly type and of a handsome rosy material, probably quartz, the hole abruptly becomes smaller near the end away from the fracture, and the circular marks of drilling are polished or worn away at the end where the fracture began, tho they are plainly

---

[1]Baer: Preliminary Rept. on Banner-stones, Am. Arch., 1921, p. 445.
[2]Moorehead: Stone Orn. of the Am. Indians, Andover, Mass., 1917, p. 193.

seen in the middle of the boring. That banner-stones were used for drill balances, fire-spindle balances, pipe-stem ornaments, and personal ornaments, has also been suggested. That many of them were not destined for rough mechanical use is shown both by their form and by their delicate workmanship.

FIG. 130. Unfinished banner-stone from Lafayette Co., 6.6 inches long, author's collection no. 13.

In the discussion of the purpose of banner-stones I invite attention to the object on top of the head-dress represented in copper plates from mound C of the Etowah group, Georgia[1]. Mr. Clarence B. Moore, who recently found in "the Indian Knoll," in Ohio County, Kentucky, a large number of rectangular banner-stones associated with what he considers as probably netting needles, advances the theory that these perforated stone artifacts were used as mesh-

---

[1]Thomas: Mound Explorations, 12th Ann. Rept., Bu. of Ethn., fig. 186 and plate.
Fowke: Arch. Hist. of Ohio, Columbus, 1902, figs. 302 and 303.
Beuchat: Archéologie Américaine, Paris, 1912, figs. 56 and 57.

spacers or sizers¹. Some of the smaller banner-stones with small perforations, such as figures 136 and 138, may be classed as beads.

The large unfinished bipinnate stone shown in figure 130 is of the double-bladed type; its two wings are brought to a relatively sharp edge. In this piece the perforation has not been begun. The material is a hard quartzite. In general it may be remarked that most of the Mississippi banner-stones are of hard material, so far as my observation goes; I have

FIG. 131. Banner-stone from Aberdeen, natural size, Geol. Survey museum.

not seen any made of slate. Another imperforate Lafayette Co. piece may be seen in the collection of Dr. H. C. Wait.

In the Aberdeen specimen presented to the Survey by Mr. B. H. MacFarland, figure 131, the two edges are less curved, so that the vertical section is more nearly rectangular; the cross-section is triangular, the back side being nearly plain. Other specimens have this general shape, except that the two faces are alike. A specimen from Holly Springs in the U. S. National Museum, no. 26,929, has an elliptical cross-section with major axis of 2.4 inches and minor axis of 1.5 inches; the perforation extends only half way thru and was made by a tubular drill. The extreme limit of the banner-stone in this

¹Moore: Some Aboriginal Sites on Green River, Ky., Philadelphia, 1916.

direction is found in the perforated ellipsoid, such as the ellipsoidal mass of iron carbonate found on the bank of the Tombigbee River at Columbus and preserved in Mr. Chapman's collection; it is perforated about half its length and

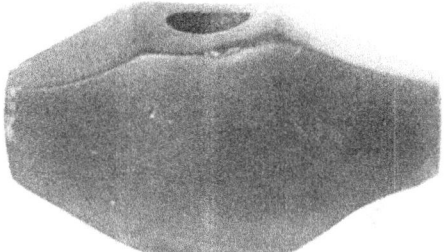

FIG. 132. Banner-stone from New Albany, natural size, Ticer collection.

may be thought of as occupying medium ground between banner-stones and tubes. In form it is not unlike the stone tube presented in figure 216 of Moorehead's *Stone Ornaments*.

FIG. 133. Banner-stone from Lafayette Co., natural size, Wait collection.

In the red banner-stone from New Albany shown in figure 132 the width of the outside of the two wings or extensions is about half that of the perforated axis.

The Lafayette County banner-stone represented in figure

133 comes to a point at the two extremities; the perforation is complete. The specimen is irregular in the bevel shown on the lower edge of one face; both ends of the hole can be readily seen at the same time. Pointed halves of this type are not infrequently found in the north-eastern part of the state.

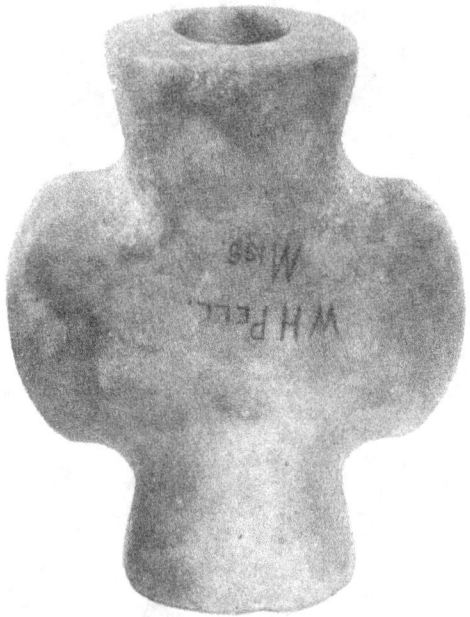

Fig. 134. Banner-stone of rose quartz, nat. size, Am. Mus. of Nat. His., N. Y., no. 1-1821. Photo. by Am. Mus. of Nat. Hist.

the weakness produced by perforation evidently being responsible for the broken condition of many specimens.

In figures 134 and 135 is shown a less common type of banner-stone. In these pieces the perforated axis is longer than the lateral axis, the lateral part of the stone taking more or less the form of a cross-bar similar to the longer bar of the stone except that it is not perforated. The finish is excellent in both pieces; the former bears the name of W. H. Pell, the latter comes from the vicinity of Corinth. Moorehead in his

Stone Ornaments classes such pieces with the tubes, with the remark that they may be tubes or small winged objects according to one's point of view.

The little specimen from Columbus, figure 136, is similar to these, except that the second bar is not so well developed and that the piece has the rudiments of a third bar at right angles to the other two. It is a handsome piece of particolored stone, and its small size, delicacy of workmanship,

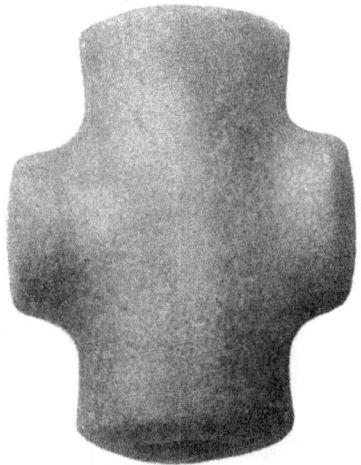

FIG. 135. Banner-stone from Corinth, nat. size, Gift collection.

and narrow perforation suggest that it might be classed among the beads.

The rectangular piece shown in figure 137 has the perforated bar larger and more angular than the transverse bar; both are of the same length. Here again the perforation extends only half way thru and was made with a tubular drill.

A small lunate banner-stone or ornament from Columbus is reproduced in figure 138; it is of uniform thickness and has a small perforation similar to that of a bead. This form seems to be scarce in the state.

Other banner-stones from Mississippi are pictured by Squier and Davis[1]; one of these has the form of a pick-ax. The authors state that it is clear both from their form and from the material that they were not designed for use, but may be regarded as simply for ornament or display.

Banner-stones with the projections carved into animal designs are unusual. Culin[2] cites and illustrates a fragment of a banner-stone of jasper carved to represent a frog (fig.

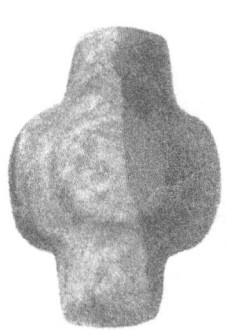 

FIG. 136. Banner-stone or bead from Columbus, nat. size, property of Mr. Hopkins.

FIG. 137. Banner-stone of quartzite, nat. size, U. S. Nat. Mus., no. 255,302. Photograph by U. S. N. M.

139). It was collected many years ago by Dr. M. W. Dickeson in one of the Ferguson mounds in Jefferson County.

The unfinished banner-stone represented in figure 140 shows the method of drilling employed in many cases. The boring has proceeded but a short distance and a core is still standing in the hole; evidently it was made with a tubular drill, probably a piece of cane, with sand as the cutting agent. There is a similar tho larger banner-stone in the department of Archives at Jackson showing the hole and core in about the same stage of advancement as in the author's specimen just

[1]Squier and Davis: Anc. Mon. of Miss. Valley, Washington, D. C., 1848, fig. 114.
[2]Culin: Dickeson Collection of Am. Antiquities, Philadelphia, 1900, pl. 13.

mentioned. The other edge of figure 140 is almost as interesting as the edge shown in the illustration; on it the artisan made a few attempts to begin drilling and left a few circles;

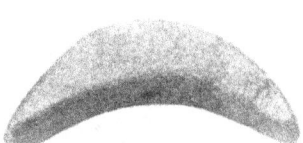
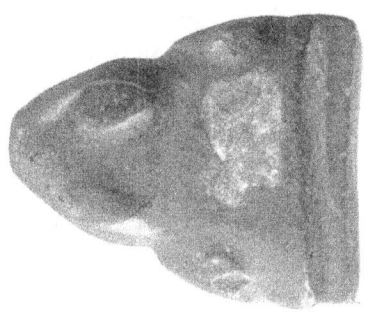

FIG. 138. Small lunate banner-stone or ornament, natural size, Columbus, Chapman collection.

FIG. 139. Half of banner-stone, frog design, Jefferson Co., nat. size, Dickeson col. no. 14,344. From Culin, plate 13.

evidently it was difficult to hold the drill in place at the beginning of the process. This piece also raises a question as to

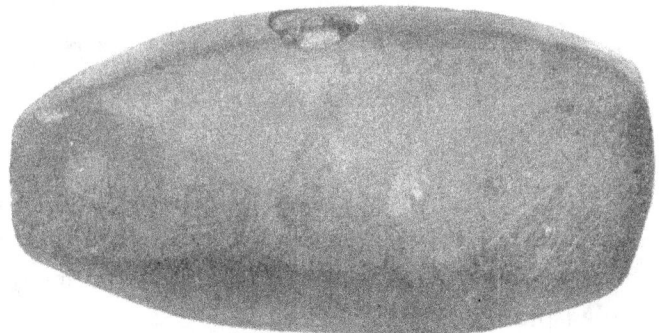

FIG. 140. Unfinished banner-stone, showing core, natural size, Alcorn Co., author's collection no. 338.

the order of finishing the banner-stone; the left end is narrow and sharper than the other end. Was the larger end to have been worked down and made symmetrical with the smaller after the finishing of the hole?

Additional evidence as to the tube method of drilling is furnished by a find that was made some years ago in a grave near New Albany in the northern part of the state. In a large brass kettle along with much relatively late material were found a piece of cane which had evidently been used as a drill and four little stone cores from drillings. These are

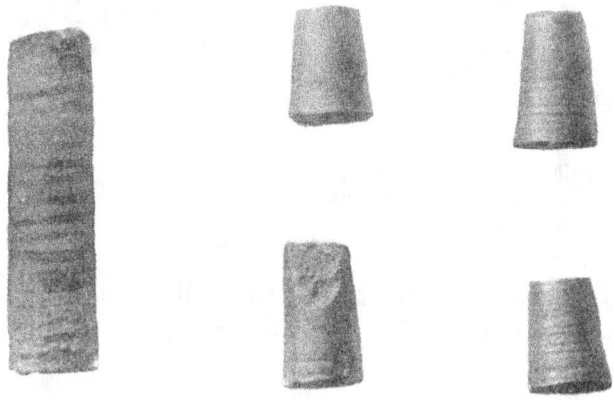

FIG. 141. Cane used for boring, and four stone cores resulting from boring, from New Albany, natural size, Ticer collection, Geol. Survey museum.

shown in natural size in figure 141. The circular striations are plainly shown on the cane and on the cores and are similar to those seen inside the perforations of banner-stones and other drilled pieces.

Several of the Mississippi banner-stones have the hole extending only half way thru the piece; in these the exterior is entirely finished. Perhaps the perforation was not to be extended further; this may be considered a reasonable assumption if we accept the supposition that these pieces were to be mounted on the end of a rod or staff.

RECTANGULAR TUBES.

In the eastern part of the state have been found several bars with square cross-section and rather large length-wise perforation. In figure 142 is shown in half size a tube 3.8 inches long with a cross-section of 1.3 inches square and a bore of one-half inch. In the middle of one side is an elevation occupying more than one-third of the length of the bar. This piece was found on the bank of the Tombigbee River at

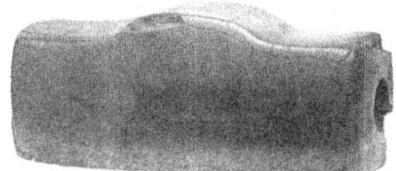

Fig. 142. Stone tube from Columbus, ½ size, Chapman collection.

Columbus, Lowndes County. The piece seems to be siderite or iron carbonate with enough pyrites or iron sulphide to crack it by oxidation. The photograph shows the cracked and broken condition of the piece.

In Aberdeen I saw a beautiful bar about 5.5 inches long, with cross-section one inch square and complete longitudinal perforation. The workmanship was perfect. Dr. J. M. Heard, the owner of the piece, reported that a neighbor boy had a similar piece, which was found with paint in it.

CIGAR-SHAPED STONES.

Another group of problematic stones is represented by the example shown in figure 143. They are here called cigar-shaped for the lack of a better name, tho they are usually more or less flattened. They may have been used as polishers. Stones of this type are fairly numerous in the state. The one here represented is 4.75 inches long; it tapers uniformly toward both ends and is flattened on one side. It was found on the Dixie plantation two miles south of Enola, Yazoo County. A specimen from Lafayette Co., no. 27 in the author's collection, is 4 inches long and made of local clay ironstone. The type grades into the flat form seen in figure 110.

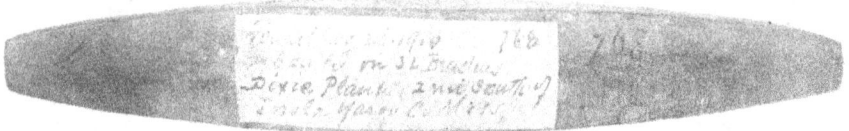

Fig. 143. Cigar-shaped stone from Yazoo Co., slightly under size, Butler collection no. 768.

CONES.

The stone objects known as cones are apparently not numerous in the state. A good example in limonite or brown hematite comes from Iuka, the gift of Robert Dyas, and is shown in figure 144. The base varies in diameter from 1.65

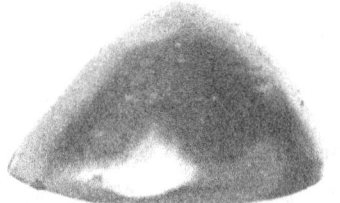

Fig. 144. Cone from Iuka, about natural size, Geol. Sur. museum no. 19.

to 1.90 inches; the height is .8 of an inch; the sides swell slightly toward the apex. It is of metallic or sub-metallic luster. A more symmetrical but flatter cone comes from Montgomery County (Ballard collection no. 30). It is of yellowish-brown shale, 1.5 inches in diameter, and half an inch high.

The purpose of such objects is not known; it has been suggested that they were used in games; as charms; and as sources of color. Hematite specimens may have been used for obtaining color in some instances, but shale pieces could hardly have been so used. Neither of the specimens cited above shows any evidence of grinding for color.

EGG-SHAPED STONES.

In figure 145 is shown a polished stone of the size and shape of a turkey-egg or goose-egg; it is 3.2 inches long. There is a slight flattening on the smaller end, so that the

Fig. 145. Egg-shaped stone from Pontotoc Co., ⅓ size, Barringer col.

piece will stand in a vertical position on that end; and a similar flattening on the side, giving the stone a horizontal position when resting on this slight face. It would therefore seem that, whatever the purpose of the stone, it was intended to assume two positions. Jones[1] describes similar stones about as large as a turkey-egg; the flattening on the end is mentioned but not the flattening on the side. He suggests their use in a weapon similar to a slung-shot.

CARVED STONES.

There are few walls and exposures of stone in Mississippi suitable for pictographs and inscriptions, and inscribed markings on small stone objects seem scarce. A good discoidal stone in the author's possession (fig. 83) has diamond-shaped

---

[1]Jones: Antiq. of Southern Indians, New York, 1893, page 372 and plate 22, no. 4.

figures upon it, possibly of a later date. A stone celt from Walls in the collection of Mr. Schubach has a U-shaped figure inscribed on one face. Cross marks are occasionally found, as upon the bottom of the problematic stone shown in

FIG. 146. Cross on stone from New Albany, natural size, Ticer col.

FIG. 147. Drawing on reverse of fig. 148 (no. 243).

figure 153. A cross on a crude stone from New Albany is of the form indicated in figure 146.

An interesting double swastika deeply carved in a stone fragment (no. 243) is shown in figure 148. On the reverse side of this fragment is a simple drawing .8 of an inch long,

FIG. 148. Double swastika, near Winona, natural size, author's collection no. 243.

of the form shown in figure 147. What other figures may have been on the unbroken stone can not now be known.

Some of the best sculpture is found on the stone pipes; among the effigies are the frog, the bear, the fish, the human figure, and fantastic creatures. The reader is referred to the chapter on pipes in this book. It would seem that independent sculpture was but little cultivated, and that human and animal images are seldom found as works of art dissociated from utilitarian objects. Two delicately carved tortoises in serpentine from the Natchez territory are shown in figures 149 and 150. A well-carved animal figure from

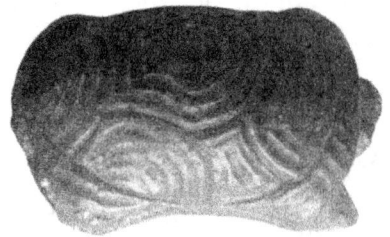

Fig. 149. Tortoise of serpentine, Adams Co., natural size, Univ. of Pa. mus. no. 14,715. From Culin.

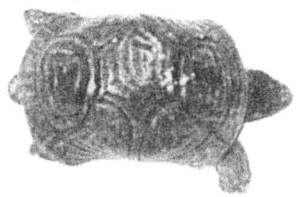

Fig. 150. Tortoise of serpentine from Natchez, natural size, Learned collection.

a mound in Jefferson County, figure 151, resembles some of those elsewhere worked into pipes. The legs and other features stand out in sharp relief. In the collection of Mr. Charles W. Clark there is a well-executed human head of

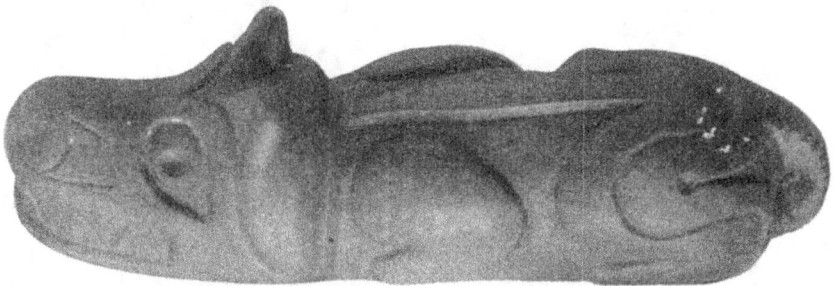

Fig. 151. Carved figure of animal, Ferguson Mounds, Jefferson Co., natural size, Univ. of Pa. museum no. 14,716. From Culin, plate 13.

diminutive size, figure 152; the face is nearly circular, but has a pointed chin; the mouth protrudes; on the forehead is carved a figure which may be a pipe or hatchet, possibly a torch; above this extends a band over the head from one side to the other, covering both ears; on this band are carved three small figures resembling tadpoles, with heads directed toward the left of the image. With this head should be compared the head of the Jefferson County pipe shown in figure 227 and that of the Yazoo County pipe shown in figures 228 and 229. The Clarksdale face may be but a fragment; if so, the re-working of the fracture has been well done.

MISCELLANEOUS.

There are various other types of stone artifacts whose purpose or use can be only conjectured. The one pictured

FIG. 152. Stone face from Clarksdale, natural size, Clark collection.

FIG. 153. Problematic stone from a grave near Nettleton, natural size. Geol. Survey museum, no. 106, 12 G. B. H.

in figure 153 is unusual. It has a rectangular base of 2.25 by 1.7 inches and an elliptical top with major axis of 1.8 and minor axis of 1.15 inches; the height is 1.15 inches, the body between the upper and lower planes being somewhat concaved. The surface of the base is divided into four parts by two straight lines crossing each other in the middle. I should be inclined to call this piece a smoothing-stone were it not for these two incised lines on the base. The stone was found in a grave near Nettleton, along with some pestles, leaf-shaped flints, and considerable other material.

CHAPTER V.

AGRICULTURAL AND DOMESTIC IMPLEMENTS.

The aborigines had a limited knowledge of agriculture; of this we have evidence in the stone implements that have come down to us, and in the testimony of the early travellers and explorers concerning the cultivation and consumption of maize or Indian corn. No doubt many of the agricultural implements were made of wood, but these have long since disappeared; others were probably made of large shells; implements of stone are still relatively abundant, and good examples may be found in most parts of the state.

Fig. 154. Chert hoe, Yazoo Co., slightly less than ¼ size, Butler collection no. 142.

Figure 154 is an example of the usual type of notched stone implements called hoes. It is 6.5 inches high by 5.4 inches wide, and deeply notched on both sides. The edge or bottom of the hoe is polished by use, as is the case in many of the notched hoes and unnotched spades. This implement was found at Benton, Yazoo County (Butler collection no. 142).

A similar implement, tho not so perfect, is shown in the first piece in figure 155, which was found by Dr. Davies near Walls, in the north-western part of the state. The illustration is on the same scale as the preceding one from Yazoo County, namely, slightly less than one-fourth size. It shows less use than the two unnotched spades in the same figure, being less highly polished about the cutting edge. The second piece in this group is of the fan-tail type: it has an unusually wide flare at the bottom and comes to a point at the top. It is highly polished by use at the bottom and in its making was chipped all the way to the top. The third piece of this group, likewise an unnotched spade, is completely worked on the lower part and has the characteristic glossy digging edge, but has the upper part left largely in an unfinished or unflaked condition; it was probably somewhat longer

FIG. 155. Hoe and spades, Walls, slightly less than ¼ size, Davies col.

originally. All three are from the collection of Dr. J. A. Davies of Walls and came from the immediate vicinity.

The Clarksdale district has furnished five good examples of this kind of agricultural implement. All are in the collection of Mr. Charles W. Clark of Clarksdale. They are illustrated in figure 156, which is on the same scale as the two preceding illustrations, the longest spade being 10.7 inches long. All are unnotched but no two are exactly alike. The first and fourth have rather straight digging edges; the third is a very common type of spade. Another fine spade from the Delta, 11.25 by 5.5 inches, is owned by Mr. Gift of Corinth.

These implements are rather scarce in Mississippi but farther up in the Mississippi Valley are much more numer-

FIG. 156. Chert spades, Clarksdale district, slightly less than ¼ size, Clark collection.

ous. Dr. Henry M. Whelpley of St. Louis has a wonderful collection of them, more than three hundred notched hoes, and several hundred unnotched hoes and spades. It is the opinion of Dr. Whelpley and Mr. Fowke that most of these hoes and spades come from the chert of Union County, Illinois, where it is said great quantities of spalls and unfinished pieces remain on the site of the old work-shops.

It is probable that local stones were much used in Missis-

Fig. 157. Crude stone piece from Itawamba Co., ⅓ size, author's collection no. 62.

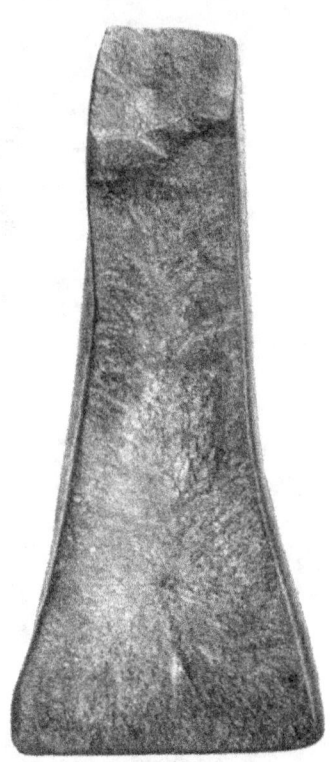

Fig. 158. Digging implement (?), Yalobusha Co., 10.5 inches long, Ballard collection no. 7.

sippi for making crude digging implements. A roughly-chipped piece of ferruginous shale 4.8 by 3.55 inches picked up by the author near the University (no. 180) seems to have been designed for such a purpose. A crude piece 9.5 by 3 inches from Tremont, Itawamba County, figure 157, has the cutting edge slightly polished. It is likewise made of a local iron claystone.

A unique object of stone is that depicted in figure 158 (Ballard collection no. 7). It is 10.5 inches long, 2.2 inches wide on one end and 4.7 inches on the other, and appears to retain largely its natural form. It is sharpened on the broad end to a smooth blunt edge and seems to have been used as a digging implement. The narrow end, tho rather sharp, seems to have been less used. Mr. Ballard obtained it from Yalobusha County.

It is no doubt impossible to assign the various uses of all the medium-sized implements of flint and chert, for there are many intermediate types. The next group shows a variety of flaked implements ranging from 4 to 5 inches long. The first piece, no. 25 (fig. 159) is of dark flint and has a few of the high projections on the front polished away, but has not been polished on the back. The second piece (fig. 160), made of light-colored chert, comes to a blunt point below and shows no sign of polishing or rubbing. The longest piece, which is 5 inches (fig. 161), is probably a digging implement, for it is highly glossed on the lower edge. It is chipped to a thin edge all along the right margin, but appears at some remote time to have had a narrow strip broken from the left margin. The fourth piece, number 67 (fig. 162), of lightly-colored chert, is slightly glossed near the edge on the front, as if by usage, but the back shows no gloss. The original surface of the stone from which this piece was chipped shows at the upper end. Both the first and third pieces are sharpened more from the rear than from the front in bringing the pieces to an edge.

When the corn was mature and dry, it became necessary to crush or grind it. This was done by means of hollow mortars in which were used pestles or mullers. The mortars vary very much in form and type, and in the quality of the stone used. As a rule the mortars are larger and heavier than the other stone implements, and therefore are less frequently found far removed from the site of their origin. Hence in parts of Mississippi where good stone is not abundant it is often difficult to find good examples of mortars.

On the other hand, local stone of poor quality was frequently used when occasions demanded, and many crude and imperfect examples were left lying on the surface. The author has picked up eight or ten in the vicinity of Oxford

FIG. 159.   FIG. 160.   FIG. 161.   FIG. 162.

Four chipped implements from north-east Miss., author's collection:

FIG. 159. Booneville, Prentiss Co., 4.3" long, no. 25.
FIG. 160. Rara Avis, Itawamba Co., 4.5" long, no. 61;
FIG. 161. Eastport, Tishomingo Co., 5" long, no. 66;
FIG. 162. Eastport, Tishomingo Co., 4.8" long, no. 67.

and the University, for the most part very crude and imperfect specimens. The depressions in most mortars are shallow; I have nowhere found in the state mortars with the very deep holes of the type so common in California. The Mississippi mortars are usually concave on both sides, though some are found that have been used on only one side.

A fine example of the primitive corn grinder is seen in figure 163. It is in the collection of Dr. Davies of Walls, and comes from the immediate vicinity, as does all of Dr. Davies's material. It is 12 inches long and 9 inches wide and irregular in outline; the thickness varies from 3 to 4 inches. It is concave on both sides.

A good sandstone specimen (no. 341 in the author's collection) comes from the vicinity of Corinth, the gift of Mr. Milton Rubel. It is approximately 7.5 inches square, 1.5 inches thick, and is doubly concave. Mr. J. E. Gift has five mortars of varying sizes from the Corinth territory. Another sandstone mortar in the author's possession, no. 188, from Lafayette County, is about 3 inches thick and has the edges

FIG. 163. Stone mortar, Walls, ¼ size, Davies collection.

of the stone more or less polished or smoothed in a peculiar way; the craters are about 4.7 inches in diameter.

An unusually regular stone mortar is illustrated in figure 164. It is nearly circular in outline with diameter varying from 8.2 to 9.8 inches and a thickness of 3 inches. It was used on both faces. This specimen was found near Mechanicsburg in Yazoo County in 1891, and is no. 371 of the Brevoort Butler collection, now in Jackson.

In the museum of Millsaps College in Jackson, Mississippi, there is an unusually fine mortar of light-colored stone, concave on both faces.

In figure 165 is shown a fine specimen of a mortar from the southern part of the state. It is nearly circular, the diameter varying from 7.8 to 8.5 inches; weight 9.5 pounds; the hollow on the back of the mortar is very similar to that on

FIG. 164. Stone mortar, Yazoo Co., ¼ size, Butler collection no. 371.

the front. It was found near Natchez and belongs to the Perrault collection, now in the Milwaukee museum. Another good mortar from the vicinity of Natchez is in the home of

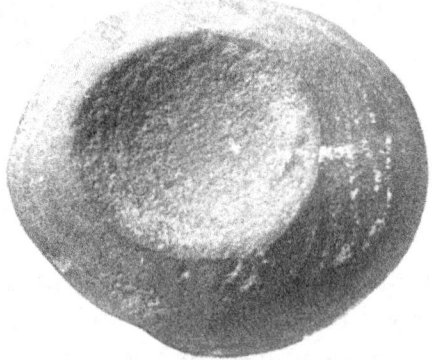

FIG. 165. Stone mortar, near Natchez, ¼ size, Perrault collection.

the Misses Stanton at Windy Hill manor; it is 14 inches long and hollowed on only one side.

Quite small mortars are found; number 12 in the author's collection is only 5 inches in its longest dimension with a maximum thickness of three inches. It has a shallow depression of scarcely 3 inches diameter on the upper face; the bottom shows the merest beginning of wear. It is from Bellefontaine, Webster Co.

To crush grain, nuts, and acorns in the mortar an instrument of percussion or trituration was necessary. Pestles or mullers of stone of various lengths and designs are found. The usual type of pestle is a cylindrical or conical stone with the grinding end larger than the upper end. Frequently these pieces are rather crude and have had but little labor expended upon their finish. The example shown in figure 166 is one of two similar pestles presented by Dr. Carmack of Iuka to the State Geological Survey. It is 4.5 inches long and of rough finish. Other examples are shorter. A rough stone bar 12.8 inches long from Nettleton, now in the Geological Survey museum, may belong to this class of implements; three other pestles were found in the same grave.

FIG. 166. Pestle from Tishomingo Co., ½ size, Geol. Survey museum, 23T.

Mullers are flatter than pestles; the prevailing type of muller has one face approximately flat, the other rounding or convex, the general horizontal outline of the stone being circular or elliptical. There are many varieties of form and the muller merges into the pestle in one direction and into the hand-hammer in the other. Many mullers were undoubtedly used as hammers also.

Four pieces in the author's collection are shown in the next group, figs. 167-170. Number 297 has the form of a flattened hemisphere, the diameter varying from 4 to 4.5

inches. The weight is 3 pounds; the finish is rough. Two large more or less elliptical pieces, numbers 445 and 262, from Lafayette County, seem to have double depressions on one side worn by the fore-finger and middle-finger; the two depressions are quite close together and the separation not very prominent. Number 262 is badly battered and has evidently been used as a hammer. These seem to be combination

FIG. 167 (no. 297).   FIG. 168 (no. 438).
FIG. 169 (no. 445).   FIG. 170 (no. 262).

Four mullers from Lafayette Co., ⅜ size, author's collection.

hammer-stones and mullers or rubbers. Number 445 weighs three and a half pounds, and number 262 three and a quarter pounds. These two stones differ from the usual hand-hammers in having a higher polish and a more swelling shape, in the character of the depressions, and in the material of which they are made, which seems to be limonite concretions. No 438, likewise of limonite, conforms more nearly to the usual hand-hammer type, tho more highly finished. It has a deep thumb depression on one face and apparently a double depression on the other.

Figure 171 represents a group of three hard stone balls. The middle one is about 3.4 inches high. All are more or less flattened on the base as if intended to rest in one position. The purpose of such stone balls is difficult to surmise; they may have been used in games; they may have been used as mullers or grinders. They vary considerably in size and finish. Most frequently they are made of a hard, flinty material. This type of crude implements seems to shade off into other types. Some are nearly globular. Number 157 of the author's collection shows the remains of a highly polished surface in the middle of the two broader faces, but has the

FIG. 171. Stone balls, Copiah Co., middle piece 3.4" high, Barringer collection.

circumference roughened, and in places battered apparently by use as a hammer. It is about 3.3 inches in diameter and has probably done duty in more than one capacity. Number 103 is of the same hard flinty material as those in figure 171 but is flattened on both top and bottom with a slight depression, thus merging towards the discoidal and hand-hammer types. It is about 2.7 inches in diameter and 1.8 inches thick. A piece from Pontotoc County somewhat larger is approximately cylindrical, being 3.3 inches in diameter and 2.2 inches in length or height. Here we have reached the crude discoidal type. A large piece in the Barringer collection from Leflore County is of the same general form but highly polished on both the bases and on the surface of the cylinder and thus falls within the class of discoidals. It is 3.9 inches in diameter and 2.5 inches in length or height and has convex instead of concave faces.

An unusual stone vessel is pictured in figure 172. It is elliptical in form with a major axis of 22 inches, the total length including the big handles being 24.5 inches, and with a minor axis of 15.25 inches. A container of this kind could have been used for many purposes. It was found in a mound about sixteen miles west by north-west of Oxford, Lafayette

Fig. 172. Stone bowl, Lafayette Co., ⅙ size, Jones collection, now in Heye museum, no. 7305. Heye photograph.

County. This mound according to local information is one of those near the confluence of Clear Creek with Tallahatchie River. The vessel was first described and pictured by Dr. Joseph Jones in his *Antiquities in Tennessee*[1]. The description is as follows:

"Col. Peyton Skipwith, of Oxford, Mississippi, obtained this remarkable vessel from a mound in the valley of the Tallahatchie River, in Northern Mississippi. When it came into his possession, it had an artistically wrought cover,

[1] Smithsonian Contrib. to Knowledge, vol. xxii, (1876) 1880, page 144, fig. 85.

which fitted accurately over the mouth of the vase. This cover was unfortunately lost during a fire which consumed the office of Col. Skipwith. The following are the dimensions: height, eleven and one half inches; long diameter, twenty-two inches; short diameter, fifteen inches; depth of bowl, eight and one-half inches; thickness of rim, one inch. On either side of the elliptical body are two projections or handles. The oval is symmetrical, and the outlines of the surface regular, with no marks of cutting instruments. The bottom of the vase is excavated, apparently with the design of rendering it

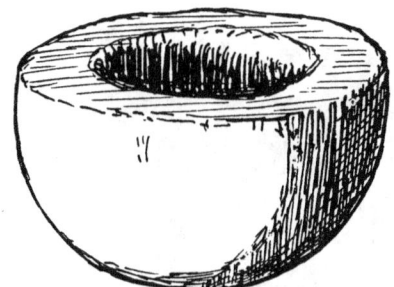
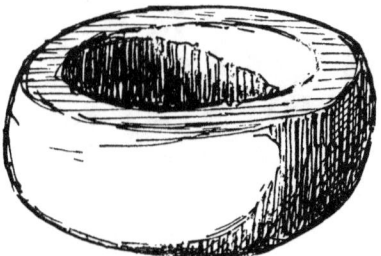

FIG. 173. Stone cup, Walls, natural size, Davies collection.

FIG. 174. Stone cup, Lafayette Co., natural size, author's col. no. 441.

lighter, and shows the marks of cutting instruments. The interior is smooth and regular. The vessel weighs over one hundred pounds, and is lifted and carried with difficulty by a strong man. It is supposed to have been used as the receptacle for the ashes of the dead."

In Natchez I saw but was unable to secure a fine stone basin or bowl which has massive handles that were hollowed out beneath. This bowl has a diameter on the outside of 18.75 inches, on the inside of 15.5 inches, the total diameter including the handles being 22.75, the total height 10.5 inches, and the depth of the bowl 8.75 inches. This vessel is finished on the outside with vertical ribs about three-eighths of an inch wide. The history of the bowl I could not learn further than that it was obtained from an old woman who had forgotten where she had obtained it. As to its Indian origin I can not be absolutely positive, as the vessel has not been thoroly cleaned and opened to inspection, and as the history is unknown.

Moore describes and illustrates two handsome stone vessels from Moundville, Alabama, of bird design and measuring about 12 and 9 inches respectively in diameter of bowl[1].

FIG. 175. Natural stone cup, Selsertown, natural size, Geol. Survey collection no. 242 (16B). Gift of Mr. Bessac.

Pretty stone cups of small size are occasionally found. They are generally called paint-cups. Figure 173 shows one from Walls. Figure 174, a still more delicate and highly polished one, is from Lafayette County, the gift of Mr. A. D. N. Lancaster to the author. A dainty little cup only eight-tenths of an inch in diameter comes from Pontotoc County (Barringer collection).

[1] Moore: Certain Aborig. Rem. Black War. River, Philadelphia, 1905, pp. 235-240.
Moore: Moundville Revisited, Philadelphia, 1907, pp. 384-387.
Holmes: in Handbook of American Archeology, Washington, 1910, II, p. 492.

The Amerind took advantage of natural formations when such were found answering his purpose, and thus no doubt often saved himself much labor. Many of the stone implements of the Cliff Dwellers of New Mexico were natural pebbles, with but slight alteration; so in Mississippi in the camp-sites and mounds are not infrequently found stones unaltered or but slightly altered by human agency. Crude celts or "wedges" are found made of natural pebbles or stones sharpened at one end; pestles are found that consist of natural stones worn at one end or at both ends, and hand-hammers have often no other alterations than the depressions on the faces. In figure 175 is pictured a natural stone cup

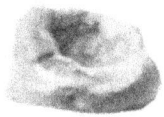 

FIG. 176. Natural cups, near Walls, longer piece about 2.4 inches, Schubach collection.

from Selsertown which is preserved in the State Geological Survey collection. A natural cup like this would certainly answer every practical purpose that an artificial cup would answer.

In figure 176 two smaller and less perfect natural cups from Walls are illustrated. The larger of the two is about 2.4 inches long.

Dr. Alfred H. Stone has a natural mortar and pestle (?) found on his plantation at Dunleith. These are shown in figure 177. It will be seen that in addition to the large opening in the mortar or cup there is also a small hole on the right. The cup is too fragile to have borne heavy pressure.

Pitted stones of the type known as cup-stones or nut-stones may be frequently picked up on the surface; they are usually of local sandstone. Figure 178 represents in natural size one of these from Lafayette County (author's collection no. 179). It has four depressions on the top, one on the bottom, one on the edge next to the observer, and one on the edge away from the observer, making in all seven of these depressions. Other than that necessary to produce the depressions the stone has had no labor expended on it.

Pitted pieces of the hammer-stone type are abundant. They are often but little more than rude stones with a

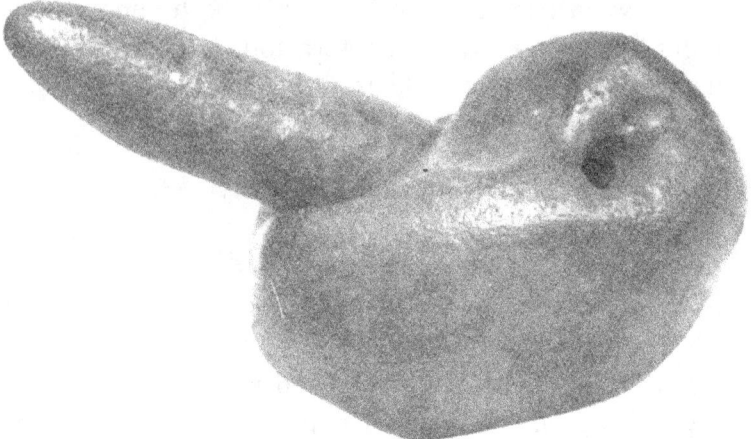

FIG. 177. Natural mortar and pestle (?), Dunleith, natural size, property of Dr. Alfred H. Stone.

depression on one or both faces, usually both. Figure 179 shows nine of these picked up by the author in excursions about Lafayette County. The scale may be had from the upper right-hand piece, the third piece on the plate, which is 2.5 inches long. It is approximately rectangular; the second piece is roughly pentagonal; the sixth piece, the last on the second row, is approximately triangular. The others are round or elliptical. All are roughly finished. They are apparently hand-hammers, the depression in the middle marking the place for the thumb on one face and for the fore-finger or middle finger or both on the other face. They are among the commonest artifacts of the state.

Thin stone plates approximately circular are occasionally found. Figure 180 represents a brown sandstone plate found on Lake George at the base of a mound in 1891. The diameter is 7.3 inches, the thickness 1.3 inches. It is highly polished (Butler collection no. 1). Figure 181 represents a

FIG. 178. Pitted stone, Lafayette Co., natural size, author's col. no. 179.

somewhat similar plate more nearly circular in outline. It belonged to the Joseph Jones collection and was transferred to the Heye Museum, where it is catalogued as number 7148; the only locality given is a mound in Mississippi. It is 7.25 inches in diameter and half an inch thick. These plates are undecorated.

Clarence B. Moore[1] describes a rather remarkable group of stone disks from Moundville, Alabama; most of them are circular, ranging in diameter from 7.25 to 12.5 inches; one

---

[1]Moore: Certain Aborig. Remains of Black Warrior River, Philadelphia, 1905.

is rectangular, with dimensions of 14 x 9.5 inches. Many of these pieces including the rectangular one are decorated with incised lines parallel with the margin and with notches. Of them Moore says: "Stone discs and slabs were found by us on many occasions at Moundville, as will be noted in this

Fig. 179. Nine hand-hammers or hammer-stones, Lafayette Co., third piece (upper right) 2.5 inches long, author's collection.

report, and in each case the disc or the slab was more or less thickly smeared with paint, sometimes cream-colored, sometimes red. . . . It seems conclusive to us that the paint on the discs and slabs is purely of aboriginal origin. The universal presence of paint upon these discs and slabs seems to offer a clue to the purpose for which they were used, and, until a better suggestion is offered, we shall consider them palettes for the mixing of paint."

DOMESTIC IMPLEMENTS.   227

FIG. 180. Sandstone plate, Lake George, ⅓ size, Butler collection no. 1.

FIG. 181. Stone plate, from a mound, ⅓ size, Joseph Jones collection, now in Heye museum, no. 7148. Heye photograph.

A remarkable stone 10 inches in diameter from near Arkansas Post, Arkansas, is described by Holmes[1] and illustrated by Moorehead[2]. It is decorated on one side with a circle

---

[1] Holmes: Certain Notched Stone Tablets, Am. Anthropologist, Jan.-Mar., 1906.
[2] Moorehead: The Stone Age in N. Am., Pt. 1, Boston, 1901, figs. 393 and 393A.

and a scalloped design, on the other with a modified circle design not infrequent on pottery and other art of the Alabama-Mississippi-Arkansas district. Compare figures 274-277. This rare Arkansas disk is unnotched.

FIG. 182. Feathered rattlesnake tablet from Issaquena Co., ½ size, in museum of Ohio Arch. and Hist. Society at Columbus. From drawing by Holmes.

One fine decorated stone disk has been found in this state (figs. 182, 183). As it has already been described by Prof. Holmes, I quote his description. Passing from the Arkansas Post disk, the design on which he thinks is probably intended to represent an open eye, he says:

"Even more remarkable are the disks with notched margins, on the face of which are engraved serpent symbols of unique design. One of these, now in the Museum of the Ohio State Archeological and Historical Society at Colum-

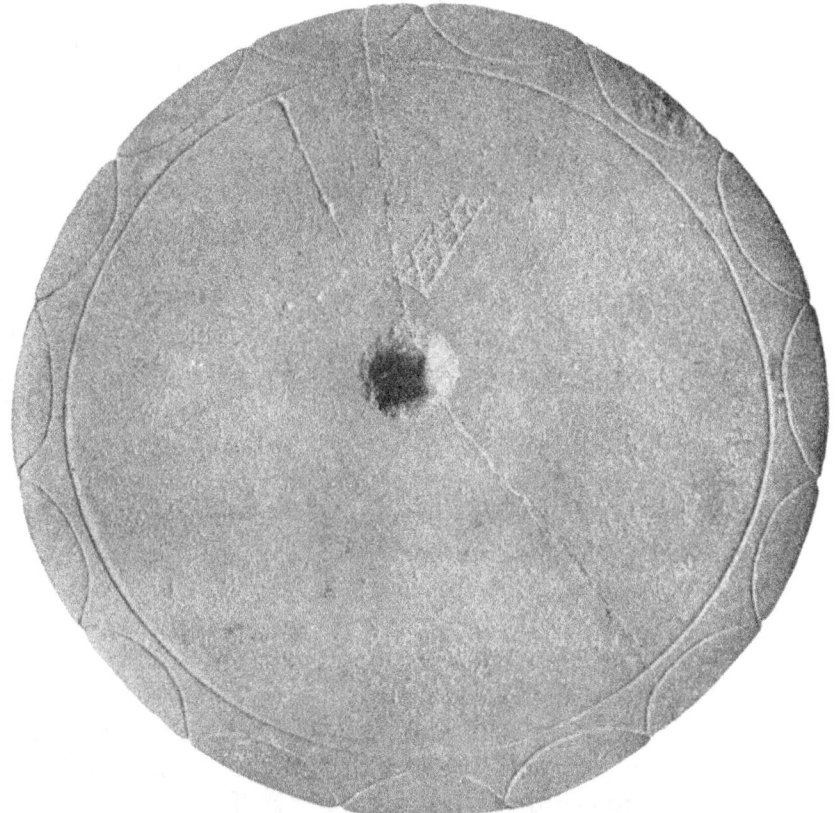

Fig. 183. Reverse or grinding surface of tablet shown in fig. 182, the mortise and markings near the center not being original features of the plate. From Holmes, Am. Anthropologist, 1906.

bus, known as the Mississippi tablet, was found in a mound near Lafayette Bayou in Issaquena County, Mississippi, in 1870. This specimen came into the possession of Marshall Anderson, from whom it was acquired by the Ohio State Archeological and Historical Society. It is made of fine-grained brownish sandstone, is discoidal in form, 8.5 inches in diameter, about one inch thick, and has smooth, slightly convex surfaces. On one face is engraved in shallow lines the representation of two interlocked rattlesnakes with heads in reverse order, facing the center from opposite sides. The serpents are the conventional, mythical, feathered rattlesnakes of the South. The heads are conventionally drawn, the mouths being furnished with teeth and tusk-like fangs. The forked tongues are indicated by flowing lines issuing from the mouths. Plumes rise from the head, and the upper surface of the body is embellished with groups of feathers alternating with scaled areas. The under surface has elementary fretwork composed of alternating sections of scaled and plain surfaces, as is usual in drawings of the mythical Serpent god in the South and South-west. One of the serpents has three rattles, the other four. The reverse side has a squarish depression near the center, probably not an original feature of the plate, and a neatly engraved border, consisting of 15 scalloped lines bordered within by an encircling band five-eighths of an inch from the margin. The margin or periphery is squarish and is divided into 15 sections by cross-lines or notches which connect with the scallops of the reverse face. Near the depression on this face is a small enclosed space filled in with crossed lines."

With this disk should be compared the double rattlesnake disk found in a mound at Moundville, Alabama, and preserved in the museum of the university of that state. It is considerably larger than the Mississippi plate and has 17 notches. Two horned rattlesnakes with heads facing outward and long protruding tongues are intertwined, the bodies encircling the disk and enclosing the representation of a hand holding in its palm an eye. A large photographic reproduction has been published by Moore[1] and there are also smaller illustrations.

---

[1] Moore: Certain Aborig. Rem. of Bl. W. River, Philadelphia, 1905, p. 136, fig. 7.

Prof. Holmes accepts Mr. Moore's conclusion that these disks were mortar plates or palettes intended for the grinding of pigments. By way of further observation he adds:

"A noteworthy feature of the engravings of the serpents and other figures on these mound tablets is the apparent maturity of the art, the intricate forms being skilfully disposed and drawn with a certain hand. These designs are not mere random products, but, like the copper ornaments, the earthen-ware decorations, and the shell engravings of the

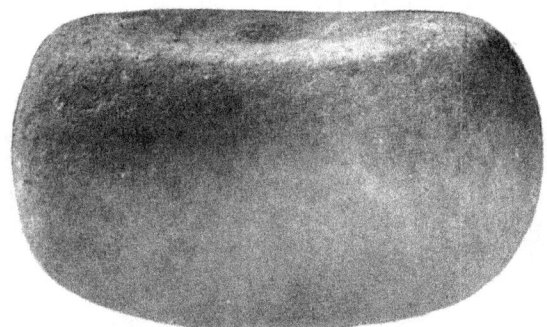

Fig. 184. Unusual stone artifact, Lafayette Co., ½ size, 5.5" x 3.1" x 3.1", Wait collection.

same region, are evidently the work of skilled artists practising a well-matured art which distinctly suggests the work of the semi-civilized nations of Mexico and Central America. These plates may be regarded as furnishing additional proof that the influence of the culture of middle America has been felt all along the northern shores of the Gulf of Mexico and has passed with diminishing force still farther to the north."

The beautiful vase from Central Guatemala published by the Heye Foundation in September, 1919, has a complicated design of interwoven figures in which two serpents are prominent.

There is a sandstone artifact of unusual form in the collection of Dr. H. C. Wait of Etta, figure 184; it was found on the surface in north-eastern Lafayette County. The form is that of a block of stone 5.5 x 3.1 x 3.1 with all the edges and corners rounded off. One of the four long faces has a curved depression, such as could now be made by holding the stone against the periphery of a revolving grind-stone of ten-inch radius. In the middle of this depression, which is also the middle of this face, is a small pit of the size of a large nut or marble. The photograph does not bring out completely the character of the stone; it is not to be confused with discoidal stones.

FIG. 185. Stone trough, from Yazoo Co., ½ size, Butler collection no. 143.

Another stone of unusual form is shown in figure 185, a granite piece 7 inches long and 2.7 inches wide with curved base and with a trough or depression in the top 3.1 inches long, 1.3 wide, and .8 deep. The depression resembles somewhat the trough of the boat-stones, but in other respects the piece is totally different.

An interesting Clarksdale specimen is shown in figure 186. It is a pillow-shaped dark green stone having a groove thru the middle of one face and a tongue projecting from one edge. The groove is of the type found in stones that were used for smoothing arrow-shafts, tho it is very uniform and highly polished. In places it shows the effects of friction. The tongue may have been used as a rabbet for cutting grooves. It has on its outer margin a series of incised marks uniformly spaced and uniformly inclined at about 45 degrees. The shoulders of the rabbet show longitudinal striations, as if from use.

 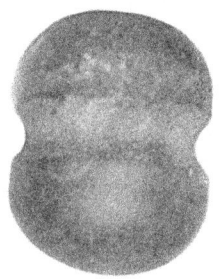

Fig. 186. Tongue and groove implement, Clarksdale, 2.7 x 1.6 inches, Clark collection.

Fig. 187. Grooved maul, Clarksdale, 3 inches long, Clark collection.

A grooved stone hammer-head or maul is shown in figure 187. The groove passes completely around the cylindrical body of this hammer, which is three inches long. The type

Fig. 188. Cloth impression, Walls, natural size, Schubach collection.

is not very common in the state. Mr. F. M. Chapman of Columbus has a fine one nearly 5 inches long and weighing two and a third pounds; the ends are somewhat more pointed and the roughly pecked groove lacks a little of going completely around the body of the implement. Moorehead figures a piece in the collection of Mr. W. P. Agee at Hope, Arkansas, which is very similar to Mr. Clark's Mississippi piece, and expresses the belief that such implements were used as weapons[1].

This chapter closes with a reproduction of an impression of prehistoric cloth or woven material from Walls, figure 188. As the impression is reproduced in natural size it will be seen that the weave of the fabric is rather coarse. At the right-hand of the illustration may be seen a decided bend or turn in the direction of the woven fabric.

---

[1]Moorehead: Stone Age in North America, Part 1, page 230, figure 212.

CHAPTER VI.

PIPES.

The practice of smoking the tobacco plant seems to have been widespread among the aborigines of America. A well-known relief sculpture of Palenque, Yucatan, shows an Amerind in the act of smoking. An engraved slab of limestone in the museum of the Tennessee Historical Society at Nashville shows among other designs a prehistoric figure smoking an elbow pipe[1]. Columbus mentioned smoking among the native Americans. Many early writers and travelers, as Las Casas, Antonio de Solís, Clavigero, John Smith, Adair, Marquette, Father Biard, and Du Pratz, made mention of tobacco and the custom of smoking. LeJeune in 1633 referred to the native Amerinds as "unhappy infidels, who spend their life in smoke and their eternity in flames"! The reader who is further interested in the early references to tobacco and smoking may consult McGuire's monograph on the subject of pipes and smoking[2].

The distribution of prehistoric pipes in the territory of the present United States likewise confirms the statement that the practice of smoking was widespread; there is scarcely a state in the Union where they have not been found. Pipes are more abundant however in the eastern states; tubular pipes abound in the Pacific coast states; catlinite pipes prevail in the states about the head-waters of the Mississippi River.

The pipe was of great ceremonial importance among the Amerinds; the calumet was smoked as a token of peace in

---
[1] See a reproduction of this slab in Thruston's Antiquities of Tenn., plate ii.
[2] McGuire: Pipes and Smoking Customs of the Am. Aborigines, Washington, 1899.

the ratification of treaties, and on other important occasions.

The first pipes would seem to have been straight tubes; the process of evolution was gradual: the end of the pipe away from the smoker became enlarged for the bowl; the right line of the tube was gradually bent until it came to be a

FIG. 189.   Clay pipe from Adams Co., nat. size, State Geological Survey museum.

right angle; the bowl and stem received various decorations until the highest ornamental types were worked out.

The rectangular type of pipe is shown in figures 189 and 190. The former is a clay pipe of compact design, two inches high, with conical bowl and stem-hole at right angles to each other. It was found near Palestine, Adams Co., in the vicinity of Natchez, in the south-western part of the state, and was presented to the Survey by Mr. F. T. Bessac. The simplest form of this design would be a cube with the two openings at right angles; the piece under discussion may be thought of as a cube with one edge removed to make the elbow.

The sandstone pipe shown in figure 190 is of slender proportions and has the bowl-opening considerably larger than the stem-hole, the two intersecting not quite at right angles. It is of rough finish and has suffered injury about the edge of the bowl. The cross-section thruout is two inches. It is

FIG. 190. Sandstone pipe from Montgomery Co., somewhat over ½ size, Ballard collection.

of coarse yellowish-brown sandstone and came from the Poor Farm, near Winona, Montgomery Co.

By rounding the edges of a pipe like figure 190 there would result a design of the type represented in figures 191 and 192. This type has its two parts cylindrical or slightly conical, the bowl end being generally somewhat larger than the other end and the bowl-opening considerably larger than the stem-opening. The angle of the two parts is greater than a right angle. The base of the Corinth pipe (fig. 191) is slightly flattened.

The pipe shown in figure 192 was found by Mr. J. B.

Johnson on his farm at Walnut Grove, Leake Co., Miss., in 1923, and presented to the Archives museum at Jackson. The length is 4 inches, the height 3 inches; the material an igneous rock of greenish hue. The openings are large and conical, with the circles resulting from boring showing plainly in the

FIG. 191. Stone pipe from Corinth, nat. size, Gift collection.

bowl. This pipe is unique in that the bowl was bored a little too deep and as a result the bottom of the pipe was pierced. The rim of the bowl is unfortunately broken.

Figure 193 represents a more ornate and highly finished stone pipe; it comes from Church Hill in Jefferson Co. The openings are large and at right angles; the mouth of the gracefully rounded bowl is surrounded by a lip or rounded rim; the union of the bowl and stem is sharply indicated by an incised line. This specimen was obtained by Mr. C. B. Moore from Mr. T. G. Wood, and was probably uncovered by the plow.

Two pottery pipes from Walls, DeSoto Co., are shown in figures 194 and 195. The former has a funnel-shaped bowl; the latter is decorated with a notched ridge on each side of the

FIG. 192. Stone pipe from Leake Co., natural size, Archives museum, Jackson, no. 2222.

stem parallel with its axis, and with incised markings on the bowl parallel with its axis.

An unusual type is presented in figure 196, a stone pipe with ovate bowl resting on top of a relatively narrow stem and separated from it by a deep constriction. Both the external form of the bowl and the opening are sharply ovate, the broad end being toward the smoker and rising somewhat above the general level. The stem projects backward under the bowl and has a rather small perforation. The pipe shows no indication of having been used. It was found by Mr. V. C. Kincannon in a mound on Mr. W. L. Joyner's place at Tupelo, and was presented by the former.

A fine example of stemless pipe is seen in figure 197. This little specimen is slightly over an inch and a half high and is

Fig. 193. Sandstone pipe from Church Hill, Jefferson Co., nat. size, Acad. of Nat. Sc., Philadelphia. From Moore, p. 377.

cylindrical in form ending in a hemispherical base with somewhat increased diameter. Both openings are conical and show the circles resulting from boring; the bowl is .8 of an inch in diameter, the stem-hole .55 of an inch. Similar stemless pipes have been found in Georgia, Tennessee, Kentucky, Virginia, Ohio, Wisconsin, and elsewhere. This one was found near Eldorado, Warren Co., where a number of good archeological specimens have been exhumed, and was presented by Mr. W. H. Russell to Dr. J. A. K. Birchett, of Vicksburg, in whose collection it remains.

FIG. 194. Clay Pipe, Walls, ¾ size, Davies collection.

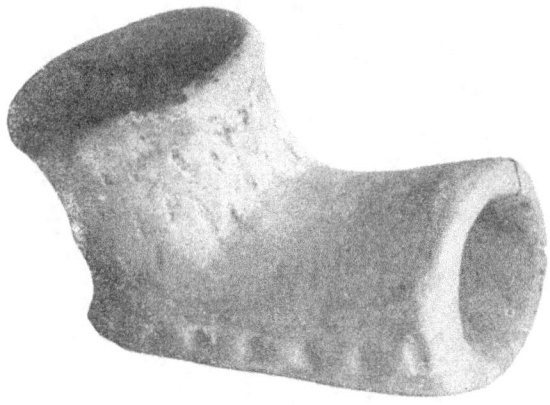

FIG. 195. Clay pipe, Walls, ¾ size, Davies collection.

A stone pipe of crude workmanship found near Columbus (fig. 198) is interesting because it has the appearance of having been made from a hammer-stone, tho the evidence is not conclusive. The outline is elliptical with the major axis 3.75 inches and the minor axis 3.2 inches long; the height is 2.2 inches. The bowl-opening is slightly elliptical.

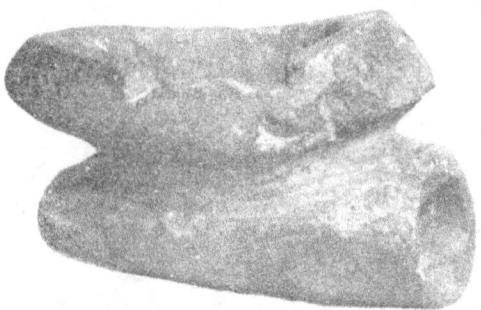 

FIG. 196. Stone pipe from Tupelo, natural size, author's collection no. 463.

FIG. 197. Stone pipe from Eldorado, nat. size, Birchett.

On the bottom, opposite the bowl, is a small pit; on the end opposite the stem-hole is inscribed a small cross.

FIG. 198. Crude stone pipe from vicinity of Columbus, ⅔ size, Chapman collection.

Somewhat similar to the preceding, tho more nearly cylindrical along its major axis, is the biconical sandstone pipe obtained in 1924 from the White Apple village site by the survey of the Natchez mounds by the Phillips Academy with the co-operation of the Geological Survey of Mississippi (fig.

199). The upper face is somewhat concave and the farther end somewhat larger than the nearer end. The length is slightly over 3 inches.

The clay pipe shown in figure 200 has the bowl leaning backward at a considerable angle and the stem cylinder continued backward under the bowl, the stem-hole being rather small. The length is 2.35 inches, the height 2.25 inches. It was found in 1896 in an addition to Yazoo City.

FIG. 199. Stone pipe from White Apple village, near Natchez, ⅔ size, Geol. Survey museum.

The pottery pipe from Lake St. Joseph near Vicksburg, Warren Co. (fig. 201) has the stem edges re-inforced by projecting ridges and the bowl orifice by a projecting lip. The length is 3.25 inches. It belonged to the Albert L. Addis collection, and is now no. 4-7276 of the museum of the American Indian, Heye Foundation, New York.

Disk pipes seem to be rare in the state. A small one is shown in figure 202; the disk surrounding the bowl is 2.1 inches in diameter. It is of clay and was found near Natchez and belongs to the Perrault collection. Two somewhat similar clay pipes from Citico, near Chattanooga, Tenn., are shown by Moore[1]; another still more nearly resembling the Natchez specimen is from Kentucky[2].

Fig. 203 is a clay pipe with belt of semicircular cross-section surrounding the bowl and with the base somewhat expanded. It likewise came from the vicinity of Natchez and belongs to the Perrault collection, recently transferred to the Milwaukee Public Museum.

Fig. 200. Clay pipe, Yazoo City, nat. size, Butler collection, no. 1650.

In both the clay and the stone pipes the maker often attempted the representation of some animal figure. The favorite effigies in the Mississippi pipes are the human being, the bear, and the frog or toad. The representations are for the most part crude, and sometimes the zoology is uncertain; a few, however, are not without merit as works of art.

A unique clay pipe is shown in figure 204; it would seem to represent a bear-paw, tho it may possibly be intended for

---
[1] Moore: Aborig. Sites on Tenn. River, Philadelphia, 1915, p. 377.
[2] Young: The Prehistoric Men of Ky., Louisville, 1910, p. 296.

the human foot; it has five toes. Thruston shows both a pipe and a pot from Tennessee with the design of a human leg and foot. The Mississippi specimen is 4.4 inches long by 3 inches wide. It was found in Coahoma Co. near Clarksdale, and is in the collection of Mr. Charles W. Clark.

A crude human face of oval outline is shown in the clay

FIG. 201. Pottery pipe, Lake St. Joseph, near Vicksburg, about nat. size, Heye museum, no. 4-7276.

pipe represented by figure 205. This piece was originally painted red; patches of color may be seen in the illustration over the right eye and about the left eye; the eyes and mouth are represented by mere depressions. The stem of this piece has been broken away, leaving only the bowl, which faced from the smoker as most pipes did. The inside of the bowl shows the black resulting from smoking. It is a product of the early Walls culture.

A more artistic effigy is the clay pipe of frog design shown in figure 206. The body rests upon the folded legs;

the eyes, nose, and mouth are clearly indicated. The large bowl rests in the middle of the back and bears evidence that the pipe has been used. The large stem-opening takes the

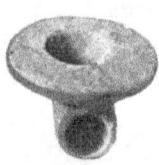

FIG. 202. Disk pipe of clay, vicinity of Natchez, about ⅓ size, Perrault col.

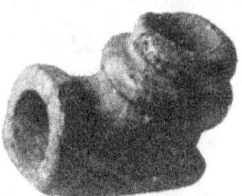

FIG. 203. Clay pipe, vicinity of Natchez, about ⅓ size, Perrault collection.

place of the tail. The pipe is 4.5 inches long and 2.5 inches high. It is in the collection of Mr. Victor C. Barringer. This

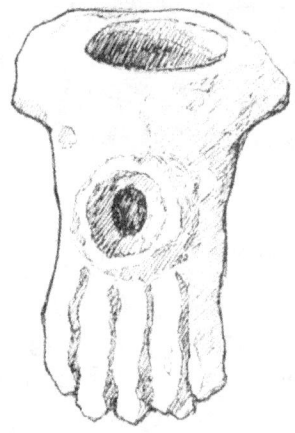

FIG. 204. Bear-claw (?) pipe of clay, Clarksdale, ½ size, Clark collection, at Clarksdale.

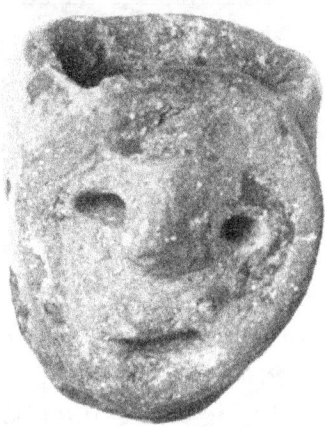

FIG. 205. Clay pipe, human face, Walls, nat. size. Originally painted red. Davies collection.

specimen is somewhat similar to a Virginia pipe described and pictured by McGuire (page 537, fig. 155).

Figure 207 is an earthen-ware pipe found by Clarence B. Moore on the surface of one of the low mounds of the great

Lake George group. According to Mr. Moore, from whom this illustration is taken, it probably represents a wolf or a dog. It stands erect on four legs and the bowl rests on the shoulders. The ware is shell-tempered; the modeling is without artistic merit.

Two views of a double-stemmed pipe are shown in figures 208 and 209. The pipe is of yellowish brown clay, rudely

FIG. 206. Clay pipe, frog design, nat. size, Barringer collection.

polished. The figure seems to be intended to represent a bear, tho there are two knobs on each side of the head, as if one pair represented horns and the other ears; possibly antlers were intended by the knobs and expanded surfaces beneath it. Across the nose are three parallel lines. The bowl is in the back and has the rim slightly elevated; the two stem-holes are behind; all of the openings are conical and of about the same size. The pipe is 5 inches long and 3.5 inches high. It came from a mound in Coahoma Co. and was presented to the U. S. National Museum by the Hon. J. L. Alcorn. A drawing of this specimen is given by McGuire in his monograph on pipes (page 538, fig. 156).

Pipes with double stem-holes are not common in Mississippi; only one other is represented in this book, the Choctaw calumet shown in figure 237, and that is of a very differ-

FIG. 207. Pipe of earthen-ware from mound near George Lake, nat. size, Philadelphia Acad. of Sc. From Moore, p. 592.

ent type. In the Dickeson collection in the University of Pennsylvania museum there is a facsimile of a rectangular sandstone pipe with two bowls and two orifices on stems (no. 14,308); a human face is carved in relief in front. The length of the facsimile is 4.6 inches. The original was found in a small mound in Pine Ridge, Jefferson Co. Double-stemmed pipes are sometimes called bridegroom pipes, a name derived however from a European custom, not from an American custom. A fine example from Middle Tennessee is shown by West in figure 95 of his book on pipes. This specimen is in limestone, is 7 inches long, 6 inches high, and weighs 5.5 pounds. It has two human heads opposite each

FIG. 208. Clay pipe with two stem-openings from Coahoma Co., length 5 inches, height 3.5, U. S. Nat. Museum no. 11,649. Photograph by Museum.

other, one looking from each smoker (and consequently one looking toward each smoker).

A number of excellent massive stone effigy pipes have been unearthed in Mississippi. They face away from the smoker, have flat bases, and for the most part have conical or conoidal openings. A fine specimen of this ancient stone-carving is shown in figure 210. The effigy is that of the front half of a frog's body. The bowl is just behind the eyes, which are represented by two prominent knobs or elevations. The stem-hole is in the rear. The mouth is prominent. The right foot has three toes; the left foot is not completely worked out. A small pebble which seems to be a natural part of the mass may be intended for the right nostril; the left nostril is not indicated. The figure is somewhat

FIG. 209. Rear view of preceding pipe. Photograph by U. S. N. M.

lop-sided. The material of which it is made is a dark heavy sandstone. The pipe is 6.25 inches long, 4.6 inches high, and weighs 5.75 pounds. This fine piece of primitive art was unearthed by Mr. R. L. Bartholomew from a slight elevation on the railroad about a mile north of Lake Cormorant. The place is only five or six miles from the rich Walls burying-grounds; the pipe may therefore be considered as belonging to the ancient Walls culture. The left side of the pipe was pictured in the Memphis *Commercial Appeal* of January 18, 1914, which was about the date of discovery.

Another fine frog pipe is shown in figure 211; it was plowed up near Marks, Quitman Co., eighteen or twenty years ago and preserved by Mr. Marks. The effigy is of

FIG. 210. Stone pipe of frog design from Lake Cormorant, ⅔ size, property of Mr. Bartholomew.

compact sandstone, is 5.65 inches high, and weighs 6 pounds. The upper part of the body is worked out in detail, whereas the legs are only slightly indicated. The biconical openings are in the back and rear.

An enormous weathered sandstone pipe found near Port Gibson, Claiborne County (fig. 212) is owned by the museum of the American Indian in New York. It is the effigy of a frog or toad, with bowl in the back. The Port Gibson pipe is 11.7 inches long and weighs 19 pounds.

Another good zoömorphic pipe is shown in figure 213; it probably represents a bear. Here the details are indistinct and the relief low. The rim of the bowl is slightly elevated. The greatest length of the pipe is 4.25 inches. This pipe was

Fig. 211. Sandstone pipe of frog design from Marks, Quitman Co., ⅔ size, property of Mr. Johns.

collected at Dundee, Tunica Co., by William H. Harrison and is now in the Heye Museum (no. 6605). There is an interesting group of mounds at Dundee, the four larger forming approximately a semicircle.

A very fine effigy pipe of the massive kind is shown in figure 214. This represents a human being crouching on his knees; the feet are turned back under the body; the shoulders, chest, and chin are thrown far forward. The eyes and nose are fairly well executed, the ears are too long, the mouth is coarse and protruding. The hands rest upon the hips; the right hand has the fingers well executed; there are four bands about the upper arm just above the elbow. On

FIG. 212. Port Gibson frog pipe of sandstone, scale ⅖, length 11.7 inches, weight 19 pounds. Heye museum no. 7294.

the left side the arm is not polished; the arm-bands are not finished; the hand is merely blocked out, the fingers not being indicated. It will be recalled that in the case of the frog represented in figure 210 the right toes are finished but the left are not. The height of the pipe is 4 inches; the base is flat, as is generally the case with the great heavy pipes. This pipe was plowed up near Clarksdale, Coahoma Co., and is in the collection of Mr. Charles W. Clark.

Mr. Clark has a still larger stone pipe with squatting human image, but it is unfortunately badly mutilated. The stone has a hard seam running thru it which stands out prominently above the surrounding surface, indicating considerable weathering and age.

Fig. 213. Stone pipe probably representing a bear, Dundee, Tunica Co., natural size, Heye museum no. 6605.

A cruder piece than Mr. Clark's fine effigy is the sandstone pipe shown in figure 215; length 5.75 inches, weight 2.9 pounds. It represents a human figure on all-fours. The legs are in medium relief; the head is poorly wrought, and there is no neck. The conical openings do not project beyond the surface. It was found at the river edge near Quitman's

Landing above Natchez. A map and drawings of the mounds in this region as they appeared to Dickeson in 1843 are given by Culin. Another massive sandstone pipe, this one unornamented, was found among the boulders at Ellis Cliffs, a short distance below Natchez, and obtained by Dickeson (no. 14,309); length 4.6 inches, weight 3.5 pounds.

FIG. 214. Stone pipe, human figure, nearly ¾ size, Clarksdale, Clark collection.

While excavating a ridge at Shadyside Landing above Greenville, Washington Co., Mr. Clarence B. Moore found along with some skeletons and pottery an effigy pipe of limestone[1] (figures 216, 217), representing a human figure crouching on hands and knees. The fine swelling bowl rises considerably above the back and is crowned by a well-

[1] Moore: Some Aborig. Sites on Miss. River, Philadelphia, 1911, p. 390, plate 29.

wrought rim. The head is a human head with lion-like features. The hands rest on the knees. The legs are folded under the body, the calves and heels showing prominently, and the spreading toes almost resembling wings. Moore says: "The pipe lay on its side directly beneath the bones, which had somewhat disintegrated the parts of the pipe in

Fig. 215. Sandstone pipe representing human figure on all-fours. Quitman's Landing, Adams Co., ⅖ size, weight 2 lbs. 14 oz., Dickeson collection, University of Pennsylvania museum no. 14,714.

contact with them. Both sides of the pipe are shown in the plate, the one injured by the bones being easily distinguishable." The pipe should be compared with the Selsertown pipes in the following illustrations.

These five interesting limestone pipes of uniform type, found in the Selsertown plateau, were obtained by Mr. Vincent Perrault of Natchez, who sold them in 1916 or 1917 to the Milwaukee Public Museum, where they bear the num-

FIG. 216. Limestone pipe, Shadyside Landing, Washington Co., slightly under size, Philadelphia Acad. of Science. After Moore, plate 29. See next figure.

FIG. 217. Another view of the preceding pipe. After Moore, plate 29.

bers 16,205 to 16,209, accession number 5390 (figures 218-226). They are all effigy pipes of the rectangular, flat-based, biconical type; the bowl is in the back of the figure, the stem-opening in the rear. The material is a yellowish fossiliferous limestone, probably of the Vicksburg formation.

Pipes 16,205 (figures 218, 223, and 224) and 16,206 (figure 222) are winged serpents. They are badly mutilated, especially about the head, and it is difficult to decipher all their details; the two are very similar; the head in each stands at an angle of about forty-five degrees, and has a rounded nose in the middle of the face. They seem to be similar to the mythical serpent heads found in the pottery of Walls (figures 289 to 291) and elsewhere. The necks are thick, the latter image scarcely having a neck at all. The rectangular sides of both images are each covered by a wing which is made of feathers (?) resembling rattlesnake tails, each part on the former and plainer image having three rattles and a button. The uppermost feather of the two wings is more nearly on the back of the image than on the side, extending up to the rim of the bowl. The lowest feather is of about half length only, being shortened apparently to make room for the hind claw. Each of the two creatures is provided with two pairs of bird claws, unfortunately somewhat mutilated. The rear claws show fairly well in figure 223; the claws are best preserved on the left side of the latter effigy, no. 16,206. The continuation of the body of the image consists of a slender snake design in low relief lying on the body of the pipe. This detail of no. 16,205 is shown in the accompanying drawing (fig. 224). The tail begins just above the stem-opening, completely encircles this opening clock-wise, passes to the top of the pipe, encircles the bowl in the contrary direction, and terminates in a set of rattles resting upon the back of the creature's head. The surface of this snake consists of spaces alternately plain and covered

Fig. 218 (no. 16,205) Fig. 219 (no. 16,208) Fig. 220 (no. 16,207) Fig. 221 (no. 16,209) Fig. 222 (no. 16,206)

The Selsertown pipes, front and rear views, ¼ size, Perrault col. now in Milwaukee. See also figures 223, 224, 225, 226.

with scales. In the latter pipe, no. 16,206, the serpent tail lying upon the back of the image is not so distinct and the

Fig. 223. Winged serpent pipe, Selsertown, ⅔ size, Milwaukee Public museum no. 16,205. See also figures 218 and 224.

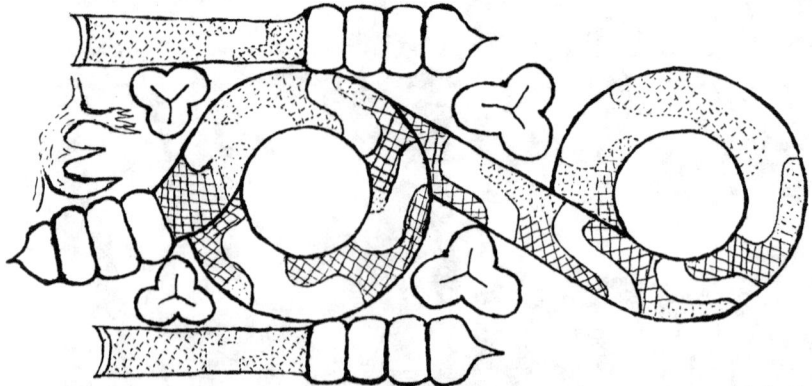

Fig. 224. Drawing of top and rear of winged serpent pipe shown in figures 218 and 223, ⅔ size (dotted parts supplied), Milwaukee Public museum no. 16,205.

rattles do not appear on the neck and head of the image. In the case of the former effigy there is further ornamentation on the rear and sides of the head, part of which I am unable to decipher. On the back of this there are also four little ornaments of trefoil design filling the spaces between the wings and the winding snake. It may be of interest to compare the claw-feet on these two pipes with the claw-feet on two fighting human figures engraved on a shell gorget from Sevierville, Tennessee[1], and with the two claw-hands on a human figure engraved on a shell gorget from Moundville, Alabama[2].

Pipe no. 16,208, shown in figures 219 and 225, is the effigy of a man crouching with elbows on knees and arms folded across the breast. The execution of the face is better than usual; the lips protrude; the forehead seems to be flattened; the ears are prominent. Two bands extend from the top of the head down to the flat bent back passing outside of the two conical holes. The legs are folded back under the body, as in the Washington County pipe shown in figures 216 and 217; the calves and heels are well defined; the toes are not separated. This is the only one of the five pipes in which the back is not horizontal or nearly so. This figure as the two following stands upon a thin plate or pedestal which is an integral part of the carving. The height is 5.5 inches, the length about the same, the weight 2.9 pounds.

Pipe no. 16,207, shown in figures 220 and 226, has the head of a bird, with round eyes and prominent hooked beak. There are two tufts on top of the head extending a short distance backward. Three bands cross the neck and breast. The wings and feathers are conventional, being represented by longitudinal bands crossed at intervals by slightly oblique lines, tho the first two rows of feathers on the wings and back are rounded. The forked tail of the bird is superposed over the left wing and turned up edgewise, no doubt as a

---

[1] Holmes: Art in Shell, Washington, 1883, pp. 301 and fol., plates 74 and 75.
[2] Moore: Moundville Revisited, Philadelphia, 1907, page 398, fig. 98.

result of the artist's limitations. The image rests upon a thin pedestal or support, and there are no indications of feet or claws. The mouth of the bowl is slightly elevated above the back of the effigy. The height is 4.7 inches, the length

Fig. 225. Limestone pipe, human effigy, Selsertown, ⅔ size, Milwaukee Public museum no. 16,208. See also fig. 219.

6.25 inches, the weight 2.75 pounds. The image is probably intended for an owl or hawk.

Pipe no. 16,209, figure 221, is an animal or monster of some kind fiercely showing its teeth. The front feet grasp the edge of the support or base-plate, the hind feet rest upon the plate. There are circles or rings upon the shoulders, sides, hips, and thighs. A band encircles the two conical openings and terminates upon the head of the image; this is no doubt the tail of the animal, which may be a snake, as in the first and last pipes of this group, tho the markings and rattles, if they existed, are now obliterated. The height is 5 inches, the length somewhat over 6 inches, the weight 3.1 pounds.

Fig. 226. Limestone pipe, bird effigy, Selsertown, ⅔ size, Milwaukee Public museum no. 16,207. See also fig. 220.

In the Butler collection at Jackson there are two mutilated limestone pipes from a mound at the mouth of Lake George, Yazoo Co., which altho inferior seem to belong to this class. Squier and Davis[1] describe and picture a pipe which is similar in many respects to the Selsertown pipes, especially to no. 16,209. "This unique relic was ploughed up on the banks of the Yazoo River in the State of Mississippi. It is composed of clay, smoothly moulded and burned, and represents some animal, *couchant,* lips corrugated and exhibiting

[1] Ancient Monuments of the Miss. Valley, Washington, 1847, page 193, fig. 75.

its teeth as if in anger or defiance. .... The attitude is alike natural and spirited." The claws grasp the base-plate, as in figure 221. The circular hole beneath the body is unusual. The five Selsertown pieces tho of limestone look very much like clay, and I suggest the possibility of an error in the identification of the Yazoo County pipe as burnt clay.

The nearest congeners to the Selsertown pipes outside the state are probably the pipes found at Moundville, Alabama, and described and illustrated by Thruston[1] and Clarence B. Moore[2]; and a limestone pipe from Hot Springs, Arkansas, described and illustrated by McGuire[3].

In several of the Southern states is found a type of image pipe which consists of a human being holding in outstretched hands a bowl or pot, which vessel constitutes the bowl of the pipe. Several of these have been described from Georgia and Tennessee. The reader may also compare the frontispiece and figure 87 in West's monograph on pipes.

Figure 227 shows a good specimen of this type from south-west Mississippi. This sandstone piece represents a seated human figure holding a pipe in the hands; the chin rests upon the bowl of the pipe just below the rim; the figure hence faces the smoker. The head is represented as flattened; the markings on the head should be compared with those in the next illustration and in other pieces cited in connection with it. The pipe is 5.4 inches high. It belongs to the Dickeson collection, and was published by Culin.

A remarkable image pipe is shown in figures 228 and 229. It represents a naked savage seated, with the hands resting upon the knees, and the legs folded beneath the

---

[1] Thruston: Antiquities of Tennessee, Cincinnati, 1897, page 187, fig. 84.
[2] Moore: Certain Aborig. Remains, Black Warrior River, Philadelphia, 1905; pp. 131 and 132, figs. 1 to 3, p. 234, figs. 165 and 166.
Moore: Moundville Revisited, Philadelphia, 1907, pp. 388 and 389, figs. 80 to 85.
[3] McGuire: Pipes and Sm. Cust. of the Am. Ab., Washington, 1899, p. 539, fig. 158.

body. The arms are carved partly in the round, the elbows standing out from the body. The neck is thick and short, the lips coarse, the cheeks prominent, the eyes somewhat slanting. The scalp is decorated with a series of panels or divisions, which may or may not be intended to represent

FIG. 227. Sandstone pipe, from the Ferguson mounds, Jefferson Co., ⅖ size, Dickeson collection, Univ. of Pa. museum no. 14,328. From Culin, plate 12.

the hair; they are longer in the rear and come down almost to points. On the back of the head is a knot or tuft. About the lower part of the ears are circular projections with radial markings, no doubt intended to represent ear-rings or ear-plugs. On the forehead is one of the rectangular panels and beneath it a hatchet-shaped or pipe-shaped figure. The two conical openings are in the rear of the body; the bowl is between the shoulders and the stem-hole about the middle of

Fig. 228. Stone pipe, Sunflower mound, Eldorado, Yazoo Co., 9 inches high, property of Mrs. Causey.

the back. This fine image pipe is 9 inches high and 5 inches broad. It was found in Sunflower mound on the Mayben Place, Yazoo Co.

FIG. 229. Another view of fig. 228, showing bowl, stem, head decoration, and ear decoration.

A comparison of this pipe with the large image from the Etowah group of mounds in Georgia illustrated by Moorehead in the *Stone Age in North America,* figure 426 is interesting. The latter piece is 21 inches high and weighs 56.5 pounds; the resemblance in form is striking. The Eldorado pipe is an inch taller than the unique tubular effigy pipe from the Adena mound, near Chillicothe, Ohio, described by Mills[1] and reproduced by Fowke[2] and Moorehead[3]. In that specimen the ear-rings stand out at right angles to the head. A large female image from Georgia described by Jones[4] shows the ears perforated but without the rings. The head decoration of the Eldorado specimen invites especial study; it should be compared with other Mississippi specimens, such as the preceding pipe from Jefferson County shown in figure 227; the stone face from Clarksdale shown in figure 152; and the pottery head from Walls shown in figure 295; in the latter piece the right side of the scalp is divided into rectangles as in the Yazoo County pipe, whereas the left side is marked by a series of semicircles centering in the top of the head; a twist of hair hangs down the back forming a small handle. The head adornment of the Yazoo County pipe may also be compared with that of an 8-inch effigy pipe from Moundville, Alabama, figured by Moore[5], with that of the Etowah specimen from Georgia just cited, and with that from Muskogee in Dr. Whelpley's collection[6].

Platform or monitor pipes have not been found in great numbers in Mississippi. Mr. George A. West[7] describes and pictures one from a mound in DeSoto County, in the northwestern part of the state; it was purchased from a dealer. It "is of calcareous limestone 4 inches high, with a wide, irregular flange around the bowl cavity and a partly broken base 2 inches wide. The stem-hole is drilled thru on the side of the

---

[1]Mills: Excav. of Adena Mound, Ohio Arch. Soc. Pub., vol. x, pp. 475-478.
[2]Fowke: Arch. Hist. of Ohio, Columbus, 1902, frontispiece, and pp. 596 and 617.
[3]Moorehead: Stone Age in North Am., Boston and N. Y., 1910, fig. 499.
[4]Jones: Antiquities of the Southern Indians, N. Y., 1873, p. 432, pl. xxvi.
[5]Moore: Cert. Aborig. Rem., Bl. W. River, Philadelphia, 1905, figs. 131 and 132.
[6]Moorehead: The Stone Age in N. Am., II, Boston and N. Y., 1910, p. 86, fig. 494.
[7]West: The Aborig. Pipes of Wis., Wis. Archeologist, 1905, page 119, fig. 102.

base instead of following its center." Dr. Charles Peabody[1] quotes two of clay from Coahoma County: "Three rude clay pipes were found; two of the platform or monitor class.

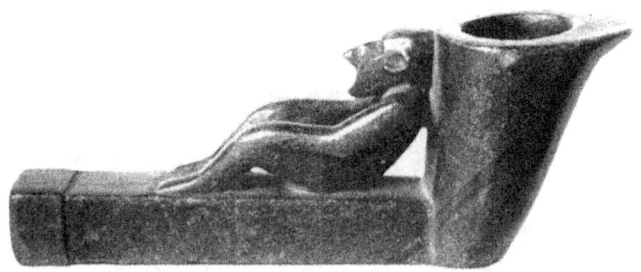

FIG. 230. Steatite pipe, with reclining figure on stem, Natchez, 9/10 size, Dickeson collection, Univ. of Pa. museum no. 14,304.

. . . One has a series of notches encircling all that is left of the platform." There is a cast of a monitor-shaped

FIG. 231. Steatite pipe, with bear on stem, largest of Ferguson mounds, Jefferson Co., 9/10 size, Dickeson collection, Univ. of Pa. museum no. 14,305.

pipe from the Tombigbee River in Mississippi in the Dickeson collection[2] in Philadelphia, no. 14,329.

Several steatite pipes were obtained by Dickeson in the vicinity of Natchez. Those shown in figures 230 and 231 have the cross-sections of the stems square and of the bowls round. A human figure reclines upon the longer stem, a bear

[1] Peabody: Expl. of Mounds, Coahoma Co., Miss., Cambridge, Mass., 1904, p. 40.
[2] Culin: The Dickeson Collection, Philadelphia, 1900, page 165.

stands upon the shorter stem; both face the smoker. The angle of stem and bowl is in each case considerably more

FIG. 232. Steatite pipe, head of alligator gar-fish, Ferguson mound, Jefferson Co., 9/10 size, Dickeson collection, Univ. of Pa. mus. no. 14,327.

than 90 degrees. A third steatite pipe (fig. 332) represents the head of an alligator gar-fish; it was found in one of the Ferguson mounds in Jefferson County, above Natchez[1]. The

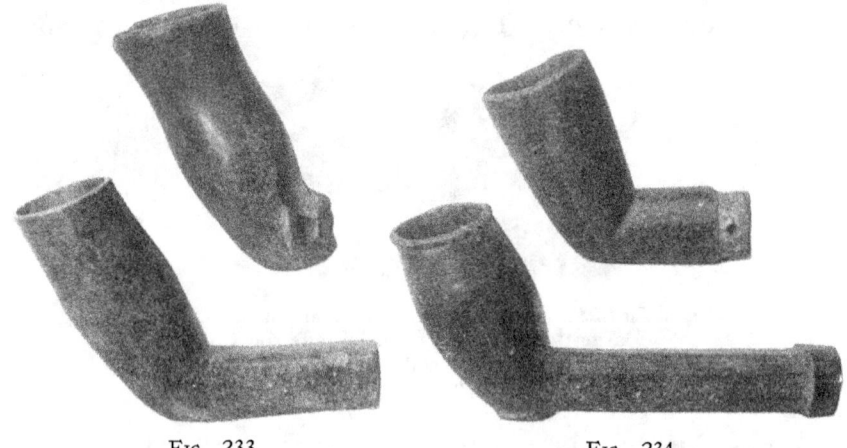

FIG. 233.   FIG. 234.
FIG. 235.   FIG. 236.
Four stone pipes from Tupelo, 2/3 size, author's collection.

length of these pipes is respectively 3.75, 2.5, and 3 inches. They probably belong to a late period of art, and may be thought of in connection with the diminutive serpentine tortoises from Natchez shown in figures 149 and 150.

[1]Culin: The Dickeson Collection of Am. Antiq., Philadelphia, 1900, page 137.

Four delicate stone pipes from Tupelo are shown in figures 233-236. The first (fig. 233) has had the stem broken away and been re-bored just above the original hole. The second (fig. 234) has a short octagonal stem which is almost

FIG. 237. Stone pipe of tomahawk design, with two stem-openings, Millsaps College museum, about natural size.

rounded and has been re-worked at the end. The third (fig. 235) has a longer square stem. The fourth (fig. 236) has a slight prolongation below the bowl with long octagonal stem enlarged at the end. All have an angle of about 120 degrees.

A stone pipe of tomahawk or hatchet design is represented in figure 237. The bar has a length of 2.2 inches, and is perforated from one end to the other; it thus has two stemholes. The height of the pipe is 3.9 inches. The lower part represents the blade of the tomahawk. This calumet was presented some years ago by a Central Mississippi Choctaw, Simpson Tubby, to Millsaps College, and is no doubt of late date. A red catlinite pipe of tomahawk design obtained from a Sioux chief in Dakota Territory is pictured by Thruston[1]; a similar catlinite pipe obtained from an Indian chief in Minnesota in 1880 is shown by West[2].

Late metal tomahawk pipes or pipe tomahawks are occasionally found in Mississippi; one is illustrated and described in the chapter on post-Columbian material, figure 350.

[1] Thruston: Antiquities of Tennessee, Cincinnati, 1897, page 210, fig. 114.
[2] West: Aboriginal Pipes of Wisconsin, Madison, 1905, page 67, fig. 14.

CHAPTER VII.

SHELL, BONE, AND COPPER.

An abundance of shells, both marine and fresh-water, were available in this territory for the use of the aboriginal inhabitants. No doubt many shells were used in their original forms as scraping and digging implements and as cups and dippers. Others were cut and worked into various ornaments and useful implements. As shell-fishes furnished an important part of the food of the Amerind in many places, shell-mounds or refuse-heaps accumulated; many of these are still found along the coast of the Gulf of Mexico and along the course of the larger rivers.

Shell was a favorite material for the manufacture of beads. Numerous shell beads of cylindrical type are shown natural size in figure 238; they vary in length up to three-tenths of an inch; some are irregular in form. They came from a grave in the vicinity of Columbus. In the early Colonial days wampum was used as a medium of exchange or money.

Other types of shell beads are shown in figures 239 and 240; the circular beads in figure 239 were taken from a mound ten miles north of Yazoo City in 1892 by Brevoort Butler; the thick flat beads in figure 240 were taken from a mound in Coahoma County by Charles W. Clark. It is scarcely necessary to remark that the string of these beads as shown in the three illustrations is recent.

After trade relations were established with the whites, quantities of beads of Caucasian manufacture were traded to the red men. An illustration of these trade beads is given in the chapter on modern material, figure 346.

Methods of making larger pendants from shells are shown in figures 241 and 242. The Aberdeen specimen is a fossil shell around the neck of which an artificial constriction

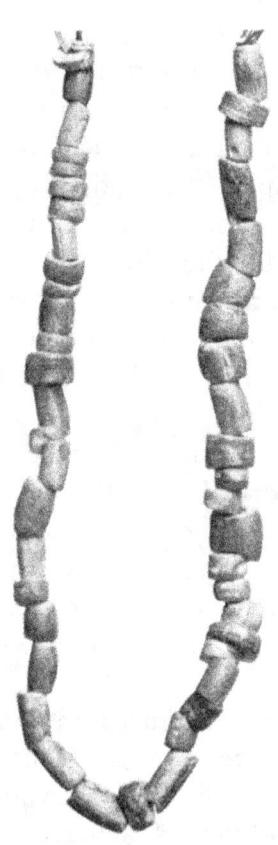

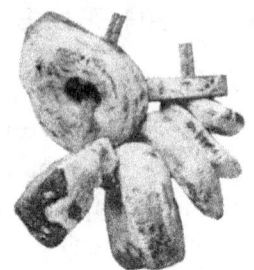

FIG. 239. Shell beads from Yazoo Co., nat. size, Butler collection.

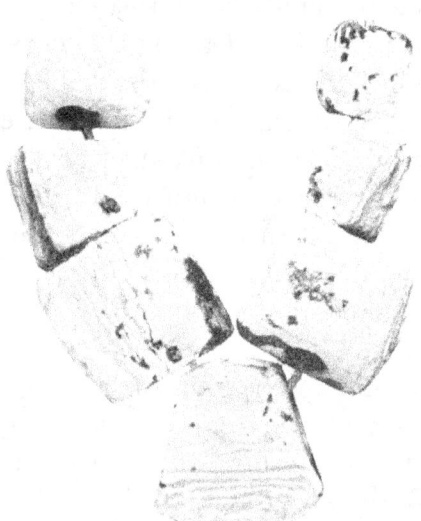

FIG. 238. Shell beads from Columbus, natural size, Chapman collection.

FIG. 240. Shell beads from Oliver, Coahoma Co., nat. size, Clark collection.

has been made. Its length is 1.8 inches. It was collected by Mr. B. H. McFarland, and presented by him to the State Geological Survey. Figure 242 is the columella of a shell, the end of which has been perforated for suspension. It is a Coahoma County specimen, taken from a mound by Mr. Charles W. Clark.

Two pretty shell ornaments from the graves at Walls are shown in figure 243. They are apparently the columellas of large univalve shells.

In figures 244 and 245 is shown a type of shell ornaments which may possibly have been used as hair-pins but more

Fig. 241. Shell pendant from Aberdeen, nat. size, Miss. Geol. Survey museum.

Fig. 242. Pendant from the column of a shell, Coahoma Co., nat. size, Clark collection.

probably as ear-plugs. The pieces illustrated here have a disk about 1.2 inches in diameter attached toward one side to a reduced shaft, the whole measuring about two inches in length. When found such pieces are often in pairs, one on each side of the head. The ear-disk or ear-plug is often shown in original Amerindian art; for instance in the Yazoo County pipe shown in this book in figures 228 and 229 and in the drawings on shell gorgets and copper plates from Georgia, Tennessee, Kentucky, and Missouri. Occasionally the perforated ears are shown without ornaments. Early writers speak of the pierced ears of the Indians, and tell us

Fig. 243. Two shell ornaments from Walls, natural size, Davies collection.

Fig. 244. Two ear-ornaments (?) of shell from Columbus, natural size, Chapman collection.

Fig. 245. Two views of a shell ornament from Walls, nat. size, Schubach collection.

that the men sometimes greatly enlarged the perforations.

Figure 246 represents a somewhat different type of ear-plug; it is a simple shell pin with a shaft attached to the center of the head and having a circular cross-section. The total length is only an inch and a quarter. Moore pictures two of this type each "having a single perforation near the end worn back of the ear, probably for more secure attachment."[1] They were found buried with a child in the Rose Mound, Cross County, Arkansas. Many child-burials in this mound were accompanied by two shell ear-plugs. Examples of the unsymmetrical type with perforated point are reported

FIG. 246. Shell ear-plug from Walls, nat. size, Davies collection.

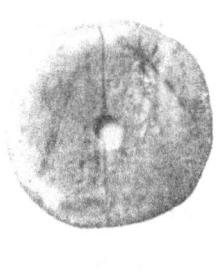

FIG. 247. Two perforated shell disks from the vicinity of Louisville, natural size, Wood collection.

from Tennessee.[2] There are likewise ear-plugs of antler and of clay; for an illustration of the latter see figure 338.

Mr. C. L. Wood of Columbus found in a grave near Louisville, Winston County, two shell disks with central

---

[1] Moore: Antiq. of the St. Francis, W. and Bl. Rivers, Ark., Phila., 1910, p. 282.
[2] Macurdy: Mounds of Eastern Tenn., Washington, 1917, page 65, fig. 13.
Thruston: Antiquities of Tennessee, Cincinnati, 1897, page 316.

perforation in each; one is somewhat over two inches in diameter, the other half that size (fig. 247). The material is polished on both sides. Some disks from Arkansas have the hole entering and emerging from the same side, thus leaving the reverse face of the ornament unbroken by the perforation.[1]

Engraved shell gorgets, which have been found in such abundance in Tennessee and other nearby states, have not as yet been discovered in numbers in Mississippi; further search should be made for them.

Moore[2] describes a crude one which he found at Commerce, Tunica Co.: "On the chest was a face-shaped gorget about 5 inches long, made from the body whorl of the conch *(Fulgur perversum)*. This ornament has two holes for suspension at the top or broader end. The decoration consists of a scallop-like carving on the lower ends of both lateral margins, and traces of workmanship intended to represent a nose and mouth on one flat side."

A fine example, with bird design, is shown in figure 248. It has already been fully described by Holmes[3], whose description I here quote:

"We know that the Natchez and the Creeks included the bird among their deities, and by the relics placed within his sepulchers we know that it held an important place in the esteem of the mound-builder. Our prehistoric peoples seem to have taken special delight in carving its form in wood and stone, in modeling it in clay, in fashioning it in copper and gold, and in engraving it upon shell. One of the most interesting of all specimens preserved to us is illustrated in plate lviii. The design with which this relic is embellished pos-

---

[1] Moore: Antiquities of the St. Francis, etc., page 285, fig. 13.
[2] Moore: Some Aborig. Sites on Miss. River, Philadelphia, 1911, pp. 412, 413.
[3] Holmes: Art in Shell, 2nd Ann. Rept. of Bureau of Ethn., 1883, pp. 281-283.

sesses no little artistic excellence, and doubtless embodies some one of the many charming myths of the heavens.

"I am perfectly well aware that a scientific writer should guard against the tendency to indulge in flights of fancy,

FIG. 248. Shell gorget from Miss., nat. size, U. S. Nat. Museum. From 2nd Ann. Report of Bureau of American Ethnology, plate 58.

but as the myths of the American aborigines are highly poetical, and abound in lofty rhetorical figures, there can be no good reason why their graphic art should not echo some of these rhythmical passages. To the thoughtful mind it will be apparent that, although this design is not necessarily full of occult mysteries, every line has its purpose and every figure its significance. Yet of these very works one writer has ventured the opinion that 'they do but express the individual fancy of those by whom they were made'; that they are even without 'indications of any intelligent design or pictographic idea.' I do not assume to interpret these designs; they are not to be interpreted. Besides, there is no advantage to be gained by an interpretation. We have hundreds of primitive myths within our easy reach that are as interesting and as instructive as these could be. All I desire is to elevate these works from the category of trinkets to what I believe is their rightful place—the serious art of a people with great capacity for loftier works. What the gorgets themselves were, or of what particular value to their possessors, aside from simple ornament, must be, in a measure, a matter of conjecture. They were hardly less than the totems of clans, the insignia of rulers, or the potent charms of a priesthood.

"The gorget in question is unfortunately without a pedigree. It reached the National Museum through the agency of Mr. C. F. Williams, and is labeled 'Mississippi.' On its face, however, there is sufficient evidence to establish its aboriginal origin. The form of the object, the character of the design, and the evident age of the specimen, all bespeak the mound-builder. It was in all probability obtained from one of the multitude of ancient sepulchers that abound in the State of Mississippi. The disk is four and a quarter inches in diameter, and is made from a large heavy specimen of the *Busycon perversum*. It has been smoothly dressed on both sides, but is now considerably stained and pitted. The design has in this case been engraved upon the convex side, the concave surface being plain. The perforations are placed near the margin and are considerably worn by the cord of suspension. In the center is a nearly symmetrical cross of the Greek type, inclosed in a circle one and one-fourth inches in diameter. The spaces between the arms are emblazoned with groups of radiating lines. Placed at regular intervals on the outside of the circle are twelve pointed pyramidal rays ornamented with transverse lines. The whole design presents a remarkable combination of the two symbols, the cross and the sun. Surrounding this interesting symbol is another of a somewhat mysterious nature. A square framework of four continuous parallel lines, symmetrically looped at the corners, incloses the central symbol, the inner line touching the tips of the pyramidal rays. Outside of this again are the four symbolic birds placed against the side of the square opposite the arms of the cross. These birds, or rather birds' heads, are carefully drawn after what, to the artist, must have been a well-recognized model. The mouth is open, and the mandibles long, slender, and straight. The eye is represented by a circlet which incloses a small conical pit intended to represent the iris, a striated and pointed crest springs from the back of the head and neck, and two lines extend from the eye, down the neck, to the base of the figure. In seeking an original for this bird, we find that it has perhaps more points of resemblance to the ivory-billed woodpecker than to any other species. It is not impossible, however, that the heron or swan may have been intended. That some particular bird served as a model is attested by the fact that other specimens, from mounds in various parts of Tennessee, exhibit similar figures. I have been able to find six of these specimens, all of which vary to some extent from the type described, but only in detail, workmanship, or finish."

Since Professor Holmes wrote this description in 1881 (published in 1883), many more of these bird gorgets have been found in the Mississippi Valley, some of them strikingly similar to the one pictured here. Other favorite gorget types are the spider design, the rattlesnake design, and the human figure, the latter often with a discoidal stone in the hand. The similarity of the engravings on some of these gorgets to ancient Mexican art has frequently been noted.

Bone, tooth, stag-horn, tortoise-shell, and other hard animal parts were used by the Indians in the manufacture of implements and ornaments. Artifacts of such material were

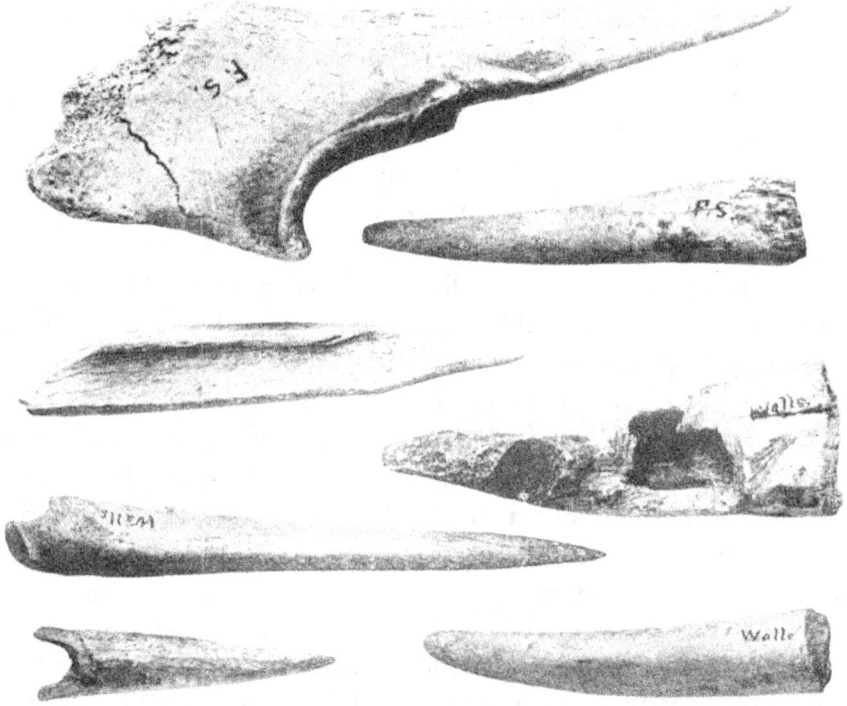

FIGS. 249, 251, 253, 255   FIGS. 250, 252, 254

Bone and antler pieces from Walls, DeSoto Co., about ¾ size, Davies and Schubach collections.

much more durable than those of wood but less enduring than those of stone and clay. Projectile points and piercing implements were often made of bone and antler and many of these have been preserved. The following two groups of illustrations, the former from De Soto County, the latter from Coahoma County, show some of the forms. Figure 249 is a favorite type of bone awl or punch made from the ulna of a deer; a similar piece is shown in figure 257. Figures 250, 252, and 254 are blunt tines of stag-horn; such pieces are frequently broken at a constriction cut some distance from the tip, as figure 254. Figures 251, 253, 256, and 258 are sharp bone awls, the last three quite slender. Figure 255

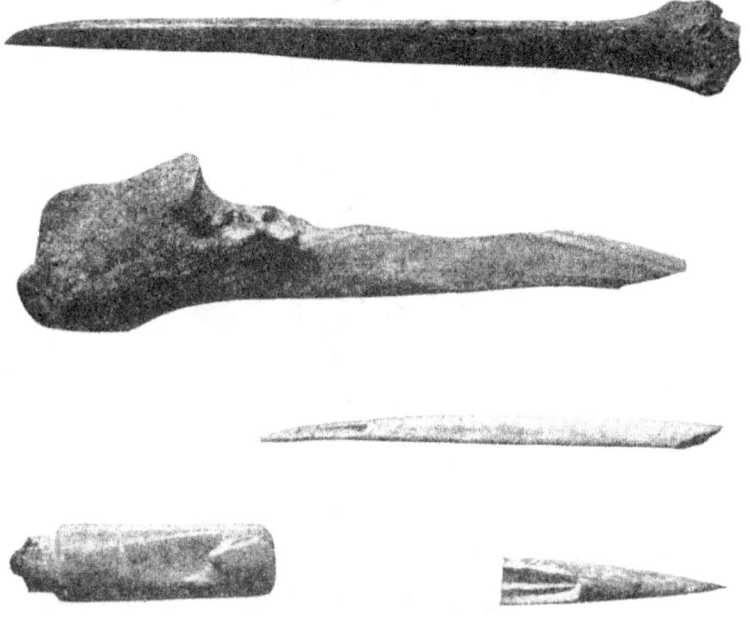

FIGS. 257, 259   FIGS. 256, 258, 260

Bone objects from Coahoma Co., about ⅗ size, Peabody museum. From Peabody, plate 20.

is a sharp arrow-point of antler, and figure 260 a sharp arrow-point of bone. Moore[1] pictures a human vertebra from Kentucky transfixed by a spear-point of antler 3.9 inches long, and accompanies the illustration with a description by Dr. W. G. Miller. The piece shown in figure 259 with a hook near one end on the side toward the observer and part of the tenon cut on the other end is described by

---

[1] Moore: Some Aborig. Sites on Green River, Ky., Phila., 1916, page 478, fig. 20.

Dr. Peabody as a bone specimen of doubtful authenticity which may be a fragment of an atlatl or throwing-stick. The reader may compare the notched implements from Kentucky pictured and described by Moore in the work just quoted and

Fig. 261. Copper celt from University, slightly over ½ size, property of Dr. Ralph Muckenfuss.

considered by him as netting needles. Many bone and antler implements were uncovered by Dr. Peabody in his former excavations in Coahoma County and in his later excavations near Alligator, in Bolivar County; some of the latter are in the Survey museum at the University of Mississippi.

Manufactured objects of native copper have not thus far been found in abundance in this state, perhaps due in some degree at least to the great distance from the principal sources of supply in the Lake Superior region. There are no copper objects from Mississippi in the United States National Museum. The beads of rolled copper found in the graves in the north-eastern part of the state are probably post-Columbian, the metal bells pictured in a later chapter (fig. 352) are almost certainly so.

A copper celt 7.3 inches long and weighing 2.1 pounds (fig. 261), found a few years ago by Dr. A. M. Muckenfuss beneath the soil near his residence on the campus of the University of Mississippi, near Oxford, has every appearance of being ancient Indian work. The polished cutting edge is rounded and considerably broader than the poll of the ax. There is indication of helving at a remote period. The celt resembles closely those found in Ohio and other states, but owing to the circumstance of its discovery near the foundation of a building in a public place it is difficult to be absolutely positive as to its genuineness.

CHAPTER VIII.

POTTERY.

Pottery is so important in the life of a primitive people and the forms which it takes are so varied that the author of this study deems it desirable to present a large number of illustrations. The greater number of these illustrations have never been published before, practically all for the northern group are new; eighteen for the southern group were kindly furnished by Mr. Clarence B. Moore; a few are from other sources and are properly acknowledged. Clay pipes are treated in the chapter on pipes; other forms of earthen-ware are treated in this chapter.

The Mississippi pottery occurs in both mounds and graves, and great quantities of fragments are scattered over many a field. There is no difference between that of the graves and that of the mounds. The custom of burying vessels with the dead has added greatly to the supply which the archeologist finds for study. Unfortunately many pieces fall to fragments when taken from the moist earth.

The quality of the Southern pottery is excellent for primitive art; it is not quite equal perhaps to that of the Cliff-dwellers and Pueblo Indians of the West, except in variety, but surpasses that of the aborigines of the North. Much of it, of course, is crude. In form there is much variety in the Mississippi pottery; in fact no two pieces are exactly alike. Bowls, basins, vases, jars, bottles, and pots abound, both decorated and undecorated. The handled dipper, common in the West, seldom occurs. Many effigy vessels are found; these include the figure of the fish, frog, tortoise, reptile, bird, bear, and other lower animals, the human figure, and mythical conceptions. Plant decoration is very scarce, if occurring at all. Geometrical designs are frequently used for ornamentation. Decoration is almost always exterior; there is very little of the interior ornamentation so common in the Western pottery. The potter's wheel was unknown; all work was made by hand or by molding. Patterns were sometimes stamped on vessels by a modeling paddle or form.

It should be borne in mind that the vast majority of all the pottery unearthed is plain and lacking in artistic merit.

Most of the earthen-ware thus far found in Mississippi falls within two of the groups or classes distinguished by Holmes[1] in his excellent work on Eastern pottery: first, pottery of the Middle Mississippi Valley, and, second, pottery of the Lower Mississippi Valley. Memphis, Tennessee, or Pecan Point, Arkansas, some miles above Memphis, may be taken as the center of the Middle Mississippi Valley group. "Apparently its greatest and most striking development centers about the contiguous portions of Arkansas, Missouri, Illinois, Kentucky, and Tennessee." Mississippi pottery at the time this was written had not been studied. Vicksburg, Mississippi, may be taken as approximately representing the center of the Lower Mississippi Valley group. Holmes does not designate the boundary between these two groups; Moore[2] suggests that the Arkansas River and an imaginary line extending eastward from its mouth be considered as such. That suggestion is followed in this book.

While in general the characteristics of these two groups are largely the same, certain differences may be remarked: (1) Incised decoration is perhaps less frequent in the middle group, more frequent in the lower group, including the use of the scroll. (2) Decoration in red and polychrome is more common tho not abundant in the middle province, less

---
[1] Holmes: Aborig. Pottery of the Eastern U. S., 20th Ann. Rept. of Bu. of Ethn., Washington, 1903.
[2] Moore: Some Aborig. Sites on Miss. River, Philadelphia, 1911, page 370.

common in the lower, while solid black is perhaps more common in the lower. (3) The use of effigy figures including the human effigy is more common in the middle than in the lower group. (4) Bottle forms are more frequent in the middle group than in the lower.

A short distance below Memphis, Tennessee, in the northwest corner of Mississippi, in the vicinity of Walls, there are aboriginal burial fields which have yielded rich returns in ancient pottery. This territory has been briefly described in the chapter on mounds and earth-works. Dr. J. A. Davies and Mr. Fred. Schubach have done considerable digging in this field, and it is largely thru their kindness that I have been able to study the pottery of this ancient culture. Unfortunately it has been necessary to write at a distance from their collections. At some future time I trust that I may be able to give a fuller account of the Walls culture than is possible at this time and in this volume. The quantity of pottery taken from this field is immense. Many of the whole vessels have been only superficially examined. The great mass of broken material has not been restored or studied.

In the Walls material there is a large amount of plain undecorated earthen-ware together with a smaller proportion of more or less artistic ware. There are relatively few red and polychrome vessels, and but little criss-cross decoration. There are many good pieces with incised designs, some of these in volutes and spirals. The triskele and tetraskele are sometimes used as decorations. Many pieces have semi-circular arches and arcades just under the rim of the vessel. Animal effigies are very common, including the fantastic serpent design. This ware is often tempered with broken shells. The culture resembles very closely that of eastern Arkansas, as illustrated in the works of Holmes and Moore and exhibited in the collection in the Cossitt Library in Mem-

POTTERY. 289

phis. The Mississippi River would seem to have been but a small barrier to intercourse among these primitive people.

Small clay disks are frequently found about Walls; many of these are made from broken fragments of pottery (fig. 262, top row). Some disks are perforated in the center (middle row). There are also found clay balls of small size;

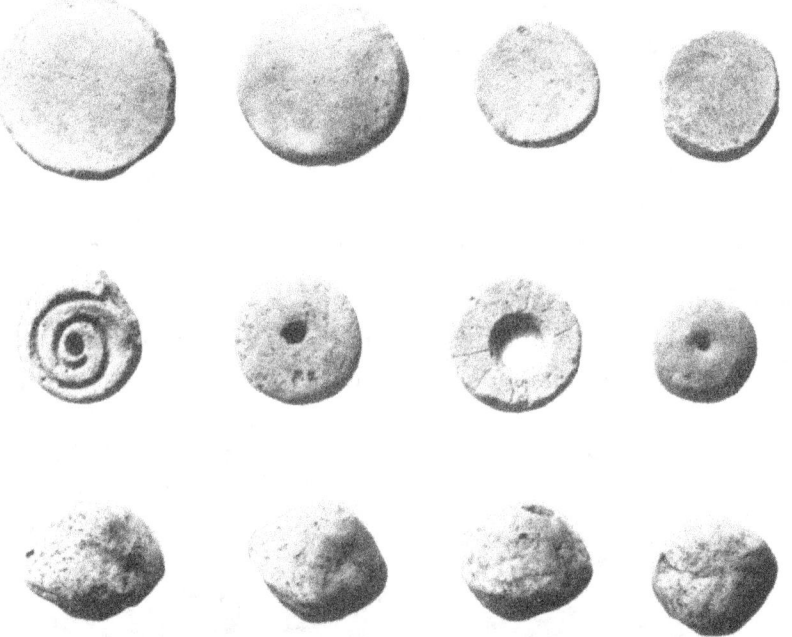

FIG. 262. Objects of clay from Walls, scale ⅖, Schubach collection.

and peculiar clay objects made in the form of two cones placed base to base (bottom row).

Figure 263 shows a number of flat earthen-ware vessels, the largest 10 inches in diameter. This type of platter must have been of every-day use, judging from the frequency of occurrence and the plainness of the ware. Some of the pieces are decorated with indentations or beaded work around the lip.

A number of open clay vessels have perforations around the edge; the one shown in figure 264 has two pairs of holes, as if for suspension; the one shown in figure 265 has eight

FIG. 263. Plain clay basins or bowls from Walls, scale ⅕, Davies col.

elongated perforations around the rim at approximately equal intervals. Some have horizontal perforations.

The Walls burials yield a rather large number of medium-

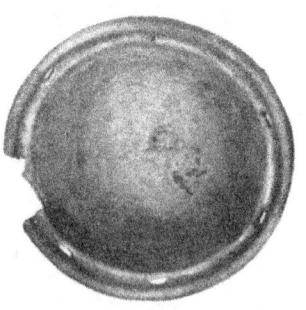

FIG. 264. Vessel with two pairs of holes from Walls, Davies collection.

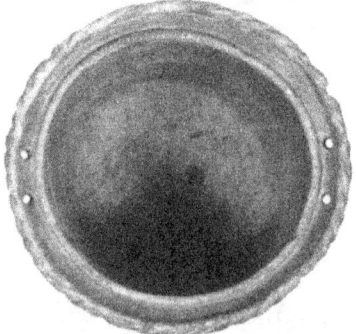

FIG. 265. Vessel with 8 holes in the circumference from Walls, Davies collection.

sized pots with semicircular relief arches below the rim (figs. 266, 267, 268). Some of these pots have columns or piers in relief supporting the arches. Many have ears or loops, always too small to receive a finger. The ears vary in number, some vessels having two, some four, others still more; in some vessels two perforated ears alternate with two solid projections.

Fig. 266. Clay pot with shell-tempering from Walls, diameter 7.5 inches, Davies collection.

In figure 266 beneath the beaded rim is a series of semicircular or somewhat flat arches, and beneath these, vertical

Fig. 267. Pot with semicircular arches and incised spirals from Walls, diameter 6 inches, Davies collection.

incised lines separated by a field of hachures, inclined to the right in one, to the left in the other. The shell-tempering shows very plainly in the photograph.

In figures 267 and 268 the pot is covered with four series

of spiral volutes, some of the lines from one spiral passing by a reversed curve into the next. In figure 268 the body of

Fig. 268. Pot with semicircular arches and incised spirals from Walls, diameter 6.6 inches, Davies collection.

the vessel covered by the four volutes is swollen into four lobes. In the four triangles formed above the spirals in

Fig. 269. Bowl with nodes from Walls, diameter 4.7 inches, Davies collection.

figure 267 are so many small circles inclosing each a tetraskele; in the same positions in figure 268 are four small circles inclosing each a plain cross. The incised lines in these two vessels are rather deep.

Figure 269 represents a pot of brown ware heavily shell-tempered. The two loop handles or ears are broader than usual. The distinguishing feature of this pot is the decoration made of thickly studded nodes or projections. The height of the vessel is 3.6 inches, the diameter 4.7 inches, the diameter of the mouth 3.3 inches.

Figures 270 and 271 have globular bodies and large necks;

FIG. 270. Clay vessel with 4 small ears from Walls, height 6 inches, Davies collection.

FIG. 271. Clay vessel with 4 depressions from Walls, height 7.5 inches, Davies collection.

there are no decorations other than the four tiny ears on figure 270 and the four circular depressions on the bowl of figure 271.

The pyramid type of vessel top is shown in the piece of brown ware illustrated in figure 272. The circular opening is on the side, and may represent the human mouth, tho no other human features are shown in this particular piece. This pyramid effect is often combined with the human head in the handles or ears of pottery, as in figure 311. Compare also figure 345, where the opening of the vessel corresponds to the human mouth; and figure 46, vessel 94, from Bradley

Place, Arkansas, in Moore[1]; it is very similar to a vessel in Mr. Schubach's collection from Walls (not shown here). The gourd type of vessel has the opening on the side, sometimes with a curved neck and with ribs. Vessels with animal heads have the opening sometimes on the back of the head or back of the neck, as in a fine vessel in Mr. Schubach's collection, or in the image vessel from Yazoo Co., Mississippi, shown by Thomas.[2]

FIG. 272. Vessel surmounted with a pyramid, Walls, height 4.7 inches, diam. 5.5 inches, scale ½, Davies collection.

The bowl of figure 273 is represented as if inclosed in a network of cord. Clay vessels are sometimes so carried by primitive people. There are three horizontal bands in relief, the top and bottom ones twisted to represent cord, the middle one beaded or knotted. These horizontal bands are connected at intervals by vertical ones, those in the upper tier alternating with those of the lower. The dimensions in inches are: height 7.5, height of neck 1.5, circumference 29, diameter of

[1] Moore: Some Aboriginal Sites on Miss. River, Philadelphia, 1911, page 436.
[2] Thomas: 12th Ann. Rept. of the Bureau of Am. Ethnology, page 263, figure 164.

mouth 2.75. A similar piece from the Arkansas side of the river is shown by Moore.[1]

The jars figured in 274, 276 and 277 have a peculiar collar in relief about the neck of the vessel. This symbol in its

FIG. 273. Vessel with decoration in imitation of cord, Walls, height 7.5 inches, circumference 29 inches, Davies collection.

entirety may be described as composed of a small circle or ellipse surrounded by another figure consisting of a circle with two projecting opposite points made by small reverse curves. In the pottery shown here the mouth of the vessel makes the inner circle. One would be inclined to think this symbol a conventionalized eye were it not for the fact that when occurring on the side of vessels the pointed axis is ver-

[1] Moore: Some Aborig. Sites on Miss. River, Philadelphia, 1911, page 439, fig. 49.

tical. The symbol is fairly common in the middle Mississippi valley district and occurs not only on pottery but occasionally

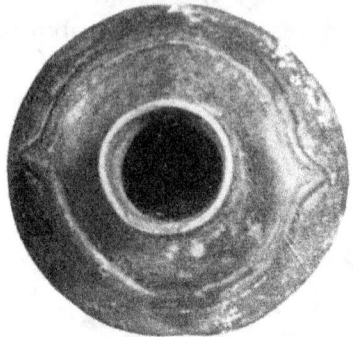

FIG. 274. Jar with relief collar surrounding neck, Walls, diam. 7.2 inches, Davies collection.

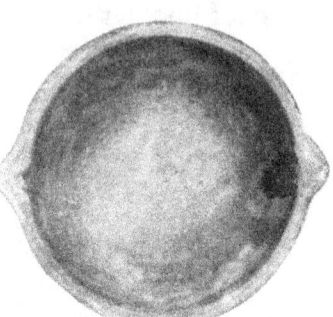

FIG. 275. Bowl in form of the collar of the preceding vessel, Walls, diam. 7 inches, Davies collection.

FIG. 276. Jar with relief collar about neck, Walls, height 8 inches, circumference 35 inches, Davies col.

ı sheet-copper (Moundville, Ala., Moore), and on stone Arkansas Post, Ark., Moorehead). Sometimes the outline a bowl is determined by this form, as in figure 275. The jar shown in figure 277 has an incised criss-cross rail-fence design between the inner and outer circle, that is, between the neck and the collar.

An interesting incised vessel is shown in figure 278 with details in 279 and 280. It is 5.5 inches high, 6.6 inches in diameter, and has a broad neck in the form of a truncated

FIG. 277. Jar with incised criss-cross ornamentation between collar and neck, Walls, diam. 7 inches, Davies collection.

cone, 4.1 inches in diameter at the top. The bottom of the vessel is a notched circular plate 4 inches in diameter with an inner circle and tetraskele or modified swastika design. The decoration on the neck of the vase (fig. 279) consists of an incised human head facing a hand. The head has an open mouth with protruding pointed tongue, and from over the brow hangs a fillet with criss-cross ornamentation. The hand is wide open with two concentric figures in the palm and with fingers of criss-cross shading. Beneath the hand is a figure probably representing the long-bones. This series of crude drawings occurs four times in encircling the neck of the vessel. On the bowl of the vessel is a complicated scroll design with criss-cross work, recurring six times (fig. 280). Moore[1] shows a vessel from Pecan Point, Ark., with human faces,

Fig. 278. Incised vessel from Walls, height 5.5 inches, Davies collection. See details in figures 279 and 280.

hands, and long-bones, all in relief, and cites another from Blytheville, Ark.

Another interesting vessel with incised decoration is shown in figures 281 and 282; it is somewhat smaller than the preceding vessel and differs from it in that the larger part of

[1]Moore: Some Aborig. Sites on Miss. River, Philadelphia, 1911, page 462, fig. 69.

Fig. 279. Part of design on neck of fig. 278, same scale. P. W. (Above.)

Fig. 280. Part of design on bowl of fig. 278, same scale. P. W. (Below.)

Fig. 281. Incised vessel from Walls, height 5.1 inches, circumference 16 inches, Davies collection. See detail in fig. 282.

Fig. 282. Detail of decoration on preceding vessel (fig. 281), same scale. P. W.

the conical neck is upward. The vessel is somewhat over 5 inches in height and in diameter. It stands upon a globular

FIG. 283. A dozen plain bottles from Walls, scale about ½, Davies collection.

bottom which has a circle about 1.7 inches in diameter inclosing a tetraskelion. The distinguishing feature of this vessel is that the original dark finish of the ware is cut away to make the decoration, which is consequently lighter than the remaining surface (fig. 282). This decoration consists of a series of seven interlocking whorls or scrolls with rays shooting off toward the top and toward the bottom. The number

FIG. 284. "Tea-pot" type of earthen-ware from Walls, diameter of largest vessel 10 inches, scale ⅕, Davies collection.

of rays toward the neck is uniformly two for each whorl, but the number shooting toward the bottom varies from one to three to the whorl: there are three whorls with one ray, three with two, and one with three. There are five tetraskeles separating the whorls above, two being missing. The large lobes left above and below this decoration resemble somewhat the petals of large flowers, tho apparently they are not intended as such.

Pots of the bottle type abound at Walls. A selection of plain examples is given in figure 283, some of the forms being quite graceful. The middle piece in the top row is 9.25 high.

The "tea-pot" variety of vessel is shown in figure 284. Each of the three has a little knob on the exterior of the vessel opposite the spout. This knob probably represents the head in the evolution of this variety of pottery from an ani-

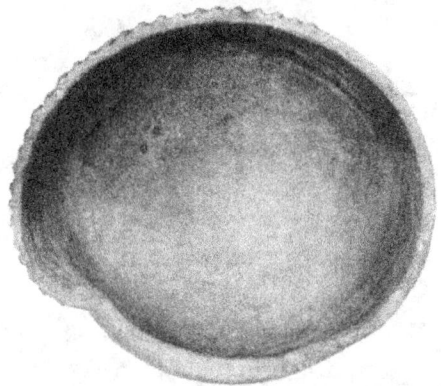

FIG. 285. Shell-shaped vessel of clay from Walls, length 5.75 inches, Davies collection.

mal form, the spout being the tail. A fine example of red ware from Mississippi, which evidently shows an intermediate step in this evolution, is shown by Holmes[1]; in it the knob is replaced by the head of a tortoise or other reptile and the vessel stands on four feet[2]. The "tea-pot" variety is not very abundant in this section. The author formerly had one in plain red ware about 7.5 or 8 inches in diameter from the Edwards place on the east side of the Sunflower River about 12 miles south of Clarksdale. Peabody illustrates two vessels

---

[1] Holmes: Aborig. Pot. of Eastern U. S., 20th Ann. Rept. of Bu. of Am. Ethn., Washington, 1903, pl. xl, b, text on page 94.
[2] Compare also such pieces as the Rose Mound vessel no. 185 from Ark. shown by Moore in the Antiq. of St. Francis, etc., pl. xviii.

of this type from Oliver in plate 14. A "tea-pot" vessel with frog surrounding the neck is shown in figure 324.

Animal life such as abounded in the vicinity is frequently represented in the remains of the Walls culture. The representations are not of high artistic value; indeed we are not always quite sure of the potter's zoology. In the following pages several illustrations of animal life will be given.

Mention has already been made of the Amerind's use of

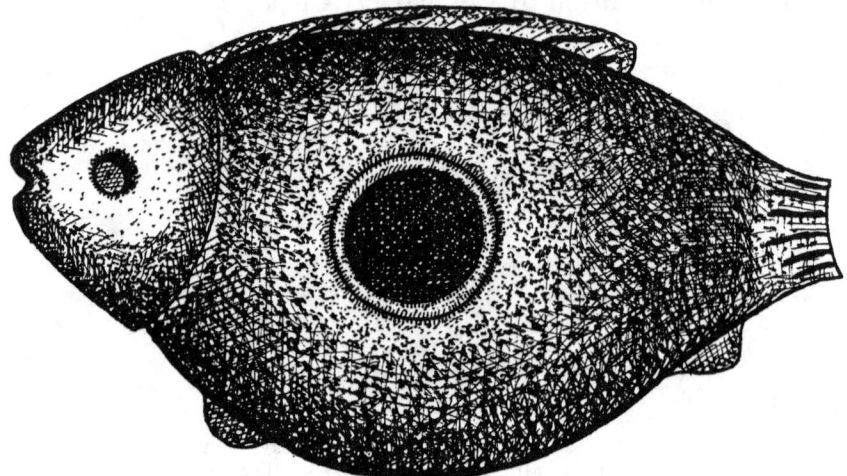

FIG. 286. Fish vessel from Walls, with opening toward observer, length 13.75 inches, height of bottle neck 2.25 inches, Schubach collection. R. M.

shells for vessels. So familiar was he with them in this capacity that he sometimes reproduced or imitated them in clay. Figure 285 shows a good example from Walls. There is also a larger shell-shaped vessel in the Davies collection. Moore[1] pictures two from Neblett Landing, his figures 15 and 21 not being reproduced here. An example from Sunflower County is illustrated by Thomas[2].

The fish was no doubt a large item in the food of the aborigines, and it figures prominently in his plastic art. Fig.

---

[1]Moore: Some Aborig. Sites on Miss. River, Philadelphia, 1911, figures 15, 21.
[2]Thomas: 12th Ann. Rept. of the Bureau of American Ethn., page 259, figure 160.

286 shows a large fish vessel found by Mr. Schubach near Walls, De Soto County. The illustration shows the fish in normal position; to show the vessel upright the fish must lie on its right side. Dorsal and ventral fins are both present. The circular neck of the vessel is over two inches high.

Figure 287 is also a fish-shaped vessel from the Davies collection at Walls, the general outline being more nearly round than in the preceding. Part of the tail has been broken away. There are four fish vessels in this collection. Peabody shows a rare fish form from the Oliver mound in plate 14.

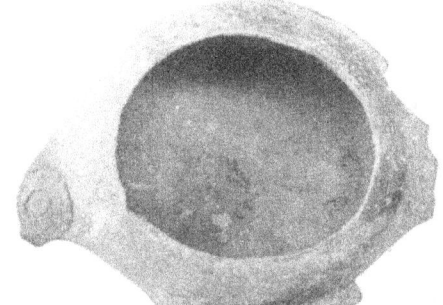

Fig. 287. Fish bowl from Walls, present length 7.5 inches, Davies collection.

Fig. 288. Effigy vessel from Walls, greater circumference 18.5 inches, total height 5.25 inches, Davies col.

Figure 288 is the effigy of some strutting animal, possibly the tortoise, tho the head belongs to the group of fantastic heads shown in the following figures. The body is elliptical; the opening is in the middle of the back; the tail has been broken away; the legs are short and heavy.

The serpent seems to have been a conspicuous creature in Indian life; it is often found in aboriginal decoration. The rattlesnake design on stone has already been mentioned in connection with tablets (fig. 182) and pipes (figs. 218, 222, 223, 224). In pottery the grotesque serpent head often forms one handle of a vessel and the curled tail the opposite handle, as in figs. 289, 290. The number of lines down each side of the neck is usually three. The bowl constitutes the body of the monster, the greater diameter of the bowl in the two figures just cited being cross-wise to the axis of the animal. The height of the bowl in each case is slightly more than half the total height. Figure 291 represents a somewhat different type of this design. The slenderness and height of the ani-

Fig. 289. Mythical serpent bowl from Walls, total width 9.28 inches, total height 6.9 inches, Davies collection.

mal heads, both real and fantastic, on the rims of vessels made them easily broken; accordingly many separated heads are found. See illustrations in figures 305 to 310.

The frog or toad was scarcely less popular than the serpent. Some fine massive frog pipes of stone have already been presented in the chapter on pipes. An unusual frog pipe of earthen-ware is also described in the same chapter of this book (fig. 206).

A number of good frog pots have been taken from the graves near Walls. Figure 292 shows a fine one with head turned toward the observer. The legs stand out in strong relief on the globular surface of the bowl; the claws are fully developed, and shade off into the surface. The circumference of the bowl over the legs is 32 inches, the height 6.75 inches, the diameter of the opening 4.75 inches.

There is an interesting frog pot of a different design in Mr. Schubach's collection (fig. 293). A neck rises above the

Fig. 290. Mythical serpent bowl from Walls, total width 10 inches, total height 8.25 inches, Davies collection.

bowl about one-third the height of the latter, and a series of four small handles spring from the bowl to the rim of the neck. The frog has a rattle in its head; such rattles are not infrequent in animal and human heads used as handles of pottery (fig. 295, for instance).

In figure 294 the top of the head is on a level with the edge of the bowl. The legs stand out in high relief. A short projection shows in the rear. The vessel is 4.5 inches long to the tip of the nose.

Figure 295 represents a fine pot with broad opening and notched or beaded rim. Broad expanses mark each of the four legs; the ears are tall and prominent; there is a pointed mouth instead of the broad mouth of the usual frog pot. The potter may have been trying to represent a bat, the broad expanses on the legs being a crude conventional effort to

Fig. 291. Serpent pot from Walls, total width 5.25 inches, Schubach collection. R. M.

show the wing membranes. A small vessel from Bear Point, Alabama, has the broad expanse on the legs but a more typical frog head, and is called by Holmes[1] a frog vessel. The Mississippi vessel is here placed below a typical frog vessel for comparison. One observer suggests that a wild-cat or lynx was intended. There is a rattle in the head of this animal, as in figure 293. There is another bat pot in the col-

---
[1]Holmes: Aborig. Pot. of the East. U. S., Washington, 1903, p. 107 and pl. lvi, e.

POTTERY. 309

lection, in which the animal is represented as clinging with its four feet to the edge of the vessel.

A common form of open bowl has a bird's head on one

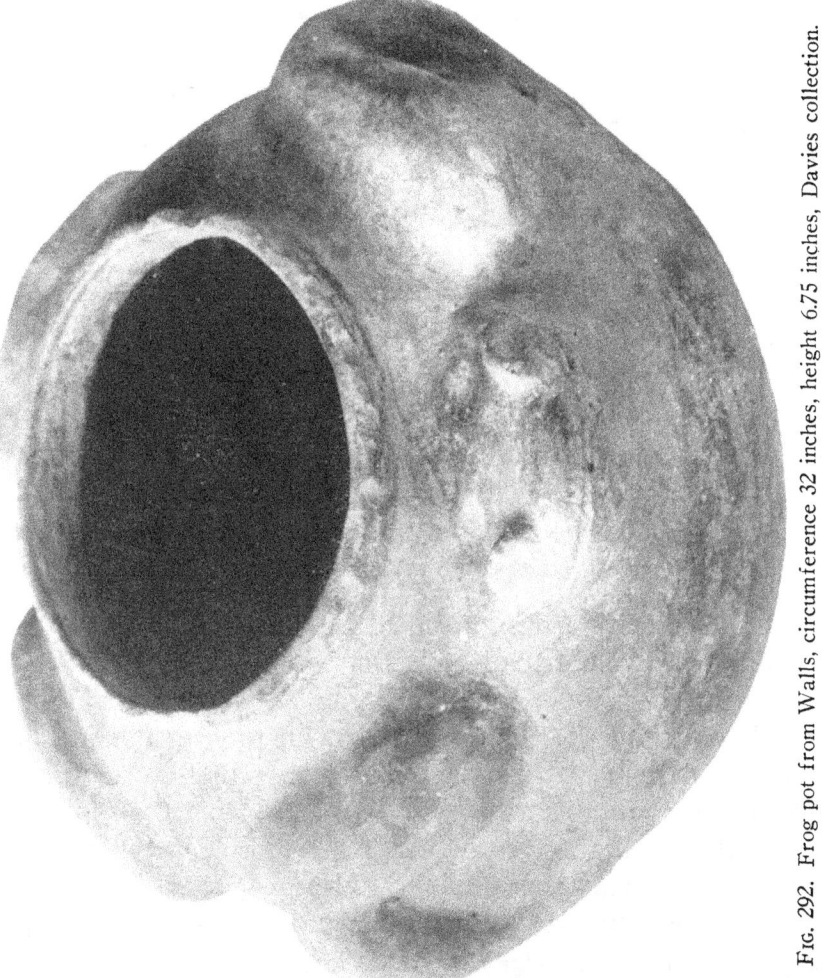

FIG. 292. Frog pot from Walls, circumference 32 inches, height 6.75 inches, Davies collection.

side of the vessel and a tail or feet on the opposite side. The tail is often rudimentary. Human heads occur sometimes instead of bird heads. Some of these varieties are shown on the following pages. Figure 296 has a bird's head looking back over the bowl towards the tail and prominent feet. On the sides are crude incised representations of wings. Figure 300 has a human head with prominent nose and with hair rolled up in a knot behind. There are three incised bands around the bowl and two circles or ellipses on the tail. The smaller human bowl, figure 298, is similar to the larger, but without the incised bands around the bowl.

FIG. 293. Frog vessel with four handles from Walls, total length 6.5 inches, scale ½, Schubach collection. R. M.

Figure 301 is a design on the bowl of a fine bottle from Walls in Mr. Schubach's collection. This would seem to be an illustration of the double ivory-billed woodpecker design, which Moore has pictured in both of his monographs dealing with Moundville, Alabama. The two pairs of wings are given more prominence in the Walls example than in those from Moundville, while the heads are more conventionalized than in the Alabama examples. Here as in the Moundville woodpeckers the tails are the most prominent feature and might be mistaken for a pair of wings. Each tail in the Walls figure has five pointed feathers at the end and bears two small concentric circles connected by four radiuses. The conventional head of the bird extends up some distance on the tall neck of the bottle. Moore, describing one of the Moundville

POTTERY. 311

FIG. 294. Frog pot from Walls, slightly reduced, Davies collection.

FIG. 295. Bat (?) pot from Walls, length to tip of nose 5.75 inches, Davies col.

decorations, says:[1] "The bird shown in the design has been

[1]Moore: Certain Aborig. Rem., Bl. War. River, Philadelphia, 1905, page 138.

Fig. 296. Bird bowl from Walls, greatest length 6.5 inches, Davies collection.

Fig. 297. Effigy bowl, Walls, greatest length 7.25 inches, Davies collection.

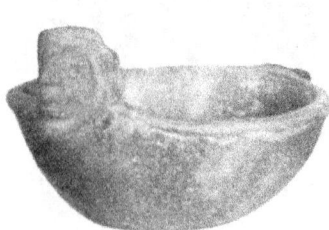

Fig. 298. Bowl with human head, Walls, greatest length 7 inches.

Fig. 299. Bird bowl from Walls, greatest length 5.5 inches.

identified by Mr. Witmer Stone, of the Academy of Natural Science, as the ivory-billed woodpecker *(Campephilus princi-*

Fig. 300. Bowl with human head, Walls, greatest length 9 inches.

palis), a bird now found in one part of Mississippi and in parts of Florida, but having ranged well north of Mound-

Fig. 301. Design on bottle from Walls, ½ size (length 7.5 inches), Schubach collection. P. W.

ville in former times. . . . When spread, the tail of the woodpecker is used by the bird to prop itself up and thus steady it at its work. This feature would no doubt strike the aboriginal eye and thus cause it to attach more importance to the tail of the woodpecker than to its wings." Perhaps the

Fig. 302. Opossum (?) bottle from Walls, height 5 inches, Davies collection.

Fig. 303. Opossum (?) pot from Walls, height 3.5 inches, Davies collection.

pileated woodpecker *(Ceophloeus pileatus)* is intended in the Walls design; it is now far more common in Mississippi.

Miss Wright's ink drawing was made from a pencil drawing by Mr. Kornick; the author has not had an opportunity to compare it with the original, which is no longer within reach. The reader may compare this double-bird design with the quadruple design on the shell gorget shown in figure 248.

The two vessels shown in figures 302 and 303 are probably intended to represent the opossum *(Didelphys virginiana)*, tho one can not be sure. Each has prominent ears and

FIG. 304. Vessel with bear-paw decoration from Walls, height 5.4 inches, circumference 25.5 inches, Davies collection.

a long thin nose ridge. Mr. Schubach has a vessel from the same locality which he believes represents the raccoon *(Procyon lotor)*.

A large handsome vessel with bear-claw decoration is shown in figure 304. Four feet with toes downward occur on the upper surface of the well-shaped bowl and four feet with toes upward decorate the lower surface. There is no other decoration except the beaded collar about the base of the neck.

316 ARCHEOLOGY OF MISSISSIPPI.

A group of pottery handles in the form of animal heads is shown on this page. The first, figure 305 (author's collection no. 206), is a squirrel head from a mound near Indianola; the remaining five are from Walls. Figure 306 is a

FIG. 305. Squirrel.　　FIG. 306. Bear.　　FIG. 307. Rabbit.
FIG. 308. Owl (?)　　FIG. 309. Wolf (?)　　FIG. 310. Deer (?)

Animal heads broken from the rim of clay vessels, all from Walls, Davies col., except the squirrel, 305, which is from Indianola, author's col., about ⅔ size.

bear head. Figure 307 is a rabbit head. The squirrel and rabbit seem to figure very little in the primitive art of this section, tho the animals are abundant. Figure 308 is probably a tufted owl; the eyes and beak are quite prominent.

Figure 309 has fierce teeth and a turned-up nose; it may be intended for a wolf or an imaginary monster. The type shown in figure 310 is relatively frequent; the snout is round and prominent, showing the nostrils; the eyes stand out boldly; there are two prominent projections above the head representing either ears or antlers. The deer is possibly intended, tho the vessels having these heads have coiled serpent tails. The type certainly connects closely with the mythical serpent type already shown (figs. 289-291). There is usually a tetraskele on the back of the head and three lines ascend the neck on each side.

Another favorite rim decoration or handle is the human head surmounted by a tall four-sided pyramid (fig. 311). The ribs of the pyramid are often notched. The heads are usually crude and sometimes contain rattles. This design is sometimes used for the crown of closed vessels; see the discussion in connection with fig. 272.

Another human head from the rim of a utensil is shown in figure 312. The face looks toward the bowl; the lips, nose, chin, and ears are prominent. The hair is parted in the middle and twisted into a strand forming a loop-handle behind the neck. On the right side of the head the hair (or covering?) is represented by two series of parallel lines crossing at right angles; on the left side by a series of concentric semicircles. Compare the tops of the heads on the pipes shown in figures 227-229. There are four deeply incised lines circling the vessel just below the rim.

FIG. 311. Pyramidal human head from Walls, natural size, Schubach collection.

Double vessels are found infrequently in this territory. A good one from the graves at Walls is shown in figure 313.

Two vases are united by their bowls and also by a cross bar between the necks. The height is 3.75 inches, the total width 7.25 inches, the circumference of each bowl about 12.5 inches. The vessel is of good plain workmanship. There are two other double pots in Dr. Davies' collection, one quite large,

Fig. 312. Human head from rim of a broken vessel from Walls, nat. size, Davies collection.

one small. Mr. Charles W. Clarke has a double bottle 5.5 inches high from Coahoma County.

Triple vessels are perhaps still less common. A fine example in several colors is shown in figure 314. This triple bottle is from the graves at Walls, and was unfortunately broken in excavation. This piece consists of three bottles with individual necks, these three necks uniting to form one neck for the whole vessel. Part of the neck is missing. The colors used are red, white, and yellowish brown, arranged in spirals or circles on two bottles and vertically on the third. The upper part above the union of the three necks is red. The present height is 11.5 inches, the total height was probably 12 or 13 inches; the circumference of the individual bottles is about 13.5 inches; the total circumference 25.5 inches. There

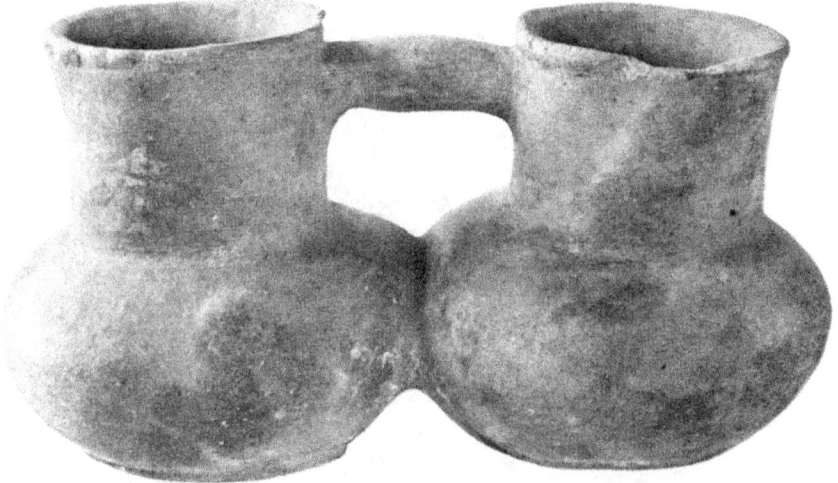

Fig. 313. Double earthen-ware vessel from Walls, height 3.75 inches, total width 7.25 inches. Davies collection.

is another fine triple pot in Dr. Davies' collection. See also the triple vessel from Oliver (fig. 315). There are relatively few red or polychrome pieces among the Walls vessels.

[The preceding incomplete account of the Walls pottery was written before Dr. Davies gave his archeological collection to the University of Mississippi. The material has since been installed in our museum, and the work of cataloguing it is in progress. It is hoped that a complete study of this valuable collection may be published later.]

Dr. Charles Peabody during his work in Coahoma County in 1901 and 1902 found the following pottery:

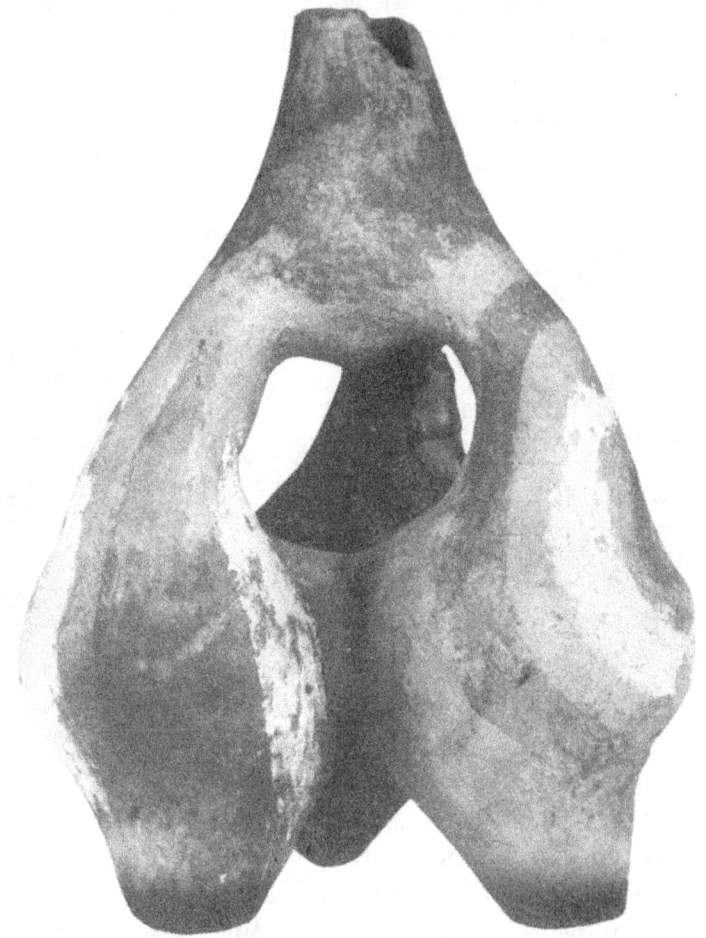

Fig. 314. Triple polychrome bottle from Walls, present height 11.5 inches, probable height 12 or 13 inches, Davies collection.

41 bowls, 20 pot-shaped vessels,
5 wide-mouthed bottles, 7 long-necked bottles,

in all 73 pieces, of which more than half are of the bowl type. Twenty-three of these pieces are shown in plates xii to xvi inclusive of his detailed monograph[1]. The greater number are uncolored, but slips of black, red, or red and white occur. Decorations by incision and in relief are found: primitive criss-cross designs, ray-like symbols, geometric rectangular figures, scrolls, conventional knobs, and animal forms. Two

FIG. 315. Triple bottle, height 6.1 inches.
FIG. 316. Bottle, height 7.25 inches.   FIG. 317. Bottle, height 6.75 inches.
Three bottles from Oliver, Coahoma Co., Peabody museum. From Peabody, pl. xv.

of the so-called "tea-pot" vessels and a good fish design are shown in plate xiv.

The triple bottle (fig. 315) and the two pattern vases (figs. 316 and 317) are reproduced from Dr. Peabody's monograph. The triple bottle was found in the cemetery mound

[1]Peabody: Exploration of Mounds, Coahoma Co., Miss., Cambridge, Mass., 1904.

of the Oliver group (fig. 18); it is 6.1 inches high and covered with red slip.

The bottles represented in figures 316 and 317 were taken from the Oliver mound by Dr. Peabody. They have a body of red with a pattern of intertwined figures in white. The second is slightly smaller than the first.

Burnt clay, often with cane impressions, is frequently found in mounds and in the earth. Such fragments are parts of floors and walls of huts or other structures where cane was

FIG. 318. Burnt clay with cane impressions, Charleston, Tallahatchie Co., scale ⅖, author's collection nos. 210 and 211.

used as a framework. The larger piece in figure 318 shows the impression of a cane crossing the canes at right angles.

We now pass to the south of the mouth of the Arkansas River and into the Lower Mississippi Valley territory. Some of the differences between the pottery of the Middle and of the Lower Mississippi Valley group were mentioned at the beginning of this chapter. The territory is largely that occupied by the Yazoos, the Natchez, and other smaller tribes at the beginning of the historic period. Mr. Clarence B. Moore has done much archeological work in this region and has kindly furnished me with a number of illustrations; the following twenty pages draw largely upon his published material[1].

---

[1] Moore: Certain Mounds of Ark. and of Miss., Philadelphia, 1908.
Some Aborig. Sites on Miss. River, Philadelphia, 1911.

An account of Moore's investigations near Neblett Landing, a short distance below Rosedale, in Bolivar County, is first given. He found ninety-seven earthen-ware vessels there, twenty-four unbroken or nearly so, most of the remainder in poor condition. His estimate of the pottery is summed up as follows:

The ware from this mound is not of the best, and no ves-

FIG. 319. Vessel from Neblett Landing, Bolivar Co., height 3.6 inches, Moore collection no. 52. From Moore, fig. 23.

sel shows a polished surface. A few of the vessels exhibit fairly graceful modeling and some diversity of form, tho, curiously enough, the bottle is present in but few instances. A favorite form of vessel is one somewhat resembling an inverted, truncated cone, which is represented among the vessels found no fewer than thirty-seven times, with various modifications, of course.

Decoration is a marked feature of the pottery, only nine of the ninety-seven vessels found being entirely without it.

The decoration in the main consists of line-work (engraved, incised, or trailed) fairly well executed in some instances, but much of it of mediocre or inferior workmanship. There is great repetition of design on the ware; the partly interlocked scroll, the current scroll, the spiral, festooned lines, and loops surrounding circles. Decoration in color is present on but

FIG. 320. Vase from Neblett Landing, Bolivar Co., height 4 inches, Moore collection no. 5. From Moore, fig. 18.

two vessels from this place, a design in red and white in each instance.

Figure 319 represents a bottle of light brown ware, with short thick neck and heavy rim. The body bears an incised decoration composed of a series of circles and scrolls.

Figure 320 is a vessel of compound form representing a cylindrical bowl set on a kind of saucer. The incised decoration is based mainly on the horizontal circle and the scroll. There is a single hole for suspension on two opposite sides.

The lip of the saucer has a series of indentations, giving a beaded effect.

Figure 321 is a bowl 8.3 inches in diameter bearing by way of decoration on the inside a circle of solid red pigment

FIG. 321. Interior of bowl from Neblett Landing, Bolivar Co., diameter 8.3 inches, Moore collection no. 28. Reduced from Moore, fig. 16.

from which extends four arms in red, forming a cross. The background is pigment of cream color. The exterior decoration is a cross of cream color with arms expanding somewhat toward the extremities, and having a background of red.

The other bowl showing color is also pictured by Moore (page 394, figure 15, vessel 56). It is a large shell-shaped

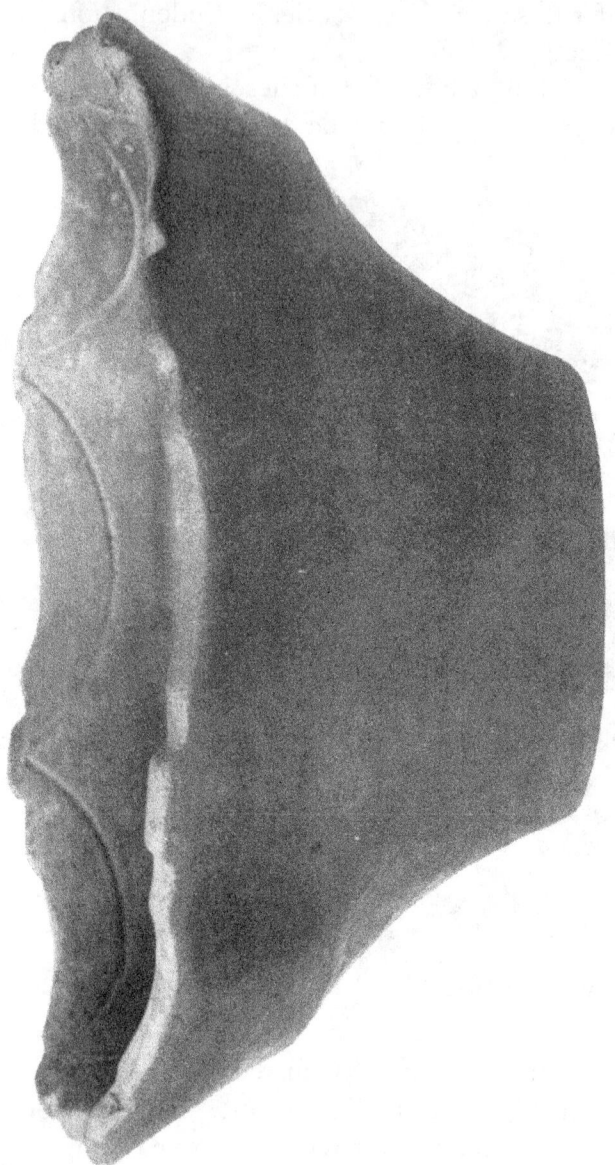

Fig. 322. Bowl from Neblett Landing, Bolivar Co., diameter 6 inches, Moore collection no. 90. From Moore, figure 20.

bowl having a coating of cherry-colored pigment on the inside, now partly worn away, and on the outside a well-pre-

Fig. 323. Bowl from Neblett Landing, Bolivar Co., diameter 8.3 inches, Moore collection no. 71. From Moore, fig. 19.

served design, hour-glass in shape, perhaps current scrolls united, in white pigment on a background of cherry.

Two other shell-shaped vessels from Neblett Landing are

Fig. 324. Frog "tea-pot" vessel from Neblett Landing, height 5.9 inches. Moore col. no. 22. From Moore, fig. 17.

Fig. 325. Effigy vessel from Neblett Landing, Bolivar Co., height 4.1 inches, Moore collection no. 65. From Moore, fig. 22.

also described by Moore, the one illustrated by him as figure 21 (page 398) having an external incised decoration based on the swastika.

Two good open bowls of the form prevailing in the Neblett Landing site are shown in figures 322 and 323. The former has a graceful modified scallop finish on the rim, and an incised festoon decoration in the interior; the latter bears on the body an incised design consisting of a well-known combination in which a current scroll has each of its loops arranged to include a circle.

Examples of effigy vessels from Neblett Landing are shown in figures 324 and 325; the former is a variant of the

FIG. 326. Vessel from Shadyside Landing, Washington Co., height 3.5 inches, Moore collection no. 3. From Moore, fig. 14.

"tea-pot" type in that it has a modeled frog upholding the neck of the vessel; the latter is a bottle of inferior ware, having projecting from one side a tail, and from the other side the mutilated head of a bird or of a quadruped. On two sides of the bottle are rude incised designs, possibly representing wings.

Moore found comparatively little pottery in his excavations in Washington Co. The small vessel shown in figure

POTTERY.   331

326 has a round opening and a square flat base, on which are a number of concentric incised squares. The body of the vessel has incised encircling lines connected by short oblique

FIG. 327. Bottle with inscribed drawing of a bird, from a mound at Bear Creek, scale ⅔, height 6.5 inches, greatest circumference 20.5 inches. Collected by Capt. W. P. Hall. Davenport Acad. of Sc., acc. no. 6706. (Figured in 4th Ann. Rept., Bur. of Am. Ethn., p. 432, fig. 461. Figured in 20th Ann. Rept., Bur. of Am. Ethn., pl. li, opp. p. 102.) Photograph by the Davenport Academy.

lines. On each side near the rim are two small circular holes one above the other.

In figure 327 is shown in a larger illustration a bottle

already twice presented by Dr. Holmes. It has been for many years in the Museum of the Davenport Academy of Science. Dr. Holmes's earlier description of this excellent piece is here quoted: "The paste is silicious, fine-grained, and quite hard.

Fig. 328. Vessel from Mound D, Peaster Place, Holmes Co., height 5.2 inches, Moore collection. From Moore, fig. 2.

The color is slightly ferruginous and clouded with fire stains from the baking. The body is ornamented with the engraved figure of a bird apparently intended for an eagle. The head, with its notched and strongly curved beak and conventionalized crest, occupies one side. The wings may be seen at the right and left, while the tail appears on the side opposite the head. The flattened base of the vessel occupies the place of the body. The lines have been scratched with a sharp point in the hardened clay. Certain spaces in the plumes, wings, and tail are filled in with reticulated lines."

Fig. 329. Pot from Anderson Landing, Sharkey Co., height 3.25 inches, Moore collection no. 1. From Moore, fig. 3.

The bottle was obtained by Captain W. P. Hall from a mound at Bear Creek, a former postoffice in Humphreys County, ten miles north of Belzoni.

Figure 328 is a vessel which was found inverted in a low mound on the Peaster place in Holmes Co. It has a thick rim and a series of incised spiral decorations.

The pot represented in figure 329 was found by Moore near the surface of a mound near Anderson Landing on Sunflower River in Sharkey Co., and is made of yellow ware without shell-tempering. This vessel, whose parts have been put together by the archeologist, has a quadrilateral body with rounded corners, on which is a decoration partly punc-

FIG. 330. Vessel from Anderson Landing, Sharkey Co., height 3.9 inches, Moore collection no. 3. From Moore, fig. 4. See detail in next figure.

tate and partly produced by the trailing of a broad-pointed implement. Below the upper margin of the vessel is a circular band of evenly made reticulated lines, and an encircling line of imprints, made with the end of a blunt tool.

In the same mound, about the base, was found in frag-

POTTERY. 335

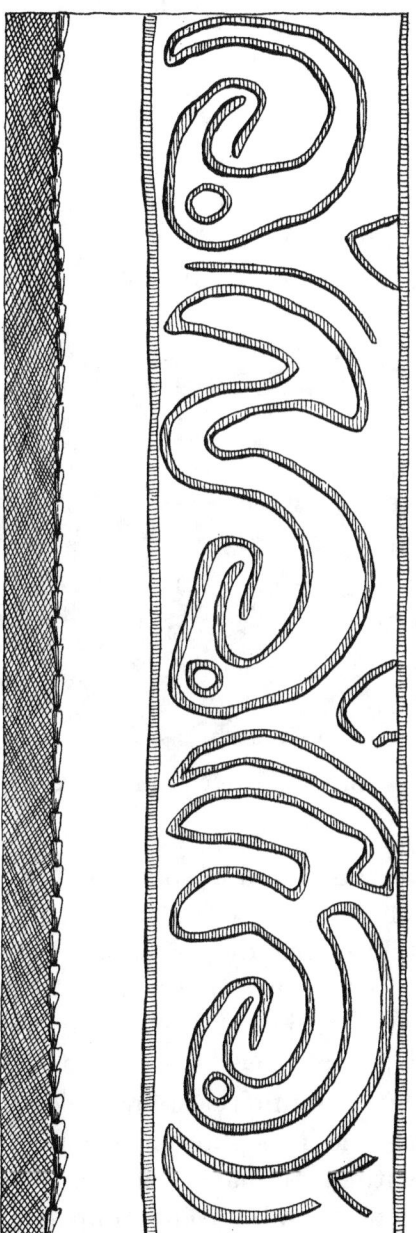

FIG. 331. Serpent (?) decoration on the preceding vessel, fig. 330, ½ size. From Moore, fig. 5.

ments the vessel shown in figure 330. The vessel is of yellow ware and without shell-tempering. Below the rim is a rude cross-hatch decoration, while the body of the vessel has a primitive trailed design, three times repeated, showing a serpent (fig. 331).

Thomas[1] shows in his figure 164 a small red image vessel from the large Champlin mound near Yazoo City, Yazoo Co., with the opening in the back of the neck.

Fig. 332. Bowl from Glass, Warren Co., diameter 6.3 inches, Moore collection no. 6. From Moore., fig. 10.

Among the vessels found in some excavations near Cary, Sharkey Co., by the present writer in 1921, was one beautiful piece unfortunately in fragments, unusual in that the mouth was not circular but elliptical, the axes being 2.4 and 1.6 inches. The decoration is somewhat elaborate, consisting of two horizontal ears, an incised line around the mouth, below which is a festoon of semicircles, and below this a group of four horizontal incised lines, interlocked at each end by down-turned curves with a similar series of incised lines with up-turned curves, presumably four groups in all, and between

[1] Thomas: Mound Explorations, 12th Ann. Rept., Bu. of American Ethnology, p. 263.

POTTERY. 337

the interlockings an irregular figure. The incomplete vessel is in the Geological Survey museum at the University.

Moore[1] in his investigations in Warren Co. in the winter of 1910-11 found eighty-one earthen-ware vessels in the

FIG. 333. Vessel from Glass, Warren Co., height 6 inches, Moore collection no. 7. Reduced from Moore, fig. 6.

mounds a short distance below Vicksburg, thirty-five from Glass, and forty-six from Oak Bend Landing. A summary of his work at these two sites is given in this book in the chapter on mounds.

Moore gives the following characteristics of the ware from Glass: it contains little if any shell-tempering; is fairly

[1] Moore: Some Aboriginal Sites on Miss. River, Philadelphia, 1911, pp. 378-88.

338   ARCHEOLOGY OF MISSISSIPPI.

FIG. 334. Vessel from Glass, Warren Co., height 4.3 inches, Moore collection no. 1. From Moore, fig. 8.

thin and as a rule of medium excellence; the bowl type predominates; nearly all vessels are decorated, having mostly

Fig. 335. Bottle from Glass, Warren Co., height 6 inches, Moore collection no. 18. From Moore, fig. 11.

incised or trailed decoration; the decoration is largely conventional and often based on the scroll.

The vessel shown in figure 332 is described by Moore as a

bowl of yellow ware having an incised decoration of concentric figures.

Figure 333. "This superb bottle, of thin, hard, black ware, by the exactness of the spacing and the freedom shown

Fig. 336. Pot from Glass, Warren Co., height 4.7 inches, Moore collection no. 36. Reduced from Moore, fig. 12.

in the execution of the design, is in the front rank among vessels from the Lower Mississippi region, whose aboriginal potters, when their best efforts were exerted, excelled all others in incised decoration, in the region now known as the United States. The regularity of the lining on this vessel and the evenness of the cross-hatch work are remarkable."

POTTERY. 341

Fig. 337. Vessel from Oak Bend Landing, height 6 inches, Moore col. no. 10. From Moore, fig. 5.

Vessel no. 24, shown by Moore as figure 7 (not reproduced here), is of about the same shape and size as the one just described, and has a design of somewhat the same spirit, tho not so detailed.

Vessel no. 1, figure 334 of this book, is of hard yellow

ware, and bears an incised design based on circles, triangles, and the swastika.

Vessel no. 8, Moore's figure 9 (not shown here), has an incised design based on circles and connecting scrolls.

Figure 335 is a bottle of yellow ware, from which the upper part of the neck has been broken. A band in relief encircles the body. The faint incised decoration is based on the swastika, with trefoil figures in addition.

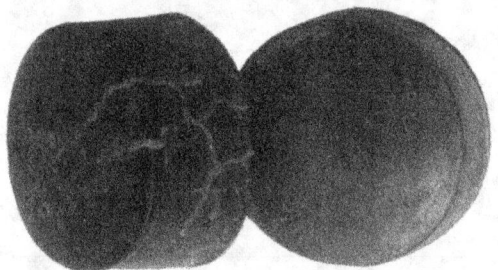

FIG. 338. Ear-plugs of clay, Oak Bend Landing, Warren Co., nat. size. From Moore, fig. 4.

Of figure 336 Moore says: "There were presented to us here fragments of a vessel which we were told had washed from a bank. This vessel is of very coarse shell-tempered ware, and entirely unlike that found by us in the mound. On each of two opposite sides of the vessel is modeled in relief a long-bodied quadruped somewhat similar to the lizard-like figures present on a vessel found at Madisonville, Ohio, and figured by Professor Holmes[1]."

Moore considers the ware of Oak Bend Landing inferior to that found in the mound near Glass, only two miles distant. Ten of the vessels are without decoration.

Figure 337 is a vessel of hard comparatively thin ware, with low wide neck. The modeling is symmetrical; the trailed decoration has been executed by a firm and practiced hand.

---

[1] Holmes: 20th Annual Report of Bureau of American Ethnology, plate clxiii, a.

In figure 338 are shown two disks of indurated clay found near a skull, but not on each side of it. The surface is polished and seems in addition to have received a coating of some dark material. The periphery of each disk shows a slight projection all the way round on each side. Presumably these objects were ear-plugs, tho the projecting parts seem inadequate to have held the ornaments in place unless they exactly fitted the opening in the lobes of the ears.

In the territory about Natchez, Adams Co., the pottery

FIG. 339. Vessel from Adams Co., near Natchez, 9 in. in diam., ⅓ size, Perrault collection (now in Milwaukee).

shows much incised decoration, frequently of scroll design. A good example is shown in figure 339. Here the scroll lines, taking their origin from circles, pass two to the neck of the bottle, two to the next circle to the right, two to the figures below near the bottom of the vessel, and two to the next circle to the left.

Another type of scroll work is seen on the bowl of bottle 340. The neck of this vessel is slightly flared at top and is about one-half the height of the bowl, that is, about one-third of the total height of the bottle.

In figure 341, broken at the neck, is shown a combination

of scroll and loop design. Unfortunately for Mississippi these three pieces have left the state.

A bottle of different form and ornamentation is presented in figure 342, found near the great Selsertown plateau in the northern part of Adams County. The material is brown ware with a small amount of shell-tempering. The height of the bottle is 7.2 inches, the neck being one-sixth of the total height and flaring somewhat at the top. The decorations consist of a series of horizontal incised lines connected and

FIG. 340. Bottle from Adams Co., ⅓ size, Perrault col. (now in Milwaukee).

FIG. 341. Vessel from Adams Co., 7 in. in diameter, ⅓ size, neck broken, Perrault collection (now in Milwaukee).

interwoven as shown in the detail in figure 343. The disregard for exact superposition of the upper part over the lower part is noticeable.

Of the 46 vessels catalogued by Stewart Culin[1] from the Dickeson collection in Philadelphia as occurring in Jefferson and Adams Counties, 30 have incised decoration, 15 being in scroll design. Only one (no. 14,175), a bowl of 7.25 inches diameter, has inside decoration, this being in the form of a festoon. It was found with a skeleton on the Lewis farm.

A flat bowl, with elongated scroll decoration, from the Lewis plantation in Adams County, is reproduced from Culin

---

[1] Culin: Dickeson Collection of American Antiquities, Philadelphia, 1900.

FIG. 342. Bottle from Selsertown, height 7.2 inches, author's collection. See detail in next figure.

in figure 344. A smaller representation of this bowl is given by Holmes[1].

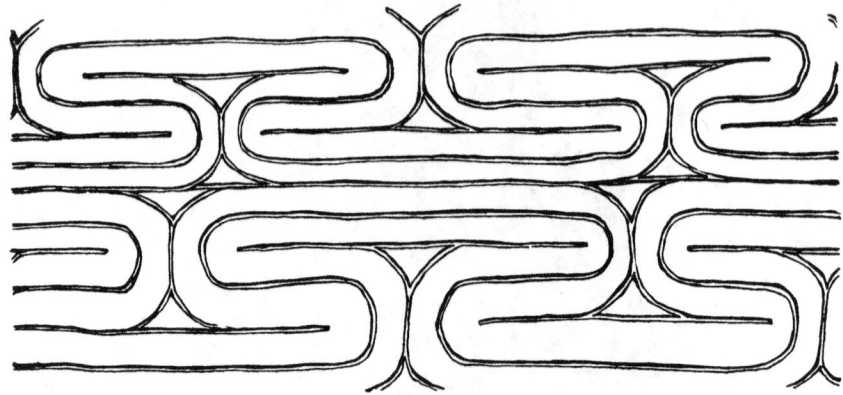

FIG. 343. Decoration on preceding bottle (fig. 342) from Selsertown, ⅓ size. P. W.

Culin and Holmes show two other South Mississippi bottles with incised scroll design, no. 14,177 from Adams Co., no. 14,184 with more flattened scroll from Jefferson Co.

FIG. 344. Bowl from Lewis mounds, Adams Co., 6 in. in diam., ½ size, Dickeson col. no. 14,201. From Culin, pl. 16.

In plate 17 of Culin's monograph is shown a small jar with incised cross-line decoration on the upper half of the vessel (no. 14,187) and a smaller jar with incised herring-

---
[1] Holmes: Aboriginal Pottery of Eastern United States, plate lii, c.

bone decoration (no. 14,205), two forms which seem to be rare in the lower Mississippi territory.

Figure 345 shows a human effigy jar of usual type. The ears and nose are in relief; the features about the eyes are incised; the mouth is made by the opening in the jar. This specimen came from the largest of the Bingaman mounds.

FIG. 345. Effigy vase, Bingaman's mounds, height 4 inches, Dickeson col. no. 14,193. From Culin, plate 16.

A bottle with unusual decoration is represented in both the *4th Annual Report of the Bureau of American Ethnology* (pp. 433 and 434) and the *20th Annual Report* (p. 106 and pl. lvi, b and c). In the earlier report it is attributed to Franklin Co., Alabama, and in the latter to Franklin Co., Mississippi; the Museum is now unable to say from which state it came. A vessel of the same height and similar ornamentation, tho with down-turned hand, was found near Nashville, Tennessee, by Thruston, who remarks (page 136): "The two vessels are so nearly alike that they appear to have been decorated in the same aboriginal paint shop."

CHAPTER IX.

POST-COLUMBIAN MATERIAL.

The Indians remained in Mississippi long after the coming of the Europeans. Until the treaties of 1832 and 1834 there were many living in the state; in 1910 there were still 1253 Indians in Mississippi; and in 1920 there were 1105, living mostly in the counties of Leake, Neshoba, Scott, and Newton. These are Choctaws and speak the Choctaw language as their mother tongue.

In the later Indian graves are not infrequently found objects of Caucasian manufacture or showing Caucasian influence, such as beads, silver ornaments, tomahawks, and other objects of bronze or brass, even cups, saucers, plates, and glass bottles. The purpose of the present chapter is to illustrate and describe a few of these later objects in order to give a general idea of them. The chapter might easily be very greatly extended.

Among the objects that traders found of value for exchange with the Amerinds were beads of glass or other composition. Personal adornment played a large part in the childish lives of these primitive people. Even yet the Choctaws in Mississippi, both men and women, wear beads. In the graves of the north-eastern part of the state about New Albany, Tupelo, and Pontotoc, and further toward the south-west near Vicksburg and Natchez, quantities of trade beads are found. In Mr. James M. Watts's collection five miles north-east of Pontotoc, I measured a string of 37 feet of those late beads, which he had put together from the graves in his vicinity. These beads vary in length from one-twentieth to one-half an inch, are of many colors, and often have spirals of color in the glass. The author's collection contains 27.5 feet of trade beads from the vicinity of Tupelo.

A good illustration of some of the variation in size, shape and color may be seen in figure 346, which shows a string from the Natchez territory. These should be compared with the prehistoric stone beads mentioned in a former chapter and shown in figures 125-128. To the post-Columbian period most probably belong also the copper beads made of thin sheet metal rolled into cylinders.

An unusual find was made some years ago in a field about three miles south-west of New Albany, Union County. A brass kettle fifteen inches in diameter and nine inches deep containing many objects was unearthed; the kettle itself is in excellent preservation but the iron handle or bail has entirely rusted away. Among the more notable things found in the large brass kettle near New Albany were:

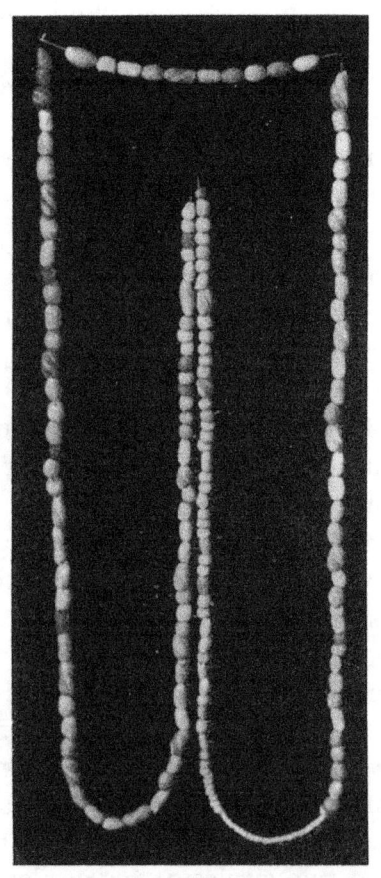

FIG. 346. Trade beads from Natchez, considerably reduced, Rufus Learned collection, Natchez.

  2 big dinner plates of chinaware; 3 saucers;
  6 china cups or bowls; 2 metal spoons;
  2 metal knives; 22 feet of trade beads;
  1 Jefferson medal of silver (figs. 348, 349);
  1 pair of silver bracelets, 2.75 inches wide;

1 pair of silver bracelets, 2 inches wide;

10 silver brooches or buckles, 1.79 to 3.94 inches in diameter (some shown in fig. 347);

quantities of silver pendants, rings, and other ornaments (some shown in fig. 347);

1 cane borer and 4 bored cores (fig. 141).

One may surmise that this was the grave of a Chickasaw chief.

There were also associated with this burial another brass kettle 7 inches in diameter and 4 inches deep, a clay pot 9 inches in diameter, some crude axes, celts, hand-hammers, some fine flints, one spear point 7.25 inches in length (fig. 30), a pendant 2 inches long (fig. 114), one banner-stone (fig. 132), several fragments of bored pieces, and a crude marked stone. The present writer cannot state that all the pieces were in one grave.

I visited this field in August, 1917, in company with Mr. Will Ticer, to whose care the preservation of this material is due and who has kindly presented it to the museum; we found on the surface potsherds, two small arrow-points, three crude mortars, numerous crude hammer-stones, and many other stones showing usage.

In the upper part of figure 347 are shown four of the ornamental silver buckles or brooches found in the grave just described. The largest is 2.25 inches in diameter and has two circles of triangular perforations and a larger circular opening in the center. The other three have only one circle of triangular perforations and the larger circular opening in the center. Each brooch has a small tongue across the central opening. The largest of the ten circular brooches (not illustrated here) is nearly four inches in diameter. These are similar to the late Louisiana ornament made from a silver dime of 1856 shown by Bushnell[1].

---

[1]Bushnell: The Choctaw of Bayou Lacomb, La., Bu. of Am. Ethn., Bull. 48, pl. 14.

POST-COLUMBIAN MATERIAL. 351

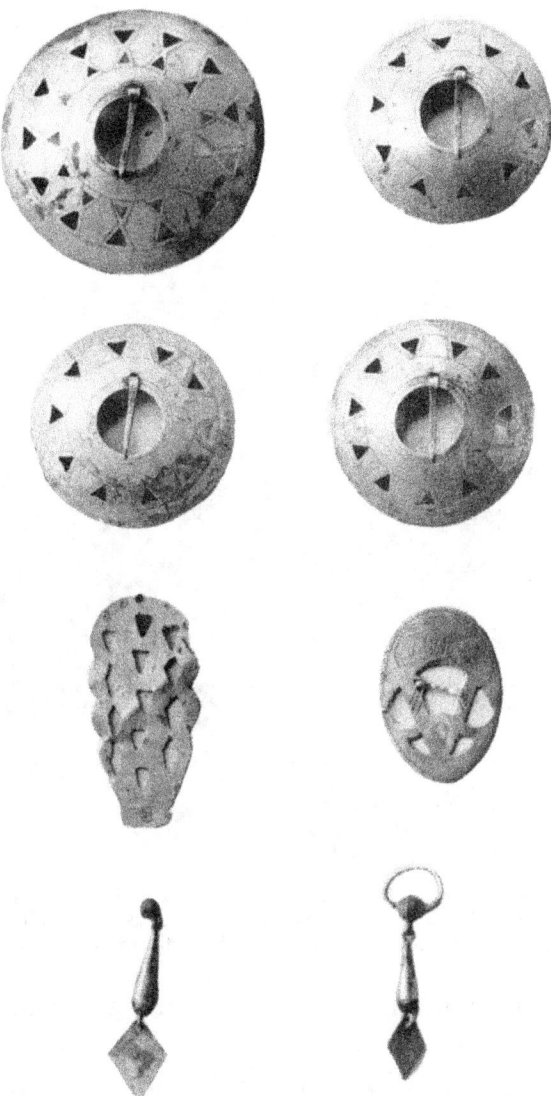

Fig. 347. Late silver ornaments from an Indian grave near New Albany, about ⅔ size, Geol. Survey museum.

The fifth piece in figure 347 is an irregular silver ornament with three rows of perforations. The sixth piece is elliptical in outline and has the name of T. Dowler engraved on the upper part and perforations in the lower part. The two bottom ornaments are silver ear-pendants with swinging plates. The first of these probably had a ring at the top similar to that of the second.

FIG. 348. Silver medal found in an Indian grave near New Albany, legend: "Th. Jefferson President of the U. S. A. D. 1801," diameter 4 inches, Geol. Survey museum, University. See fig. 349.

Of peculiar interest is the Jefferson medal (figs. 348, 349) found in this grave. It is made of two silver plates fastened together and has a diameter of 4 inches. The obverse has a profile bust portrait of Thomas Jefferson in low relief, surrounded by the inscription TH. JEFFERSON PRESIDENT OF THE U.S. A.D. 1801. The reverse of the medal has in relief two hands clasped in a hand-shake, one cuff bearing three bands with as many buttons, the other bearing a bracelet with a spreading eagle. Above the handclasp are crossed a tomahawk and calumet. The legend is PEACE AND FRIENDSHIP. Over the word PEACE a perforation has been made, no doubt by the proud possessor with a view to suspension on his person. A brief history

Fig. 349. Reverse of the Jefferson medal shown in figure 348, legend: "Peace and Friendship."

of the presidential peace medals is given in the *Handbook of American Indians* under the heading *Medals*.

Fewkes found a thin silver plate stamped with the Spanish coat of arms in a mound at Ingomar, Union Co.; associated with it was an iron knife. These were apparently in a disturbed portion of the mound, but there was a piece of greenish glass lower down in a bed of ashes undoubtedly as old as the mound itself. "Although the iron knife and silver plate offer no positive proof as to age [of the mound], the piece of glass is strong evidence that the mound was constructed after its builders had dealings with the whites."[1] For illustrations of this Spanish piece the reader is referred to Thomas[1], Dellenbaugh[2], and Beuchat[3].

The material from graves several miles north-west of Tupelo, found by a negress and preserved by Mr. C. W. Troy, is as follows:

    a pair of bronze spur-frames with the name of "John Trumbull";

    an iron tomahawk 6.5 inches long with pipe-bowl on top;

    2 pretty clay pipes of late design with angle of about 135 degrees, one about 3 inches long, the other 5.25 inches long, each with a little hole above the stem-hole and at right angles to it;

    2 metal plates 5 inches in diameter, one engraved with a picture of a house and fence, the other with a picture of a horse;

    other thin metal pieces;

    10 little thimbles with hole in top of each;

    a glass lens 2.375 inches in diameter;

    a circular metal ornament (?) with 7-pointed star connecting outer and inner circles;

    many circular brooches or pins with tongues;

    a number of buckle-shaped pieces without tongues, about 1.3 inches in diameter;

    several heart-shaped silver pieces;

    2 thin triangular pieces; a few light silver pendants;

    a small glass bottle with "Augusta, Me." on it;

    a silver cross (now missing).

Within the corporate limits of Tupelo near the Frisco

---

[1] Thomas: Mound Explorations, 12th Ann. Rept. of Bu. of Ethn., 1894, p. 275.
[2] Dellenbaugh: North Americans of Yesterday, N. Y. and London, 1906, p. 307.
[3] Beuchat: Archéologie Américaine, Paris, 1912, p. 158.

railroad were unearthed some years ago and preserved by Miss Ruth Brown objects which she lists as follows but which I have not seen:

- 2 silver bracelets about 3 inches wide;
- 2 silver bands about 6 inches wide supposed to be armlets;
- a sun-dial [?] about 1.5 inches in diameter;
- silver ear-bobs; beads;
- several silver crescents, one engraved to represent the sun;
- 3 silver crosses each with two cross-beams, one engraved with the letters "R.C." in script (all three later sold to a man in Arkansas).

The author of this book obtained in 1924 the following material from the late graves about Tupelo:

- 1 small silver disk 2.15 inches in diameter;
- 3 silver bracelets from 0.8 to 2.25 inches wide;
- 10 small silver brooches, and many parts of brooches;
- part of a silver cross with ring at top;
- fragments of silver ear-bobs;
- 2 circular silver plates over 4.5 inches in diameter, one engraved with a small tetraskele, the other with a large eagle;

FIG. 350. Bronze tomahawk, pipe design, Aberdeen, natural size. Geol. Survey museum no. 195 (13M). Presented by B. H. McFarland.

other silver pendants, circular, triangular, rectangular, heart-shaped, etc.;

27.5 feet of trade beads, no. 559;

33 inches of rolled copper beads, no. 560;

32 inches of fragments of soft light clay pipe-stems (?);

1 brass bowl with two ears, diameter 7.8 to 8 inches;

1 colored glass decanter, 8.5 inches high, no. 553;

1 metal bell 2.8 inches in diameter, 1.8 inches high, without handle;

1 tiny copper hawk-bell;

1 bowl of a brass spoon;

15 brass bracelets of C design;

1 rusty iron pot with three legs and two ears, height 7.55 inches, inner depth 5.5 inches, outer diameter 7.7 inches, no. 552;

quantities of metal gun-butts, trigger-guards, and gun ornaments, metal buttons, metal buckles, and other material;

4 small stone pipes (figs. 233-236).

Mr. James M. Watts has found north-east of Pontotoc silver pendants and other metal trinkets similar to those from Tupelo and New Albany, a string of 14 rolled copper beads each about three-fourths of an inch long, and also great quantities of trade beads.

With the coming of the white men stone implements rapidly gave way to implements of metal. Figure 350 shows a combination tomahawk and pipe, made entirely of bronze. The blade is beautifully decorated with a graceful spray of leaves. The poll of the ax terminates in a pipe-bowl. From the bottom of the bowl a small hole communicates with the eye of the tomahawk. An iron tomahawk-pipe or pipe-tomahawk is in the collection of Mr. Troy at Tupelo; Mr. Boggan of the same town also has a metal tomahawk. In the collection of Mr. Clark at Clarksdale there is a pewter tomahawk from the vicinity. Mr. West[1] pictures a pewter pipe-tomahawk collected among the Cherokee Indians over 50 (now 65) years ago and says: "This specimen was evidently intended for a pipe and not a weapon. In describing the Indians of New England in 1643, Roger Williams said: 'They have an excellent art to cast their pewter and brass into very neat artificial pipes' ". Pewter tomahawk-pipes are also recorded from New York[2] and elsewhere.

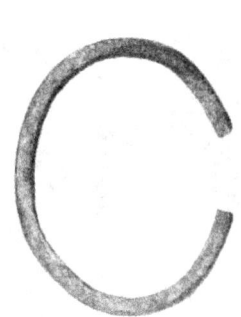

FIG. 351. Brass bracelet from Garlandsville, Jasper Co., ½ size, property of Miss Bessie Loughridge (now in new statehouse, Jackson).

FIG. 353. Choctaw basket from Central Mississippi, period about 1905, ⅛ size, author's collection.

One of eleven brass bracelets found on the arm of a skeleton in a grave at Garlandsville, Jasper Co. is shown in figure 351. This bracelet has the form of the letter C with a total height of 2.9 inches and an opening three-quarters of an inch wide; it has on the outer margin a snake-fence or zigzag design. These eleven bracelets were collected by Dr. Loughridge, along with many beads of various sizes and colors. All have disappeared except the one here pictured, which is

---
[1]West: The Aboriginal Pipes of Wisconsin, Madison, 1905, p. 60.
[2]Beauchamp: Metal. Impl. of the N. Y. Indians, Albany, 1902, p. 67 and pl. 22.

preserved in the new state-house at Jackson. It will be noted that the height of this bracelet is exactly that of the copper bracelets from Chillicothe, Ohio, illustrated and described by Squier and Davis[1]. Mr. L. P. Wulff and the author each have a number of brass or bronze bracelets from Tupelo similar to the Garlandsville pieces. They seem to have been made of heavy wire.

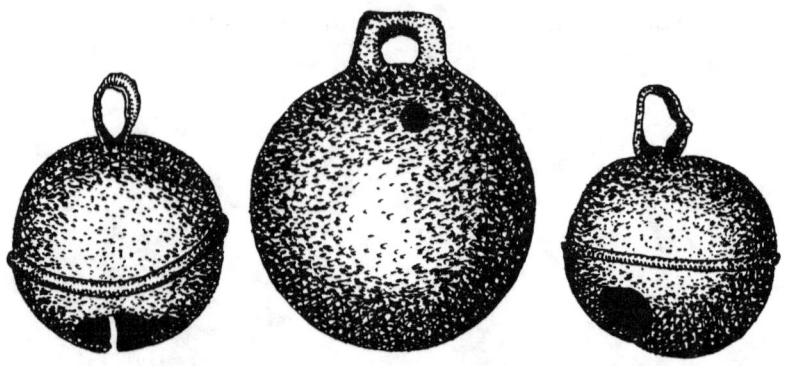

FIG. 352. Three copper bells; the two smaller ones from Mr. Clark, Clarksdale; the large one from Dr. Birchett, Vicksburg; nat. size.

Some broad silver bracelets from the graves of the northeastern part of the state are mentioned in an earlier part of this chapter.

Copper bells or rattles are occasionally found. In figure 352 three are shown in their natural sizes. The two smaller bells were taken by Mr. Charles W. Clark from a mound in Coahoma Co., near the Oliver mound; there were three in this find. The largest bell in the illustration is from the vicinity of Vicksburg and is the property of Dr. J. A. K. Birchett. The author has a tiny hawk-bell from Tupelo, not half as large as the Clarksdale specimens. Four copper rattles of the hawk-bell or sleigh-bell type, similar to the two Coahoma

---

[1]Squier and Davis: Ancient Monuments, Washington, 1848, p. 204.

County bells, were found in a mound in East Tennessee associated with the skeleton of a child[1].

The art of pottery, so far as I have learned, is no longer practiced among the Choctaws of Mississippi. The art of basketry however is still kept up. Figure 353 shows an elbow basket from the central part of the state east of Canton; it is made of split cane; some of the splints are in their natural color, others are dyed blue, others red. The arrangement

FIG. 354. Contemporary Choctaw ball-sticks from Central Mississippi, ⅛ size, author's collection.

of the splints on the handle has been somewhat disturbed. Other illustrations of Choctaw baskets may be seen in Bushnell[2] and in Mason[3]. The original art of basketry is now being vitiated by outside influences.

The old Choctaw ball game is still played in Mississippi, tho baseball is making serious inroads upon this ancient sport. Figure 354 shows a pair of present-day ball-sticks (Choctaw, *kapucha*) from the central part of the state. Each stick is made of a single piece of timber skilfully bent back upon itself and securely wrapped with a leather thong. The basket of each stick is bottomed with two leather thongs crossing at right angles, the short one re-inforced by wrap-

---
[1] Thomas: 12th Ann. Rept. of Bu. of Ethn. (1890-91), 1894, p. 376, fig. 252.
Thomas: Study of N. Am. Archæology, Cincinnati, 1903, p. 86, fig. 25.
Holmes: in Handbook of American Indians, 1907, Part I, p. 141.
[2] Bushnell: The Choctaw of Bayou Lacomb, La., Washington, 1909.
[3] Mason: Aboriginal American Basketry, Washington (1902), 1904.

ping. These sticks are 34 and 32.75 inches long respectively.

Clearings known as ball-grounds (Choctaw, *hitoka*) are still pointed out; there is a village called Ballground in Warren County north-east of Vicksburg. Dr. Eugene A. Smith camped there on October 27, 1870, and spoke of "its having been the ground of the Indian ball-play years ago."[1] Georgia also has a postoffice called Ball Ground in Cherokee County.

Stewart Culin[2] gives details of the ball-play among various tribes and shows a number of illustrations; for Mississippi he quotes the accounts of Bossu (1771), James Adair (1775), and Bernard Romans (1776); to these I add Claiborne's[3] detailed account of the Mississippi ball-game at a later date, probably about 1842 or 1843.

"An open, level piece of land is selected, and four poles are planted some two hundred yards apart, two at each end, two feet apart at their base, but inclining outwards to a width of three feet at top. From twenty to fifty players, on each side, engage in the game, which never fails to attract a crowd. The parties, respectively, assemble at the pole, and then advance, whooping and leaping, to the centre, where they lay their sticks down in two rows. These sticks are about three feet long, one end fashioned, very ingeniously, of basket-work, in the form of a hand half open, with which to catch the flying ball. The object of one party was to throw the ball through the posts, and the business of the other party was to intercept the ball, and cast it through the posts at the other extremity. After depositing their sticks, an interval of about an hour was allowed for betting. Men and women, old and young, almost without exception, staked everything they could command, blankets, leggings, ornaments, moccasins on their feet, horses, and money. When

---
[1] Smith: Manuscript field notes, 1870.
[2] Culin: Games of the N. Am. Indians, 24th Ann. Rept. Bu. of Am. Ethn., 1907.
[3] Claiborne: Miss. as a Province, Ter. and State, Jackson, Miss., 1880, pages 496-7.

two persons make a bet, the stakes are placed in the hands of a stake-holder, to be delivered to the winner. The players then post themselves along the line, and one of them, standing in the centre, tosses up the ball. The struggle then to catch the ball begins between the rivals. It must be caught only with the stick. The ball is about the size of an ordinary trap-ball, stuffed with deer-hair and covered with buckskin. Two mingos, one for each side, kept the tally. The ball had to pass twelve times through the poles. The party that succeeded first was the winner. The instant a player caught the ball it was his aim to cast it, with all his might, towards his own poles. But it was lucky if it was not snatched from him before he could throw it, or caught in an instant after he had hurled it. 'Stand from under' and 'look out' were the rules in this game. No responsibility for accident or injuries, even should such injuries be fatal. No respect for rank, or age, or sex. When the play opened, the players were supreme. If you got in their way, you were remorselessly run over. If an arm, or a leg, or a rib, head or neck, was broken in the struggle to catch or throw the ball, it was all in the game, and no one was censured. They ran like a stampeded herd of wild horses or buffalo, over everything in their way, and if one or more fell the others passed over him. As the ball would come whizzing by, with the velocity of a bullet, a player would spring four or five feet in the air to intercept it, and just as he was in the act of casting it to his own poles, or starting to run with it in that direction, a rival would seize and hurl him to the ground, clutch the ball and be, in turn, overthrown as he was about to cast it.

"One of these games sometimes lasted all day. Village played against village; clan against clan; tribe against tribe; the same rules governing in each case."

The present writer witnessed the play in Neshoba County

in 1923 and made the following notes upon the Choctaws and their game.

There were a number of Indians about camp all day. All had black hair, the women wearing the hair down the back. All spoke Choctaw; most of the men knew a little English; the women less; the children none. The women were fond of colors and displayed some of the old gaudiness; many beads were in evidence. The men wore citizens' clothing, tho with broad-brimmed hats and some display of color and of beads. Some of the girls were sufficiently civilized to be chewing gum. There prevailed a monotonous beating of drums.

For the ball-game two poles 12 or 15 feet high are planted in the earth about 100 yards apart. The object of the game is to strike the pole with the ball as often as possible and to keep the opponents from striking the opposite pole. Each player has two sticks (fig. 354) 25 to 35 inches long with a basket-like cup at one end, one of these cups being somewhat smaller than the other. With these two sticks the ball is controlled exclusively, the hands and the feet not coming directly into the game. The ball is apparently about two inches in diameter.

The game begins with a yell, the players lifting their sticks into the air and marching around the pole. Then there is a rush toward the middle of the field with a whoop and the sticks are put down radiating from the center.

Twenty-four players arrange themselves on each side. The ball is tossed into the air to begin and many sticks strike for it. Each party tries to move the ball towards its respective end of the field. Sometimes they catch the ball in midair with the two sticks; it is thrown only with the sticks, and their skill in throwing it thus is great. The ball must strike the upright pole in order to count a point. The contests for the ball are spirited and there is often an animated scramble with many sticks for it when it comes to rest on the ground.

The game lasted over two hours, during which time there was a constant thumping of the drum. Most of the players were barefooted; some wore stockings only. The costumes were varied. The influence of baseball seemed to be shown in the dress; tho a few still wore fox-tails or horse-tails.

As a sample of the Choctaw language I quote the oldest version of the creation legend unmixed with modern accretions that Halbert[1] was able to discover among the Mississippi Choctaws. It was taken down word for word in Choctaw from the lips of Pistonatubbee, who died about the close of the nineteenth century in Newton County at the age of some eighty years. The old Indian stated that in his boyhood he had often heard the story from some of the old chiefs.

Pistonatubbee's version of the creation legend:

Hopahki fehna kash hattak at atoba ammona kat Nanih Waiya yo^n atobat akohcha tok oke. Maskoki yosh tikba Nanih Waiya akohcha mat Nanih Waiya yakni banaiya yo^n illaio^{n}hofka mat shilat taha mat hashi akohchaka ilhkoli tok oke. Atuk osh Itombikbi ola ho^n afoha mat hakchuma shunka mat luak bohli tok oke.

Mihma Chelaki yosh atuklant Nanih Waiya akohcha tok oke. Mihmat yakni banaiya ya^n illaio^{n}hofka mat shilat taha mat akni at atia tok a^n iakaiyat ilhkoli tok oke. Maskoki at afohat hakchuma ashunka cha ia tok o^n, luak at itonla tok o^n, kowi at lua tok o^n Chelaki at Maskoki at atia tok a^n ik ithano mat yoshoba cha filami cha falammi imma ko^n ilhkoli tok osh falammi imma ko^n ont aioklachi tok oke.

Mihma Chikasha yosh atuchinat Nanih Waiya akocha tok oke. Mihmat yakni banaiya ya^n illaio^{n}hofka mat shilat taha mat Chelaki at atia tok a^n iakaiyat ilhkoli tok osh Chelaki at ayoshoba tok a^n ona mat filami mat Chelaki at atia tok akinli ho^n iakaiyat ilhkoli tok oke. Atuk osh Chikasha at

---
[1] Halbert: The Choctaw Creation Legend, Pub. Miss. Hist. Soc., vol. iv, Oxford, Miss., 1901, pp. 269, 270.

Chelaki ạt ont aioklachi tok a^n ona mạt Chelaki bilinka aioklachi tok oke.

Mihma Chahtah yosh ont aiushta ma Nạnih Waiya yạmma ishtaiopi akohcha tok oke. Mihmạt yakni banaiya ya^n illaio^{n}hofka mạt shilạt taha mạt kanima ik aiyo hosh yakni ilap akinli ho^n abinohli tok osh Chahta ạt aiasha hoke.

Halbert's translation of the Choctaw creation legend:

"A very long time ago the first creation of men was in Nạnih Waiya; and there they were made and there they came forth. The Muscogees first came out of Nạnih Waiya, and they then sunned themselves on Nạnih Waiya's earthen rampart, and when they got dry they went to the east. On this side of the Tombigbee, there they rested and as they were smoking tobacco they dropped some fire.

"The Cherokees next came out of Nạnih Waiya. And they sunned themselves on the earthen rampart, and when they got dry they went and followed the trail of the elder tribe. And at the place where the Muscogees had stopped and rested, and where they had smoked tobacco, there was fire and the woods were burnt, and the Cherokees could not find the Muscogees' trail, so they got lost and turned aside and went towards the north and there towards the north they settled and made a people.

"And the Chickasaws third came out of Nạnih Waiya. And then they sunned themselves on the earthen rampart, and when they got dry they went and followed the Cherokees' trail; and when they got to where the Cherokees had got lost, they turned aside and went on and followed the Cherokees' trail. And when they got to where the Cherokees had settled and made a people, they settled and made a people close to the Cherokees.

"And the Choctaws fourth and last came out of Nạnih Waiya. And they sunned themselves on the earthen rampart and when they got dry, they did not go anywhere but settled down in this very land and it is the Choctaws' home."

Many Choctaw words remain in the geographical names of Mississippi and adjoining states. The Bureau of American Ethnology has published a valuable Choctaw dictionary by Byington[1]. The same ethnologist prepared a grammar of the Choctaw Language[2], published by Dr. D. G. Brinton in Philadelphia more than fifty years ago. In addition to the speakers in Mississippi the language is spoken by fifteen or twenty thousand Indians in Oklahoma (*okla*, people, tribe; *humma, homma*, red). There is a small remnant of Choctaws in Louisiana; they have been described by Bushnell[3], who gives photographic illustrations of the people, their mode of life, and their handiwork.

The other Indian languages have disappeared from the state; some have ceased to be spoken. The Natchez Indians were early dispersed, and are practically extinct. Swanton[4] in 1907 found five persons living near Braggs, Oklahoma, who could still speak the Natchez language; the oldest of these died in the spring of 1908, leaving four. A remnant of mixed-blood Tunicas exists in Louisiana, a few speaking the old language. The Yazoos were early fused with the Chicasaws and Choctaws. The Pascagoulas are extinct. Of the Biloxis only a small number remain, including a few in Rapides Parish, La. Of the Ofos (Ofogoulas) one was still living in the year 1908, Rosa Pierette, wife of a Tunica husband near Marksville, La. The Bureau of American Ethnology has published in Bulletin 47 a dictionary of the Biloxi language by Dorsey and Swanton, with a number of myths and stories accompanied by translations of the same, and also a small Ofo dictionary; in Bulletin 68 a comparison of the Tunica, Chitimacha, and Atakapa languages.

[1]Byington: A Dict. of the Choctaw Language, Bull. 46, Washington, 1915.
[2]Byington: Grammar of the Choctaw Language, Philadelphia, 1870.
[3]Bushnell: The Choctaw of Bayou Lacomb, La., Bull. 48, Washington, 1909.
[4]Swanton: Indian Tribes of the Lower Miss. Valley, Bull. 43, Bu. of Am. Ethn.

INDEX.

All numbers refer to pages. The asterisks indicate illustrations.

Aberdeen, 10, 137*-139, 141, 142, 149*, 150, 178*, 196*, 203, 274, 275*, 355*.
Adair, James, 161, 235, 360.
Adams Co., see Natchez.
Agnew, Samuel A., 10, 11.
Agricultural implements, 209*-214*.
Alcorn Co., 182*, 201*, see also Corinth.
Alligator, 94, 160, 167, 184, 284.
American Museum of Nat. Hist., 198*.
Amory, 142, 143*.
Anderson Landing, 70, 333*-335*.
Anguilla, 80.
Animal bones in mounds, 105.
Anna, 1, 40 * 42, 46.
Antler, 282 * 284.
Arcola, 80, 81.
Arrow-heads, 125 * 144; beveled, 139*; curved, 136*, 140*; embedded, 128*, 129, 283; of antler, 282*.
Avondale mounds, 82*.
Axes, 146 * 160; grooved, 146 * 153; smooth (celts), 152 * 160*; toy, 148.
Baldwin, 11.
Ballard, E. R., 135, 136*, 137, 140*, 141*, 149, 157, 176, 177*, 190, 192*, 193, 204, 212*, 213, 237*.
Ball-game, 359-363.
Ballground, Warren Co., 174, 175*, 360.
Ball-sticks, 359*.
Banner-stones, butter-fly stones, 193 * 202; animal, 200, 201*; lunate, 199, 201*; unfinished, 195*, 196, 200, 201*.
Barringer, V. C., 47, 138*, 144*, 150*, 154*, 163*, 166, 169*, 174*, 180*, 183*, 190*, 194*, 205*, 219*, 222, 246, 247*.
Barton, C. A., vi, 121*, 122.
Baskets, 357*, 359.
Batesville, 2, 113 * 116.
Bay St. Louis, 30.
Beads, aboriginal, 188 * 193; rolled copper, 356; shell, 273, 274; trade, 348, 349*, 356.
Bear Creek, 331*, 332.
Bellefontaine, Webster Co., 217.
Bells, 285, 356, 358*.
Belmont, Tishomingo Co., 14.

Belzoni, 65.
Benton, Yazoo Co., 209*.
Bessac, F. T., v, 222*, 236*.
Beuchat, H., 195, 354.
Biloxi, 30-33.
Birchett, Dr. J. A. K., 162*, 175*, 185*, 186*, 241, 242*, 358*.
Birdsong, Dr. T. B., 47, 174.
Boat-stones, 173*-176*.
Bobo, Coahoma Co., 106.
Bone artifacts, 282 * 284.
Booneville, Prentiss Co., 214*.
Bowdre mounds, 120 * 122, 191 (bead).
Bracelets, brass, 356, 357*, 358; silver, 349, 355, 358.
Brinton, D. G., 365.
Bronze tomahawks, 355*, 356.
Brown, Miss Ruth, 355.
Bryant, Yalobusha Co., 165*.
Bunts, 136*.
Bureau of Am. Ethn., 58, 81, 82, 94, 97, 107, 182, 279*, 331, 347, 365.
Burnt Clay, 322*.
Bushnell, D. I., Jr., 350, 359, 365.
Butler Breevoort, 75, 155*, 157 * 159, 168*, 177 * 179*, 190*, 204*, 209*, 215, 216*, 225, 227*.
Butter-fly stones, see banner-stones.
Byington, Cyrus, 365.
Cairns, 4, 12*-14.
Calumet, 271*, 272.
Cane for boring, 202*.
Carey, 76-78, 336.
Carmack, Dr. F. T., 217*.
Carson mounds, see Stovall mounds.
Carved stones, 205 * 208.
Celts, 153*-159*; double-edged, 158*; of coal, 158*; of copper, 284*, 285; of petrified wood, 158.
Ceremonial stones, 161 * 208.
Champlin mounds, 58*-60, 336.
Chapman, Felix M., 139*, 147*, 151*, 152, 187*, 192*, 193, 197, 201*, 203*, 233, 242*, 274*, 276*.
Charleston, 95, 322*.

368 ARCHEOLOGY OF MISSISSIPPI.

Cheatham, Richard, 122.
Choctaw, language, 348, 362-365; creation legend, 363-5.
Chunky (chunkee)˙stones, 161 * 170.
Cigar-shaped stones, 203, 204*.
Claiborne Co., 47.
Claiborne, J. F. H., 28, 360, 361.
Clark, Clarksdale, 96-99, 103, 106, 138*, 156, 172 * 174, 180*, 187*, 207, 208*, 210, 211*, 233*, 245, 246*, 255*, 269, 273 * 275*, 303, 318, 357, 358*.
Cloth (woven fabric) impression, 233*, 234.
Coahoma Co., see Clarksdale, Oliver, Stovall.
Coffeeville, 28.
Coldwater, 132-134*, 137, 139*, 140, 181, 182*.
Columbus, 131*, 133*, 139*, 147*, 148*, 152, 156*, 157, 175, 176*, 187*, 192*, 193, 197, 199, 200*, 203*, 233, 241, 242*, 273, 274*, 276*.
Commerce, Tunica Co., 119, 120, 168, 278.
Cones, 204*.
Conglomerate artifacts, 167*, 168*.
Copiah Co., 47, 157, 166, 169*, 174*, 180*, 183*, 219*.
Copper artifacts, 284*, 285.
Cores from borings, 202*.
Corinth, 14, 132*, 134 * 136, 187*, 198, 199*, 210, 215, 237, 238*.
Cornish, Lafayette Co., 6*.
Culin, Stewart, 35, 42, 44, 45, 158, 200, 201*, 207*, 255, 265*, 270*, 344, 346*, 347*, 360.
Cup-stones, 222-225*.
Davenport Acad. of Sc., 144*, 145, 331*, 332.
Davies, Dr. J. A., 160, 172*, 180*, 185*, 209, 210*, 214, 215*, 221*, 246*, 276*, 277*, 282*, 288 * 320* (pottery).
Dear Island, 31, 32.
Delay, Lafayette Co., 138*, 221*, 222.
Delisle, Harrison Co., 30.
Dellenbaugh, F. S., 354.
Delta, Panola Co., 116.
De Soto Co., 268; see also Walls.
Dickerson, Dr. M. W., 35, 42-45, 158, 200, 201*, 248, 255, 256*, 265*, 270*, 346*.

Digging implements, 209 * 214*.
Dillville, 30.
Discoidal stones, 161 * 170.
Disks of clay, 289*; of shell, 277*, 278; of stone, 225 * 231.
Domestic implements, 215 * 234.
Dorr mounds, 100, 105.
Dorsey, James O., 365.
Drills, drilling, 200*, see perforators.
Dubbs, Tunica Co., 117.
Dumas, Tippah Co., 12.
Dundee, Tunica Co. 116, 252, 254*.
Dunleith, 82, 83, 188, 192*, 193, 223, 224*.
Du Pratz, 36, 235.
Ear-plugs, 275 * 277* (shell), 342 (clay).
Earth-walls, 3, 7, 8 (Lafayette Co.), 71, 72 (Spanish Fort), 73 (Holly Bluff), 97 (Clarksdale).
Earth-works, 1 * 124.
Eastport, Tishomingo Co., 214*.
Edinburgh, Scotland, material in, 32.
Edmonds mounds, see Oliver mounds.
Egg-shaped stones, 205*.
Eldorado, 57, 240, 242*, 266 * 269.
Elizabeth, Washington Co., 81.
Ellis Cliff, 34, 43, 159, 255.
Ellistown, 10, 11.
Embedded arrow-points, 128*, 129, 283.
Enola, Yazoo Co., 204*.
Etta, 231*, 232.
Evansville, 116.
Farabee, W. C., 100.
Ferguson mounds, 45, 46, 265*, 270*.
Foster, Adams Co., 34.
Fowke, Gerard, 125, 127, 139, 182, 195, 211, 268.
Friar's Point, 106, 107.
Fulton, Dr. R. B., 189.
Garlandsville, Jasper Co., 357*.
George Lake; see Lake George.
Gholson, A. J., 170.
Gift, J. E., 132*, 134 * 136, 187*, 199*, 215, 238*.
Glass, 50 (mounds), 336 * 342* (pottery).
Gorgets, 176-183* (stone), 278 * 282 (shell).
Gouge of slate, 159.

INDEX.

Grand Gulf, Claiborne Co. 46.
Greenville, 255; see Winterville, 83 * 88.
Greenwood, 53, 68, 69, 94.
Gulf Coast, 30-33.
Gunnison, Bolivar Co., 94.
Guntown, Lee Co., 10, 11.
Halbert, H. S., 24, 26-28, 363-365.
Handbook of Am. Indians, 128.
Hand-hammers, hammer-stones, 226*.
Harris, W. H., 143*, 144, 158, 187*, 188*.
Hansell, G. B., 10, 208.
Haynes Bluff, 53, 55, 125, 144*, 145, 174, 184*, 185.
Height of mounds, 1, 2.
Heye, George C., 129.
Heye Museum, 173, 175, 176*, 182, 183*, 186*, 220*, 225, 227*, 231, 243, 245*, 251 * 254*.
Hinsdale, Dr. W. G., 30-32.
Hoes, 209*, 210*.
Holly Bluff, Yazoo Co., 2, 72 * 74, 157*, 159.
Holly Landing, Humphreys Co., 63.
Holly Springs, Marshall Co., 196.
Hollywood, Tunica Co., 117, 120.
Holmes Co., 332*.
Holmes, W. H., 108, 127, 222, 228 * 231, 261, 278, 287, 288, 303, 308, 332, 346, 359.
Honey Island, 67, 68.
Horseshoe Lake, Warren Co., 48.
Hough, James, 93.
Hubbard Landing, Tishomingo Co., 9.
Indian languages, 348, 362-365.
Indian Mound (station), 29.
Indians in Mississippi, 348, 361-365.
Ingomar, Union Co., 1, 2, 14 * 21, 353.
Issaquena Co., 76, 228 * 231.
Iuka, Tishomingo Co., 134*, 142*, 204*, 217*.
Jackson Co., 32, 33.
Jaketown, Humphreys Co., 66.
Jefferson Co., 207*, 208, 238, 240*, 248, 269*, 346.
Jefferson medal, 349, 352*, 353*.
Jones, C. C., 146, 205, 268.
Jones, Dr. Joseph, 7, 145, 175, 220*, 225, 227*.
Keownville, Union Co., 9.

King's Crossing, 53-55.
Kingston, Adams Co., 34.
Kossuth, Alcorn Co., 14.
Lafayette Co., 4, 4 * 7*, 152*, 153*, 166*, 167, 180*, 189, 195*, 197*, 204, 215, 218*, 221*, 224 * 226*, 231*, 232.
Lake Cormorant, 124, 250, 251*.
Lake George, 2, 70, 73*, 225, 227*, 247, 248*, 263.
Lancaster, A. D. N., 221*, 222.
Lawrence Co., 189.
Learned, Rufus, 172*, 173, 186, 207*, 349*.
Lee Co., 164*, 165; see also Tupelo.
Leflore Co., 219; see Greenwood.
Leflore, Greenwood, 4, 94.
Lodi, Montgomery Co., 177*.
Logan, Prof. W. N., 23.
Louisville, Winston Co., 277*.
Love, W. A., 25*, 133*, 156*, 157.
Lowe, Dr. E. N., i, iii, v, 12, 47.
Lowndes Co., 21-23, 129, 148*, 151*, 152; see also Columbus.
Lunate stone, 199, 201*.
McCullough, W. L., 148*.
MacCurdy, G. G., 277.
McFarland, B. H., v, 10, 151, 196*, 274, 275*, 355*.
McGuire on pipes, 235, 246, 248, 264.
Madison, 29.
Magnetite plummet, 185*.
Malmaison, 94.
Marks, Quitman Co., 96, 251, 252* (pipe).
Mason, Otis T. (basketry), 359.
Mauffray, Joseph, 30.
Maul, stone, 233*.
Mechanicsburg, Yazoo Co., 215, 216*.
Melrose, Yazoo Co., 190*, 191*.
Mhoon Landing, Tunica Co., 118.
Middleton, J. D., 39.
Midnight, 64.
Miller, Miss Rebecca, 176.
Millsaps College Museum, 215, 271*, 272.
Milwaukee Pub. Museum, 244, 246*, 256, 258 * 264, 343*.
Monroe Co., 192*, 193.
Montgomery Co., see Ballard.

Moore, C. B., 9, 21-23, 32-34, 48-57, 60-76, 118-120, 169, 184*, 195, 222, 226, 240*, 246-248*, 255, 261, 268, 283, 286-288, 303, 310, 322 * 343 (pottery).
Moorehead, W. K., 46, 128. 134, 146, 175, 182, 194, 197, 198, 227, 234, 268.
Mortars, 213 * 217.
Mound Place, See Holly Bluff.
Mounds, 1-124;
  age of, 3;
  Anna (or Robson), 40 * 42;
  Cary (Sharkey Co.), 76-78;
  Champlin, 58*, 33ɔ;
  Coleman, 23;
  Ferguson, 200, 201*;
  height of 1, 2;
  in Adams Co., 33 * 45;
    Bolivar Co., 90-94;
    Clarksdale and Coahoma Co., 96 * 113;
    De Soto Co., 122 * 124;
    Issaquena and Sharkey Co., 76 * 80;
    Lafayette Co., 4 * 9;
    Lowndes Co., 21-23;
    North Central Miss., 9 * 21;
    Oktibbeha Co., 23;
    Panola Co., 113 * 116;
    Sharkey Co., 76 * 80;
    Tunica Co., 116 * 122;
    vicinity of Natchez, 33 * 45;
    Warren Co., 48-53;
    Washington Co., 80 * 90;
  Mt. Helena, 79*, 80;
  Nanih Waiya, 1, 4, 24 * 28, 363-365;
  near Batesville, 113 * 116;
    Carey, 76-78;
    Fairview Landing, 75;
    Greenwood, 69;
    Ingomar, 14 * 21, 353;
    Racetrack Landing, 69;
    Rolling Fork, 78;
    Stovall, 108 * 113;
    University, 5*;
  Oliver (Edwards), 101 * 106;
  on Gulf Coast, 30-33;
    Sunflower River, 70 * 75;
    Yazoo River, 53-69;
  purpose of 2, 3;
  Robson (Anna), 40 * 42;
  Selsertown, 36 * 38*;
  White Apple, near Natchez, 4, 34, 35.
Mullers, 213, 217, 218*.
Museum of Am. Indian, see Heye Museum.
Nanih Waiya, 1, 4, 24 * 28, 363-365.

Natchez, 33 * 45, 128*, 143, 158, 172*, 173, 184, 188, 207*, 216*, 221, 236*, 243, 244, 246*, 256, 258 * 264, 269*, 270*, 348, 349*.
Natchez Indians, 33, 35 36, 278, 365.
Natural stone cups, 222*, 223*.
Neblett Landing, 90-93, 323 * 330.
Nettleton, 10, 142, 169, 208*, 217.
New Albany, 9, 10, 129, 131*, 132*, 135*, 184*, 197*, 202*, 206*, 348, 349 * 353*, 356.
Norris, P. W., 97, 107, 108.
Noxapater, 24.
Oak Bend Landing, 48, 337, 341*, 342*.
Ocean Springs, 32.
Oliver mounds, 1, 101 * 106, 187.
Ornamental stones, 161 * 208*.
Oxford, 148, 214, 220; see also University.
Palestine, Adams Co., 236*.
Palettes, 226 * 231.
Panther Burn, 80.
Peabody, Dr. Charles, 1, 47, 94, 100 * 106, 160, 167, 184, 186, 269, 283*, 284, 305, 320*-322.
Peabody Museum, 100, 283*, 321*.
Pell, W. H., 198*.
Pendants, 183*-188*, 192*.
Perforators, 125, 140*-143*.
Perrault, Vincent, 216, 243, 244, 246*, 256, 258 * 264, 343*, 344*.
Pestles, 213, 217*.
Petrified wood, 158*, 159.
Philipp, 3, 95, 96*.
Phoenix, 57.
Pipes, 235 * 272; disk, 246; effigy, 244 * 270*; tomahawk, 271*, 272, 354 * 357.
Pitted stones, 223 * 226*.
Plates, stone, 226, 227 * 229*.
Plummets, 184*-188*.
Pocahontas, Hinds Co., 29.
Pointevent, Scuyler, 32.
Pontotoc Co., 10, 11, 144*, 150*, 152, 154*, 155, 163*, 164, 179, 180*, 183*, 205*, 222, 348, 356.
Port Gibson, 251.
Post-Columbian Material, 348 * 365.
Pottery, 286 * 347*;
  classification of, 287;
  designs on, 299*, 300*, 313*, 335*, 346*;

INDEX. 371

Pottery, double, 317-319*;
  effigy, 286, 288, 303*-318*, 328*, 329*;
  handles (heads), 316*-318*;
  of Coahoma Co., 320 * 322;
  Cossitt Library. 288;
  Lower Miss. Valley, 322 * 347*;
  Middle Miss. Valley, 287 * 322*;
  Neblett Landing, 323*-330;
  Walls, 288*-320*;
  triple, 318*-321*.
Problematic stones, 161 * 208*.
Quitman Co., 171, 172*.
Rara Avis, Itowamba Co.. 214*.
Rattlesnake tablet, 228 * 231.
Rau, Dr. Charles, 189.
Refuse-heaps, 4, 64, 72*.
Ripley, Tippah Co., 14.
Robins, Williams, 10.
Rockport, 47.
Rodney, Jefferson Co., 46.
Rolling Fork, 78, 79*.
Rosedale, Bolivar Co., 90.
Rubel, Milton, 215.
Satartia, 57.
Schubach, F., 134*, 156, 160*, 206, 223*, 233*, 276*, 282*, 294, 304*, 305, 308*, 310*, 313*, 315.
Sculpture, 206*-208*.
Selma, Adams Co., 176.
Selsertown, 2, 36 * 39, 45, 222*, 223, 256, 258 * 264, 344 * 346.
Sessumville, Oktibbeha Co., 23.
Shadyside Landing, 88, 89, 255, 257*, 258, 330*.
Shelby, Bolivar Co., 94.
Shell artifacts, 273 * 282.
Shell Bluff Landing, 68.
Shell gorgets, 275, 278 * 281.
Shell-heaps, 4, 30-32, 64.
Shellmound, Leflore Co., 95.
Sidon, Carroll Co., 95, 159*.
Silver articles, 349 * 356.
Silver City, 63, 64.
Simpson Co., 47.
Sinkers, 187*, 188.
Skipwith Peyton, 220*, 221.
Skulls from Walls, 124*.
Skulls with embedded arrow-heads, 128*, 129, 283.

Smith, Eugene A., 57, 360.
Smithsonian Institution, 182, 183*, 220.
Smoking among Indians, 235, 363, 364.
Spades, 210*-212*.
Spade-shaped stones, 170 * 173.
Spanish coat of arms, 19, 353.
Spanish Fort, 70-72*.
Spear-heads, 125, 126, 131*, 132*, 134*, 138*.
Squier and Davis, 7, 39, 93, 116, 173, 200, 263, 358.
Stag-horn artifacts, 282 * 284.
Stanton, Adams Co., 36.
Starkville, 23.
Stone, A. H., 82, 192*, 193, 223, 224*.
Stone balls, 219*.
Stone bowl, 220*, 221.
Stone cups, 221*-223*.
Stone-heaps, 12*-14.
Stone plates, 225 * 229*.
Stone trough, 232.
Stoneville, Washington Co., 81.
Stovall (Carson) mounds, 101, 108 * 113.
Sumner, Tallahatchie Co., 95.
Sunflower Co., 94.
Swanton, John R., 36, 365.
Swastika, 206*.
Tallahatchie (River). 3, 6-8, 10, 12, 220.
Tchula Lake, 61-63.
Thomas, Cyrus, 15 * 21, 58-60, 195, 294, 304, 336, 354, 359.
Thruston, G. P., 138, 146, 264, 272, 277, 347.
Ticer, Will, 12, 131*. 132*, 184*, 197*, 202*, 206*, 349 * 352*.
Tippah Co., 10, 12*-14.
Tomahawk pipe, 271*, 272, 354 * 357.
Tomahawks, 354 * 357.
Tombigbee River, 21, 197, 270.
Tremont, Itawamba Co., 148*, 212*.
Tubes, 203*.
Tunica Co., 116 * 122, 156*, 157, 254.
Tupelo, 9, 10, 240, 242*, 270*, 348, 349, 354-356, 358.
Tutwiler, 95.
Tortoises in serpentine, 207*.
Troy, C. W., 354, 356.

U. S. Nat. Museum, 170, 171*, 177*, 189, 196, 200*, 247, 249*, 250*, 279*, 285.
University, 4, 5*, 212, 214, 284*, 285.
Vance, Tallahatchie Co., 96.
Vicksburg, 53, 162*, 163, 185*, 186*, 241, 243, 245*, 348, 358*.
Wailes's Geology, 14 (cairns), 24, 26 (Nanih Waiya).
Wait, Dr. H. C., 195, 197*, 231*, 232.
Walls, De Soto Co., 122, 123*, 134*, 135, 156, 159, 160*, 168, 171, 172*, 180*, 185*, 206, 209, 210*, 214, 215*, 221*-223*, 233*, 234, 239, 241*, 245, 246*, 250, 268, 275 * 277*, 282*, 288 * 320 (pottery).
Walnut Grove, Leake Co., 238, 239*.
Walnut Lake, 117.

Watts, J. M., 348, 356.
West, G. A. (pipes), 249, 264, 268, 272, 357.
Whelpley, Dr. H. M., 211, 268.
White Apple village, 4, 34, 242, 243*.
Wilkinson Co., 143*, 144, 158, 187*, 188*.
Winona, 139*, 140 * 142, 177*, 190, 206*, 237*.
Winterville, 2, 83 * 88.
Wood, Charles L., 277*.
Woven material, 233*, 234.
Yalobusha Co., 212*, 213.
Yazoo City, 58, 243, 244*, 273.
Yazoo Co., 58-64, 155, 157, 158, 168, 178*, 209*, 232*, 268, 274*.
Young, Bennett H., 244.

THE END.

www.ingramcontent.com/pod-product-compliance
Lightning Source LLC
Chambersburg PA
CBHW071016240426
43661CB00073B/2307